POLITICAL THEORY AND
PARTISAN POLITICS

SUNY series in Political Theory: Contemporary Issues
Philip Green, Editor

POLITICAL THEORY AND PARTISAN POLITICS

Edited by

EDWARD BRYAN PORTIS, ADOLF G. GUNDERSEN, and RUTH LESSL SHIVELY

State University
of New York
Press

Published by
State University of New York Press, Albany

Printed in the United States of America

For information, address State University of New York Press,
State University Plaza, Albany, N.Y., 12246

Production by Michael Haggett
Marketing by Anne M. Valentine

Library of Congress Cataloging-in-Publication Data

Political theory and partisan politics / edited by Edward Bryan
  Portis, Adolf G. Gundersen, and Ruth Lessl Shively.
      p.   cm. — (SUNY series in political theory. Contemporary
  issues)
    Includes bibliographical references and index.
    ISBN 0-7914-4591-7 (hc. : alk. paper). — ISBN 0-7914-4592-5 (pbk.
  : alk. paper)
    1. Political science.   2. Politics, Practical.   I. Portis, Edward
  Bryan.   II. Gundersen, Adolf G., 1958–   .   III. Shively, Ruth
  Lessl.   IV. Series.
  JA71.P6314   2000
  324.7'01—dc21   99-44721
                                                         CIP

10 9 8 7 6 5 4 3 2 1

CONTENTS

ACKNOWLEDGMENTS

All of the nine chapters that form the core of this book are derived from discussion papers that were originally presented to the "Political Theory Convocation" of the department of Political Science at Texas A&M University. We would like to thank the department of Political Science and especially its chairman, Charles A. Johnson, for encouragement and support. Melissa Scheier and Joshua May helped in the preparation of the manuscript, and Anneliese Reinemayer served in effect as both adviser and manager of this project. Finally, we thank Sage Publications, Ltd., for permission to republish the essay, William E. Connolly, "Review Essay: Twilight of the Idols," *Philosophy and Social Criticism*, vol. 21 (3): 127–137, which has been substantially incorporated into Professor Connolly's contribution to this volume.

INTRODUCTION

By its very nature political theory must be more concerned with political potential than with the processes or means by which this potential, however conceived, might be realized. To theorize is to generalize, if not universalize, and the criteria by which satisfactory collective existence is assessed, because more general, have greater theoretical priority than the institutional procedures and political sentiments they rationalize. And for the same reason, these procedures and sentiments are of greater theoretical significance than the techniques that might be used to install or instill them. The purpose of this collection of essays is not to bring this bias into question, for it is entailed in theoretical endeavor itself; to be a political theorist is to be so biased. Instead, our purpose is to explore one of the consequences of the priority political theorists give to political potential over political process.

This is the marked tendency of political theorists to define politics, or at least the "political," in ways that diverge from meanings most often given the term. For most people, politics almost always refers to a type of conflict or competition. Colloquially, politics usually refers to something professional politicians are supposed to do, which is to engage in an opportunistic competition for positions of authority. At higher levels of conceptual sophistication politics typically is seen as a struggle for influence through the mobilization of constituencies, as opposed to the use of physical coercion or the control of scarce resources. Military, economic, and political competition, in other words, tend to be distinguished by the different means they employ. The fact that politics is typically seen as a form of conflict, especially when in conjunction with opportunism, certainly does much to explain the negative connotations associated with the word in popular discourse.

Political theorists do not share this disdain for the word, largely because "politics" usually means something different to them. For example, in an influential essay of an earlier decade, Christian Bay used the term "pseudopolitics" to characterize factional struggle over interests or goals unguided by universal moral priorities. Genuine politics, according to Bay, must proceed from a concern with, and therefore from a conception of, human need. Bay confidently asserted

1

that a theoretically guided political science could eventually discern basic human needs, and thereby "become a potent instrument for promoting political development in the service of human development" (Bay 1965, 51). Not only must genuinely political action be normative, but it also must be "an instrument of reason." From this perspective, however much the champions of rational human need may be forced by circumstance to resort to deceitful rhetoric, appeals to parochial interest, or compromise in order to prevail over the irrational or the malevolent, public issues are ultimately amenable to rational solution and politics is, at least ideally, a rational rather than a conflictual, partisan endeavor.

Many issues of public policy undoubtedly are matters of knowledge, and perhaps an appreciable fraction of social animosity is the result of ignorance and misunderstanding. Yet Bay's rather facile assumption that theoretically guided research will disclose an unambiguous set of rational human needs would be questioned by many if not most contemporary political theorists. And without this assumption, "genuine politics" is likely to be just as partisan, and perhaps even more conflictual than "pseudopolitics" since disagreement over the nature of the good can be at least as deep as that resulting from the clash of individual or group interests.

By extension, partisan divisions based upon competing constellations of interests, such as class conflict, are in some ways less likely to lead to serious political enmity than those based upon contradictory moral or ideological priorities. Conflict generated by divergent interests need not be "zero-sum." Indeed, within a single political jurisdiction there is almost always a significant degree of mutual dependence among competing interests. As Karl Marx himself realized, class conflict is not likely to lead to class war unless the system itself suffers from "internal contradictions" that threaten the very existence of at least one of the contestants. In the absence of such fundamental structural instability, interest conflict is amenable to mutual accommodation through negotiation and compromise. Whatever its faults, selfishness is not inherently inflexible, much less aggressive.[1]

Moral commitment, on the other hand, is not always so readily compromised. Even bargaining with like-minded counterparts of good faith can be difficult, but bargaining with the morally corrupt, dissolute, or obtuse is sordid business. And irrespective of the sincerity with which proponents of divergent moral views attempt to find some way to live together in peace, they ultimately must be committed to changing one another's minds about what is proper and necessary. That is to say, they must be so committed if politics is to be based on fixed moral commitment to human needs. It is certainly possible for groups with divergent moral commitments, or even religious beliefs, to be unconcerned with one another's priorities and practices, and this mutual indifference undoubtedly facilitates bargaining and accommodation. But this is simply another form of interest (or pseudo) politics, one in which the interests of each self interested group are determined by a common creed or identity rather than personal advantage.

Moral or ideological dispute can be deliberative only if the contestants are convinced they might prevail through public discussion and argument, that minds might be changed. This conviction makes sense if the contestants agree on fundamentals and see themselves divided primarily by matters of interpretation and implementation. We suspect that to some degree this is usually the case. Even the word partisanship, while denoting divisiveness, implies a whole of which the partisan is part, and this implication may be the source of the negative connotations the word "partisanship" carries with it. To the extent that this is so, the fact that contestants share a larger consensus compels them to consider the costs to the "whole" of unrestrained struggle, as well as consider the political costs to themselves of appearing too partisan. More important in the present context, disputants who see themselves as differing primarily in matters of interpretation are more likely to think that they can convince one another's supporters of the error of their ways and that they themselves might be mistaken. Moreover, they are likely to be justified in these assessments because a common framework provides criteria by which coherence might be assessed and alternative positions evaluated.

In the absence of agreement on fundamentals, however, ideological partisanship can be displaced by deliberation only if theoretical differences are in principle resolvable through rational discussion. Otherwise, each internally consistent theoretical system would rest upon its own supposedly self-evident conceptual axioms, impervious to criticism based on rival doctrines. Of course, if there were a set of truly self-evident conceptual premises, this situation would rarely arise, for there would be consensus on fundamentals. Yet it is the rare political theorist who believes that the basic concepts of political thought are self-evident, and not many defend the possibility that rational discussion could establish a rational consensus on fundamental concepts.

Indeed, an influential thesis concerning the nature of interpretation in political theory holds that disputes over the meaning of fundamental concepts are theoretically irresolvable: Such concepts are not simply controversial; they are "essentially contested." As this postulate was first articulated by W. B. Gallie (1962), it is the normative nature of complex concepts such as "freedom" or "democracy" that inevitably renders their meaning irredeemingly controversial. As normative concepts, their application is by definition appraisive, and real world instances are valued achievements. As complex concepts, however, they contain a number of elements that contribute to these valued achievements, and the relative weight of each element's contribution, and therefore its importance in the definition of the concept, cannot be conclusively established by rational means. As a result, their meaning will always be contested, and the contest must be to some extent political because one position is not necessarily more rational than another.[2]

There are a number of problems with the essentially contested concept thesis. One is that it assumes a degree of consensus on the general meaning of a term and refers exclusively, it seems, to problems of specification. Yet little is said about how this general consensus is secured or why it is irrelevant in evaluating the concept's specific applications. In his influential version of the thesis William E. Connolly (1974) characterizes this sort of concept as a "cluster concept" because the various attributes which contending definitions of any particular concept might use to define it cannot logically be hierarchally organized, or even exhaustively specified. But what determines whether an attribute is eligible for inclusion in any particular cluster? This apparently is a question of social usage rather than theoretical appropriateness.

Although this response certainly would not serve the purpose of theorists attempting to distinguish valid from defective usages, Connolly's version of the thesis of essentially contested concepts rests upon an additional premise that is particularly germane to the relationship between partisan politics and political theory. Instead of focusing solely upon the nature of these concepts that are supposed to be irretrievably ambiguous, Connolly also considers the nature of the reality such concepts are intended to capture and communicate. Social reality, and in particular political reality, ultimately consists of practices that are understood or presumed by the practitioners to achieve or embody meaningful ends. Without this understanding or presumption the practices do not take place. Consequently, social and political reality is necessarily a conceptual reality in the sense that it does not exist unless it is conceptualized. A social system, like a solar system, is a complex conceptual construct of a dimension of reality that presumably exists irrespective of whether a scientist attempts to capture it conceptually. The difference between these two conceptual constructs is that any particular social system inevitably comes to us "preconceptualized," and that the social scientist must in some manner incorporate this self understanding into any rational account of social and political processes. To conceptualize a social system in the same manner that natural science conceives the solar system is to dissolve one's subject matter. For if all the concepts used by the social scientist to explain unintended consequences or elucidate aspects of social interaction unknown to participants were "technical," they would be unintelligible to the participants and, hence, irrelevant as well (See Connolly 1974, 39–40).

That is to say, purely technical concepts would be irrelevant unless the social scientist were able to coax members of a given society to think in his or her terms rather than those to which they had been accustomed. And yet, this is just what social scientists do. In varying degrees, they attempt to modify existing understandings in order to more adequately achieve social ends. Because political theorists deal with the way in which these ends are understood and justified, their work tends to be controversial. Concepts like "freedom," "justice," "democracy," and even "politics" are going to be contested because they are constitutive of what people (including political scientists and theorists) think they are or at least could be. Irrespective of whether or not the meaning of such terms is *essentially* indeterminate, they will be contested in any society characterized by a significant degree of both cultural diversity and freedom of thought and expression. In these societies their meanings will not be self-evident, and public debate over their appropriate definition will not be monopolized by those committed to rational discourse.

In other words, because of the conceptual dimension of political reality, ideological partisanship will exist irrespective of whether it is possible by means of rational discourse to objectively discern valid meanings for political concepts. Bay's distinction between "pseudopolitics" and "genuine politics" masks a more fundamental, or at least more intractable tension between the discourse of theoretical inquiry and the discourse of political rhetoric. But any animosity generated by this tension is likely to be one-sided, felt only by those committed to theoretical discourse. Those engaged in attempting to mobilize support through rhetoric and ideology do not necessarily have cause either to fear or to denigrate political theory. While they are likely to consider rational discourse practically insufficient to ensure proper public policy, they need not assume that it is a bankrupt enterprise. Even in a world where collective decisions were made solely on the basis of rhetorical eloquence and emotional appeal, individual priorities would still cry out for rational justification.

In another imaginary world, however, where collective decisions were solely the result of rational deliberation, rhetorical discourse would be pointless. More to the point, if such a world is conceivable then ideological partisanship is in the last analysis pathological. Political theory would then have the potential, and even the responsibility, to displace partisan politics. We do not know, of course, what percentage of political theorists feel this way, but we are confident that to one degree or another the sentiment is widespread. Many, perhaps most political theorists see their endeavor as the search for principles of political right that in some sense transcend or at least limit political struggle. Liberal political theorists in particular tend to place a premium upon "neutrality" of one kind or another.

We are hardly the first to sense a certain enmity, or more often a dismissiveness toward political conflict among political theorists. Yet even Bernard Crick, whose influential book, *In Defense of Politics*, is devoted to the defense of politics from numerous detractors, including those who treat everything as a matter of abstract principle, does not identify politics as a form of struggle or conflict. Instead, politics is defined by its sociological function, as the activity by which conflict is managed and a diverse, pluralistic civilization is maintained (Crick 1964, 21–26). More recently, Benjamin R. Barber has assailed a collection of major political theorists for their attempts to subordinate political engagement to abstract principle (Barber 1988). Yet like Crick, Barber sees politics in terms of its potential function, although in his case the function is primarily psychological rather than sociological. For Barber, politics is the engagement through which contending individuals are able to act (or decide) collectively, despite lack of agreement on guiding standards (see Barber 1984, 120–122). Political participation requires deliberation and genuine communication, and in the process dissension is transformed into mutualism, and individuals educate themselves politically.

Managing or transforming conflict may be a worthy end, but these functional definitions of politics have two disadvantages. The first is that this kind of definition simply assumes that certain results always follow a certain kind of action; without this assumption it would be impossible to recognize any instance of the action until the results are known. Referring specifically to Barber's definition, Mark E. Warren puts the point nicely: "Clearly, a definition should not treat a possible outcome of an activity—which may or may not be realized in any given instance—as a condition of its existence" (Warren 1997, 12). More generally, to see politics as something that deals with conflict rather than a form of conflict itself would seem to rest upon the assumption either that all conflict is resolvable through deliberation, or that the only kind of conflict with which politics deals is that which can be resolved. Either version, it seems to us, denies by assumption that essential tension between theoretical and rhetorical discourse alluded to in previous paragraphs. It assumes, in other words, that rhetorical discourse can be rendered pointless. Such a world may or may not be conceivable but theorists, just because they are theorists, should not simply assume its potential existence.

Nor, on the other hand, should theorists simply assume that all important political difference is impervious to rational deliberation. A good many of those theorists who are inclined to define the political as a form of struggle, discount the role of rational dialogue because the ultimate stakes in political conflict concern collective identification and legitimacy. Collective and self-identity must reflect experience and be appropriate to the demands of the present to be plausible; but in the last analysis identity is subjectively construed, and from this perspective political freedom consists not just of the opportunity to express identity but also of the ability to alter it. Freedom, in brief, is equated with the creative act of self-definition. Because the determination of identity precedes and provides the criteria of social rationality, questions of identity cannot themselves be resolved through rational deliberation. Consequently, whatever the benefits or necessity of collective consensus, it arbitrarily advantages a portion of society while it just as arbitrarily disempowers marginal groups and deviant individuals.

Those adopting this theoretical orientation tend to see their role as one of revealing suppressed conflict by exposing the arbitrary and oppressive implications of hegemonic political understandings. In Bonnie Honig's words, "once any conception of politics and identity or agency begins to sediment, its usefulness as a lever of critique is diminished and its generative power becomes a force of constraint" (1993, 206). Theorists in search of rational principles of political right are in effect attempting to contain the capricious contingency of struggle by establishing guidelines through which it can be limited, or at least judged. In her sophisticated and insightful critique of such theoretical endeavor, Honig grants that regimes as a practical matter must have such theoretical foundations; but she argues that they are always to some degree one-sided and arbitrary, and therefore always contestable. Moreover, theoretical foundations always need contesting, because the attempt to envelop an inherently multidimensional and changing political reality within an abstract and static conceptual system inevitably forecloses political potential and provides the criteria by which some can be singled out as politically marginal or deviant. Against the theoretical role of establishing the intellectual foundations of right order, which Honig calls "virtue theory," she posits that of the *"virtù* theorists" who "seek out the rifts and fissures of foundational identities and constitutions" in order to encourage the contest of identity and difference (1993, 12–13).

By this analysis theory itself is a partisan endeavor, and each theorist must choose to be a partisan of order or a partisan of openness. Honig chooses the latter. Not, she says, because of the "benighted teleological belief" that political engagement is intrinsically meaningful, but rather because she thinks that the "displacement of politics with law or administration" threatens to "disempower and perhaps even undermine democratic institutions and citizens" (1993, 15). Perhaps so. Yet however benighted, either of these reasons would seem to rest upon the kind of theoretical postulates from which justifying foundations are construed. And however contestable, such postulates would appear to be just as unavoidable for theorists as for regimes. Irrespective of whether one chooses to use one's theoretical postulates to prescribe principles of right or to expose the limitations of alternatives, either of these activities would seem to differ in kind from that of formulating and criticizing the postulates themselves.[3] What we seem to have here is not an analysis of the nature of theory, but of alternative ways its political relevance might be brought to bear by those who chose to do so.

If so, it is not self-evident that political theory itself can be seen as just another form of partisanship, and the relationship between theoretical endeavor and partisan politics, as well as their mutual implications, remains problematic. Pointing this out has been the purpose of this introduction, and provides the justification for this book. The following chapters are organized into three parts, each corresponding to one of three different ways of conceiving of the optimal or necessary relationship between political theory and partisan political struggle. Each of these parts contains three chapters, each developing a theme to some extent divergent from those of the other two. As such, each part is characterized by a significant degree of theoretical diversity.

Traditionally political theorists have tended to see political conflict as something to be confined, if not eliminated. Political theory is often, perhaps typically seen as the search for rational principles of political order which can both justify and limit authority. To the extent that such principles do provide rational limits to political authority they furnish the intellectual underpinnings for constitutional procedures. Although the existence of partisan politics might require a relatively stable constitutional context, constitutional procedures themselves must be largely exempt from political contestation. The chapters of the first section are devoted to exploring this traditional view and its implications for both partisan politics and the political role of the political theorist. Arlene W. Saxonhouse argues that only those political theories that define a political need or function for plurality, and depreciate the ideal of harmonic unity, can support a constitutional framework for partisan politics. Donald S. Lutz maintains that political theorists have both the ability and the obligation to counsel politicians on appropriate constitutional procedures, but to effectively perform this task they must practice a non-partisan form of critical theory. Conversely, Edward Bryan Portis considers theoretical discourse potentially subversive of the doctrinal consensus necessary for constitutional order, and suggests that political theorists are ill suited to assume responsibility for the articulation and propagation of constitutional doctrine.

In the second part, the role of rational deliberation in politics is examined. Although all three authors recognize both the necessity and limitations of rational discourse in the establishment of collective priorities and public policy, they vary significantly in their assessment of the extent to which it can displace partisan political strife. Thomas A. Spragens Jr. points out that there are different modes of political rationality and that they tend to be complementary rather than competing. While few political disputes are completely resolved through rational discourse, still fewer are not in some significant way constrained, ameliorated, or transformed by reasonable debate and accommodation. Adolf G. Gundersen argues that deliberation and partisan politics are in one sense mutually exclusive endeavors, but in another they are mutually dependent; partisans must deliberate and deliberators must conclude and act before consensus is attained. Any realistic conception of deliberative democracy cannot envision the elimination of partisan politics, but it can and must institutionally limit its sphere to the final stages of decision making. Mary G. Dietz does not deny that partisan politics is a rational enterprise, but points out that its end is not to discern truth and its logical imperatives differ therefore from those of political theory. Those who presume that the aim of a rational politics must be justice or rational deliberation itself ignore the real nature of political responsibility and its irredeemably strategic character.

The third and final part considers the extent to which political theory is itself a mode of political action, and the political theorist inevitably partisan. From William E. Connolly's perspective there is no Archimedean point of rationality allowing the theorist to transcend partisanship. Moreover, the failure to admit the contestability of all standpoints undermines the openness essential for democratic responsiveness to new identities and needs challenging prevailing notions of justice. The recognition of the contestability of all conceptions of the public good, including one's own, both legitimizes and fosters an ethic of restrained partisanship. Conversely, Ruth Lessl Shively argues that political theory necessarily attempts to guide political practice, and that it is impossible to study or to engage in politics without assuming that both its practice and study have objective, rational foundations. Those who deny this, especially those who hold that political theory must be a form of partisanship because its disputes cannot be rationally resolved, inevitably contradict themselves because they must make non-partisan claims about the necessity and benefits of partisanship. Finally, John G. Gunnell maintains that both the supposed partisanship of political theory and its supposed ability to guide political practice are not much more than pretentious fantasies. On the one hand, political theory cannot presume to judge politics without alienating itself from politics, which is supposed to be its subject matter. Neither, however, can political theory plausibly claim to be a form of politics. Political theory, and more generally political science, must accept itself for what it is, a second order activity that can neither guide nor be the primary activity which is its *raison d'être*.

NOTES

1. Which is why eighteenth-century liberal philosophers relied upon interests to discipline the passions. See Hirshman, *The Passions and the Interests*, 1977.

2. For critical discussions of the essentially contested concepts thesis, see Grafstein, "A Realist Foundation," 1988; Gray, "On the Contestability," 1977; Mason, *Explaining Political Disagreement*, 1993.

3. "Philosophic truth, when it enters the market-place, changes its nature and becomes opinion, because a shifting not merely from one kind of reasoning to another, but from one way of human existence to another, has taken place" (Arendt 1967, 112).

REFERENCES

Arendt, Hannah. 1967. "Truth and Politics." In *Philosophy, Politics and Society*. Edited by Peter Laslett and W. C. Runciman. 3rd Series. Oxford: Basil Blackwell.

Barber, Benjamin R. 1984. *Strong Democracy: Participatory Politics for a New Age*. Berkeley, CA: University of California Press.

————. 1988. *The Conquest of Politics: Liberal Philosophy in Democratic Times.* Princeton, NJ: Princeton University Press.

Bay, Christian. 1965. "Politics and Pseudopolitics: A Critical Evaluation of Some Behavioral Literature." *American Political Science Review* 59:39–51.

Connolly, William E. 1974. *The Terms of Political Discourse.* Lexington, MA: D. C. Heath and Company.

Crick, Bernard. 1964. *In Defense of Politics.* Baltimore, MD: Penguin Books.

Gallie, W. B. 1962. "Essentially Contested Concepts." In *The Importance of Language.* Edited by Max Black. Englewood Cliffs, NJ: Prentice-Hall.

Grafstein, Robert. 1988. "A Realist Foundation for Essentially Contested Political Concepts." *Western Political Quarterly* 41:9–28.

Gray, John. 1977. "On the Contestability of Social and Political Concepts." *Political Theory* 5:331–48.

Hirschman, Albert O. 1977. *The Passions and the Interests: Political Arguments for Capitalism Before Its Triumph.* Princeton, NJ: Princeton University Press.

Honig, Bonnie. 1993. *Political Theory and the Displacement of Politics.* Ithaca, NY: Cornell University Press.

Mason, Andrew. 1993. *Explaining Political Disagreement.* Cambridge: Cambridge University Press.

Warren, Mark E. 1997. "What Is Political?" Presented at the annual meeting of the Western Political Science Association, Tucson, AZ.

PART I

Political Theory and the Constitutional Foundations of Partisan Politics

CHAPTER 1

Political Theorists on the Legitimacy of Partisan Politics

Arlene W. Saxonhouse

A recent book on local city government by a leading political scientist argues that for the sake of social, economic and political development, partisanship is beneficial (Eldersveld 1995). The party structure ensures the competition necessary for democratic regimes to function and the training necessary for effective political leadership. Partisanship in the city enables the city to meet the needs of its citizens in ways unlikely to occur were parties not part of its political structure. Political theorists, in contrast, are often uncomfortable with partisanship. It assumes conflict rather than harmony; it assumes that debates over policies are decided by power, rhetoric, influence rather than reason; and, by its very name, it assumes that citizens and leaders are motivated by the interests of a part rather than the welfare of the whole, irrespective of a rhetoric that may shade private interest in the language of a common good.

The editors of this volume have challenged us to consider how the political theorist may address the partisanship that lies at the heart of so many of the studies by contemporary political scientists. Have political scientists, accepting partisanship as a core concept for the study of democratic politics, removed themselves from concerns with rationality and/or virtue?[1] Have political theorists, by avoiding considerations of partisanship, in turn removed themselves from politics and the discipline of political science? As political theorists, must we learn to accept partisan politics as inherent in politics and therefore build our theories on it rather than try to transcend it, that is, must we accept differences of interests, understand their legitimacy and not work to destroy those differences? Or, one could ask whether we should even try to address the political world rationally; whether to argue for or even accept partisan politics denies politics any rationality that might assume truth as a goal and the exercise of reason as the mechanism to achieve that goal? In this latter case, a theoretical grounding for partisan politics asked for by our editors would seem to become either a contradiction in terms or a danger.

Underlying all of these adumbrations on the original questions posed by the editors of this volume is the problem of politics as conflict, disagreements among the different groups or individuals of a particular society about what the community as a whole does and what it values. Conflict is assumed and while, on the one hand, that conflict must be structured and tamed lest it lead to a war of all against all, leaving us with a life solitary, nasty, brutish, and short, or it may also, on the other hand find a theoretical justification that makes it the grounding of our political life.

In this essay, I consider how a number of the classic theorists have addressed the theoretical foundations of what we can call "partisan politics." I do this in order to explore what assumptions would be required to accept partisanship as a legitimate component of political life, even if this raises questions concerning the ultimate power of rationality and its place in the polity. To begin, though, let us look at a number of theorists who not only have done the opposite and built their political structures on the *illegitimacy* of partisan politics, but also who have structured their constitutions to ensure the absence of partisanship in the political communities they advocate. By understanding the assumptions and goals that underlie the hostility to partisanship, we can better comprehend the significance of accepting partisanship as a necessary part of the political community and not, by definition, hostile to its structure and goals.

POLITICS BEYOND THE PARTISAN:
HOBBES, PLATO, AND ROUSSEAU

Here I will consider theorists not usually associated with one another, except often as opposites: Thomas Hobbes, Plato—or rather the Socrates of Plato's *Republic*—and Jean-Jacques Rousseau. These authors provide powerful and distinctive views on the need to eliminate partisan conflict on theoretical grounds: Hobbes argues on the grounds that partisan politics is too dangerous for any political regime to endure, the Socrates of Plato's *Republic* argues on the epistemological grounds that there exists a uniform and universal Truth accessible to human intellect above partisan claims, and Rousseau argues on the grounds that partisan politics means the death of freedom in the polity. The editors have asked: "Does the existence of partisan politics, as an alternative to military struggle, depend upon a theoretically grounded set of constitutional rules or priorities?" For the authors considered in this section, who remove the partisan from their political regimes, the question of whether he (or she)[2] is to be restrained by constitutional forms never arises. Instead, partisanship as such is to be excised and a harmonious unity achieved, though each author offers a significantly different route to and justification for that unity. From their differences we can see the variety of concerns that partisanship raises for those theorizing about the political life.

As Hobbes views it, there is clearly a theoretical grounding for partisan politics in our very natures—a grounding we can recognize if we only look into ourselves, following the ancient injunction, *gnothi seauton*, know thyself. As human beings, we all seek our own interests in survival and in the pursuit of power after power. Thus, conflict based on the pursuit of self-interest simply defined as survival is *the* feature of our natural condition, that condition in which we each pursue power over others for our own individual interests. It is the fear of the deadly consequences of such conflict (whether in the experience of civil war such as the English endured in the mid-seventeenth century or of the bandit on the local roads) that so controls Hobbesian man that he constructs a polity and listens to laws that will make conflict and partisanship disappear. This enables him to move from a world that is dominated by the politics of power to one where he need not be concerned with politics or the pursuit of power. Hobbes's epistemology, based on an empiricism that denies the existence of an intersubjective truth or morality, and his psychology that asserts the pursuit of continuing motion and the predominance of pride in the panoply of human passions give theoretical grounding to existence of partisanship, but his goal is to remove it from the life of the well-constructed political community. The divisions are so great, the conflicts (as matters of life and death) so serious, that the foundation of partisan politics cannot simply be contained within a set of rules that moderate. The conflicts must be eliminated by a series of mechanisms that reconstitute the divisive many into one.

The Hobbesian solution to the threat of partisan politics is to unify, to create one body where there had been contesting parts through the innovative theory of authorization and representation. As he describes this process:

> A multitude of men, are made *one* Person, when they are by one man, or one person, represented; so that it be done with the consent of every one of the multitude in particular. For it is the *unity* of the

> representer, not the *unity* of the represented that maketh the Person
> *one*. And it is the representer that bearest the Person, and but one
> Person: And *unity*, cannot otherwise be understood in Multitude (*Le-*
> *viathan*, 104).[3]

This unity is accomplished through the process of authorization
whereby all together give up the right of "governing" themselves to
a defined individual or body of individuals. "This done, the multitude
so united in one person, is called a COMMON-WEALTH" (*Leviathan*, 109).
It is from the creation of such a unity that Hobbes moves forward to
the metaphor of the body (so elegantly portrayed in the frontispiece to
Leviathan) to capture the degree of unity accomplished through authorization. The sovereign as one body is the one "person" who "represents" them all, the parts. Thus, towards the end of the second part of
Leviathan, we find a chapter (24) with the title "Of the Nutrition, and
Procreation of a Commonwealth," and another chapter (29) that, in
recording "those things that Weaken or tend to the DISSOLUTION of a
COMMONWEALTH," discusses the "internal diseases" and *"infirmities"*
which may lead to its "perishing" (210).

The metaphor of the body reaffirms the unity that is created and
the dangers of partisan politics. The body that is thus created rhetorically by Hobbes cannot be at war with itself; in an image we find also
in Aristotle, the foot does not fight with the hand, nor the tendons
with the muscles. The body moves as one. Of course, this is just a
metaphor, but it is supported by the peculiar construction of the leviathan which theoretically not only eliminates any divisions through
authorization and representation, but also eliminates more practically
through the teachings of the laws of nature. The laws, deductions of
a reason directed towards self-preservation, encourage a sociability
that inclines us to yield partisanship for the comforts of living within
a political community. The fifth law of nature in *Leviathan*, for instance, urges "COMPLAISANCE," or *"that every man strive to accommodate*
himselfe to the rest" (*Leviathan*, 95). The laws urge equity in the use of
common property, or a willingness to submit to lot when such divisions of the common good are not possible; they urge abstention from
judgment where partiality might enter. The gentle souls whom these
laws encourage yield to the welfare of the whole rather than pursue
their partisan interests. On this, the security of the Hobbesian state is
grounded.

In a long chapter (22), Hobbes writes of "systems," by which he
understands "any numbers of men joined in one interest, or one business" (146). There are many such systems, regular or irregular, politi-

cal or private, lawful or unlawful. Among these are "factions . . . for government of religion (as of Papists, Protestants, &c.) and of state (as patricians and plebeians of old time in *Rome*, and of aristocraticals and democraticals of old time in *Greece*)" which he now describes as "unjust" and "contrary to the peace and safety of the people, and a taking a sword out of the hand of the sovereign" (154). Hobbes's concern with the danger of factions also leads to his dismissal of democracy as a viable political regime. His opposition to the rule of the many is not based on his arrogance about the questionable intellectual qualities of the many (though that is certainly there, too), but on the expectation that democracy legitimates the multitude of diverse opinions that may surface in a world where not everyone has read and digested *Leviathan*. The sovereign assembly, Hobbes warns, will listen to the counsel of those "versed more in the acquisition of wealth than of knowledge" (120). It is a sovereign divided in itself, not a source of action or stability and thus a threat to security. Partisan politics, though based in the theoretical grounding of human nature and descriptive of our natural state, can only lead to self-destruction for the humanly constructed body of the leviathan.

Socrates in the *Republic* likewise tries to exclude any form of partisanship in his construction of the just city; such conflict can only lead to the victory of and support for ignorance in its battle with philosophy. Partisan conflict occurs because we lack knowledge and because our actions are based on uncertain opinions concerning what is best for us. Such uncertain opinions lead to actions that harm rather than benefit us and a political community that allows for the flourishing of a multitude of opinions about the best life allows for lives not well lived. Politics here is not a compromise between various versions of the good life, but the assurance of the best life.

Perhaps the most vivid portrait of the consequences of partisanship for the political community as Socrates views it appears in Socrates' parable of the boat in Book 6 of the *Republic*. On this boat there are sailors who are eager to control the direction of the boat in the pursuit of their own self-interest; they attempt to seduce the tall, slightly deaf shipowner with mandrake, while the one who knows how to guide the boat, who can read the stars, stands aft staring upward and is considered useless. Likewise, Socrates evokes the image of the meeting of the Athenian assemblies where the orators debate and the young watch those skilled in speaking earn the praise of the city. The eloquence of the orators' speeches draws forth enthusiastic applause that is echoed in the surrounding hills. The brilliance of the speech, not its relationship to any truth, earns renown. Thus, the self-interested speaker, opposing other self-interested speakers, presents the model of the partisan who corrupts the young men who come to listen and who hear the applause enhanced by the echoing hills.

Socrates' worry about the sailors on the figurative boat and the speakers at the actual assembly is not the same as Hobbes's concern with the threat of violent death, but rather the assertion that this partisanship undermines the respect for and particularly the search for a Truth that may exist. The conflicts which he observes around him as partisans pursue political power arise because of ignorance of that truth. Thus, rhetoric able to sway ungrounded opinion controls the decisions of the community without reference to good of the whole or even the individual citizens within that community. Were we to have access to a Truth, and especially to be able to communicate what we had discovered, there would be no conflict, the stargazer would guide the ship, and the many, recognizing the wisdom of the wise, would gladly submit. Xenophon in his *Reminiscences of Socrates* describes conversations in which Socrates asserts that the one who knows is the one who rules—whether it be in sports, or medicine, or farming, or piloting a ship. To ignore the one who knows is to harm oneself, so it is in one's self-interest to obey the one who has the Truth. Xenophon records that when someone used say to Socrates that a tyrant could refuse to obey good counselors, Socrates would reply: "How could he refuse to obey when there is a penalty imposed on the man who disregards good counsel? For if a man disregards good counsel in some matters he will surely make a mistake; and when he makes a mistake he will be punished" (3.9).

A consequence of this view of knowledge, though, is the creation of a community that, like Hobbes's leviathan, strives towards becoming one body where the differences between individual bodies, male and female in particular, but more generally all bodies are elided. Socrates takes the epistemological assertion of a Truth and in translating that to the political world eliminates partisanship and divisions of any sort.[4] The fear of divisions and the assertion of unity leads to a number of truly ludicrous statements, such as when Socrates suggests: "Whichever city is closest to one human being [is it not governed best]? Such that whenever the finger of any of us is harmed, the whole community suffers the pain as a whole while the part is suffering" (*Republic,* 462c–d). To deny the boundaries between people, to eliminate differences whether of gender or otherwise, Socrates must in effect diminish the role of the body, ignore the physical needs of the human being, who is situated in a world of multiplicity, and create a uniformity and unity that in the end is sterile and (so far as I can tell) cannot preserve itself. The elimination of difference and thus any source of conflict from at least the ruling class creates a monstrosity which is against the bodily nature of the human being in its denial of even bodily difference and boundaries among its members. But that elimination is grounded on the rhetorical assertion that the city must direct itself towards the unified Truth that is accessible to the mind of the philosopher, that divisions and disagreements cannot surface in a world of certainty, that difference (not a static sterility) is the greatest threat to the city.

Jean-Jacques Rousseau offers yet another understanding of the dangers of partisanship and the grounds for its illegitimacy in the political world. Underlying Rousseau's proposals in the *Social Contract* is the basic concern with freedom; slavery, though very much the condition of modern man, is never legitimate and partisanship can only be understood as the attempt to enslave another, to impose one's own or a particular group's corporate will on another. We are all slaves now because we are ruled by those whose will is other than our own, because laws have come from the victory of some over the others, victories defined by the good of a part rather than the whole. The enslavement of modern man and woman comes from the divisions in modern society which were not there when men were citizens and attended to the whole and not to the part, when they enjoyed the glory and success of the state as a whole and did not pursue private pleasures and vanities. In his *Discourse on the Arts and Sciences* Rousseau imagines Fabricius, the hero of the Roman wars against Pyrrhus in the third century B.C., speaking to the Romans of a later age: The citizens of his Rome conquered the world, those of a later day became slaves of those they conquered, distracted from citizenship by the vain arts. The unity of early Rome (at least in Rousseau's fantasy of that time), directed toward the common goal of military expansion, yielded over time to the divisions and partisanship that came with attention to the Roman citizens' private lives of wealth and pleasure. The *Discourse on the Arts and Sciences* is a call to recognize how the modern world, enamored of its arts and sciences, has been tainted by the partisanship that these arts and sciences, by their very nature, encourage. By their questioning of political truths, by their focus on the happiness of the individual, they foster divisions that undermine the potential for greatness that, for example, the Romans early achieved—at least in the retelling of their history.

We may say that partisanship, according to Rousseau is, in the words of the editors of this volume, "theoretically grounded"; Rousseau recognizes only too vividly the psychological power of the particular will as against the general will: "Each individual can, as a man, have a private will contrary to or different from the general will he has as a citizen" (*Discourse*, 1.7). It is the strength of this private will (sometimes expanded to the corporate will of a group), focusing on the welfare of a part, that requires that the citizen "be forced to be free." The government, that administrative body which mediates between the citizen as sovereign and the citizen as subject, has a corporate will which, as it strengthens, threatens the survival of the legitimate state: "Just as the private will acts incessantly against the general will, so the government makes a continual effort against sovereignty" (*Discourse*, 3.10). On the other hand, Rousseau recognizes that it is the challenge of politics to overcome the particular will and the divisions among the peoples in a state and to bring about the discovery of and imposition of the general will. As he points out in a footnote: "If there were no different interests, the common interest, which would never encounter any obstacle, would scarcely be felt. Everything would run smoothly by itself and politics would cease to be an art" (*Discourse*, 2.3). Or put another way, politics is the art of overcoming partisanship. Were there no partisanship, Rousseau would not be warning us about the slavery of humankind, presenting us with the means to overcome it and urging us to cast off our chains.

Included, then, in the challenge of the political art is the removal and prevention of partisanship: "In order for the general will to be well expressed, it is therefore important that there be no partial society in the state, and that each citizen give his own opinion" (2.3). In a footnote to precisely this passage, Rousseau reminds us that Machiavelli had likewise worried in his *History of Florence* about how "divisions" through cabal and factions injure a republic; therefore, the quote from Machiavelli continues, "the legislator of a republic, since it is impossible to prevent the existence of dissensions, must at least take care to prevent the growth of factions" [II.3n, 61 (translation of the Italian, 139)]. Rousseau quotes Machiavelli's comment that "divisions" sometimes harm, but he curiously also cites Machiavelli's point that they also sometimes aid a republic. Rousseau comments only on the harm that Machiavelli identifies, not the benefit (in particular, the liberty) that such divisions may give to a republic.

Rousseau's abhorrence of partial communities, of partisan activities, dominates his *Social Contract*. While each individual may have his or her own will, the social contract makes that private person part of a "moral and collective body" and a "common *self*" (*Social Contract*, 1.6). The private will will always be fighting against the general will and Rousseau accepts that as the condition of human nature and of the political state (as Socrates does not), but for Rousseau the danger emerges when "factions, partial associations at the expense of the whole, are formed, [and] the will of each of these associations becomes general with reference to its members and particular with reference to the State. The differences become less numerous and produce a result less general" (*Social Contract*, 2.3).

Hobbes, the Socrates of the *Republic*, and Rousseau are, then, theorists for whom partisanship can have no place in the well-structured polity. For them it brings dreaded conflict and fractures the delicate political unity created through the process of authorization, it allows us to replace the pursuit of Truth with the manipulation of opinion, and it means no less than certain slavery to the will of others. Hobbes transforms the many into a body that moves as one, Rousseau's general will unites the many likewise into a common self, and Socrates destroys differences so that all say "ouch" when the finger of one is cut. For these thinkers no constitutional rules can adequately restrain the deleterious effects that come from allowing divisions or partisanship to emerge in society *nor* do they find value in the divisions themselves. Rousseau's cryptic footnote to Machiavelli with his half quote make us aware that there may be benefits to divisions in society, benefits to which he alludes, but does not develop in his *Social Contract*. Perhaps, he does this precisely because for Machiavelli those divisions lie at the heart of a republic's liberty as captured by the battles between factions comprised of the people and of the nobles. A consideration of the perspective of some other authors gives us insight into what these "aids to a republic" might be.

PARTISAN AS POLITICAL ACTOR:
ARENDT, ARISTOTLE AND MADISON

Sheldon Wolin in an essay entitled "*E Pluribus Unum*: The Representation of Difference and the Reconstruction of Collectivity" (Wolin 1989, 120–136) concludes that in American political thought, at least, *plures* never managed to achieve a theory. He looks to the history of the universalizing constitution as opposed to the *plures* of a theoretical feudalism that expressed the force and virtue of political localism. Wolin sees the issue here, as did the Anti-Federalists over two-hundred years ago, as a problem of place and individual, both of which become subsumed in the *unum* of the newly adopted constitution. While Wolin's analysis of the theoretical-historical conditions of the American founding may leave us without a sense of the justifications for divisions as opposed to the universalizing we find in an author such as Hobbes or even in Wolin's reading of Madison (though I am sure there would be debate here), there are authors who defend the *plures* and give the theoretical grounding for it. Wolin sees in the victory of the universalizing aspects of the constitution the overriding of the original democratic principles of the earlier articles of union and thus the defeat of a democratic grounding of a theory that recognizes divisions and multiplicities rather than the *unum* of an undivided sovereignty. Let us look at a few authors who exalt the multiple over the uniform and see if they give us some basis for a flourishing of democratic partisanship.

Hannah Arendt, who without question romanticizes the life of the ancient polis, nevertheless creates a model of political action that exalts the partisan, or at least the one who articulates well through debate with others' views that address the broad issues of communal life. This is the political actor who may seek glory for himself, but does so through engagement in controversies in the open about public decisions. It is conflict on this level of thought and will that transforms us from the mindless pursuers of the material necessities of our lives to the human beings who can act. Such divisions, then, which come to the fore in the public space, are necessary for our humanity. Partisanship in this sense is not to be avoided, but exercised skillfully with a focus beyond the petty concerns of everyday life to a concern with choices that polities make in their confrontations with barbarism. To enter into this debate is to demonstrate the courage of the human being to lift himself out of the struggle for mere survival. In writing of the world of the ancient polis, she notes:

> Whoever entered the political realm had first to be ready to risk his life, and too great a love for life obstructed freedom, was a sure sign of slavishness. Courage therefore became the political virtue par excellence, and only those men who possessed it could be admitted to a fellowship that was political in content and purpose and thereby transcended the mere togetherness imposed on all—slaves, barbarians, and Greeks alike—through the urgencies of life . . . by overcoming the innate urge of all living creatures for their own survival, it [the good life] was no longer bound to the biological life process (Arendt 1958, 36–37).

In a way that is similar to Wolin's criticism of the universalizing science of the American founders, Arendt criticizes the statistical methods that likewise assimilate individuals to one another and thus have the effect of "leveling out fluctuation." Arguing that "statistical uniformity is by no means a harmless scientific ideal," she worries about the immersion of the self in society and thus the failure to distinguish oneself in the arena of public action. To so distinguish oneself entails the engagement in debate and conflict, to rise out of the biological life processes. "Human plurality," she says, is "the basic condition of both action and speech" (Arendt 1958, 175). And it is this plurality that allows for the initiation of the new, the transformation of what appears to be. Without an attachment to the self, the pursuit of a public identity which earns immortality is lost. "Partisanship" here appears at its highest level, as the basis for our humanity and only a political regime that can accommodate this sort of partisanship is worthy of praise.

Arendt builds her analysis of the *plures* of human interaction on a somewhat idiosyncratic reading of Aristotle. Despite the idiosyncrasies, she does draw attention to the ways in which Aristotle is perhaps the most powerful exponent of a theory of *plures*, of a theory that enables us to conceptualize the partisan as a key player in the construction of the polity and not as the destroyer of a beauteous unity. Aristotle is known for his quotable assertion that by nature man is a political animal. By this he means that man, as the only creature who possesses speech and reason (*logos*) and can thus debate the advantageous and disadvantageous, the just and unjust, must have a realm in which that capacity can be exercised. The polis provides that realm where man exercises his rationality in the process of making choices for the collective community of the polis. Other actions, such as those that go on within the family are usually governed by inclination and lack the generality of the larger community of the polis.

This perspective leads to his comparably famous definition of the citizen as an actor—as one who engages in the offices and the judgments of the city. The citizen is a participant in the communal choices that the city makes. The definitions that Aristotle offers indicate how different his epistemological stance for the city is from Socrates'. If there were the possibility of epistemological certainty, we would be left with the Socratic philosopher king who knows the good and can benefit the polis through the exercise of that knowledge. Indeed, there are parts of Aristotle's *Politics* (e.g., 3.14–17) that suggest that Aristotle may even be encouraging such a political regime and debates among scholars concerning the *pambasileus* (king of all) and his potential role in the city certainly abound.[5] But in his discussions of the political man by nature and in his definitions of the citizen, Aristotle focuses on political knowledge as practical knowledge where the precision characteristic of theoretical knowledge is absent. Instead, we rely on *phronesis* (or judgment) rather than a certain truth. Since political choices are not determined by the scientific precision of the theoretical arts, there will need to be judgments and there will be debate about the adequacy or inadequacy of those judgments. To engage in debates is part of the political process and it derives from the different perspectives that the citizens bring to the assembly.

Aristotle readily recognized the diversity out of which the city is made, the multiplicity of members who will be part of that city, and the interests of the members of those groups (especially of the rich and the poor, but also the farmers, the fishermen, the craftsmen) that divide the city and regularly threaten its survival. He understood that the study of politics is the study of parts always in potential conflict about who should exercise power within the city and who is to be defined as the citizen who actively pursues his (or her) humanity through the exercise of reason in the assembly and the offices of the city. These divisions in society are at the core of political life, and a polity always faces the threat that those divisions can lead to such disruptions that the city undergoes a revolution and dissolves.[6]

The city is divided and therefore its security is tenuous. Even the efforts to provide constitutional safeguards are inadequate protection against the potential conflicts that arise from these necessary divisions. Much of Book 5 of the *Politics* describes the civil wars or revolutions that arise because of the divisions within the city, and much of the earlier Books, especially 3 and 4, are devoted to constructing a polity that tries to balance the partisan interests of the wealthy and the poor so that those tensions between the rich and the needy do not readily lead to factions that destroy rather than sustain the political system.

Here, where Aristotle plays the moderator between factions we see him responding to the question raised by the editors. There are constitutional arrangements that can moderate the conflicts that emerge in any political community. Aristotle is the first theorist who articulates proposals for accommodating conflict rather than excising it, as Socrates, for instance, tries to do in the founding of Callipolis in the *Republic*. Aristotle argues that arrangements like fines for the rich who do not attend the assembly and pay for the poor who do will bring both sectors of the society into the political activities of the community and thus provide a stability. He is not searching here for harmony, but a balancing. "Parts" are part of the political process; the danger is not that they exist and have influence on the direction of the polity as a whole, but that their existence leads to warfare and revolution rather than debate. Instead of trying to eliminate those differences which can become the grounds for partisanship, Aristotle can build the structure of the polity on it. He recognizes the political arena as a realm of conflict[7] and, according to him, it has to incorporate conflict in part because political knowledge is always contingent knowledge and because the active citizen, who Aristotle envisions as fulfilling human nature only when he acts by choice rather than necessity, would otherwise find no home.

Theoretically, partisanship is the key to Aristotle's vision of the city, but he also worries that as it weaves itself into the fabric of the city, it can lead to disruptions that unravel the tentative unity created by the city's *politeia*, constitution or regime. This tension is perhaps most vivid in the chapter (3.11) of the *Politics* where Aristotle explores the claims to rule of the many as opposed to the "best." Here he considers the claims that the many might have, that is, the ways in which a multiplicity of perspectives, talents, interests, can create a whole greater than the unity achieved by the one who is best. The argument is intricate and it can be read as ultimately finding the claims for the rule of the many rather than the best as uncertain (See Saxonhouse 1992, 222–24). Nevertheless, in his attempt to address this problem, Aristotle demonstrates that theoreticians must confront the divisions that comprise any political community and not abstract from those divisions, as Hobbes, Socrates, and Rousseau had tried to do. Aristotle is willing to explore the benefits of division and diverse interests and skills as he imagines the advantages, for example, of the artistic judgments of the many or of a potluck dinner which draws on the skills and interests of many rather than the meal which is "orchestrated" by the expenditure of one individual (1281b2–3).

For Aristotle there are many levels beyond wisdom and riches that divide peoples in a city. There are lifestyles, modes of economic activity, and so forth. Aristotle, as one fascinated by the many, is also fascinated by the construction of the city out of the many. The threat of a many limbed monster always is there in Aristotle's work as is the threat of *stasis* or armed revolution, but Aristotle recognizes that the complexity of the political world demands an acknowledgment of the many, of differing interests, and of the public space of the polity as the arena in which to express those interests. This makes Aristotle a theorist who places the incorporation of the diversity of human interests into the core of his political studies. His goal is never to rise above or eliminate the partisan; rather, it is to explore how best to incorporate him into the political structure so the city benefits rather than falls because of his presence. Thus, in his proposals for the best practical regime, he imagines constitutional mechanisms to draw in participation from those without resources and those with them. He does not try to dampen participation as do the theorists of stability and unity like Socrates and Hobbes, nor to make participation abstract from the private concerns of the citizen, as does Rousseau.

Finally, it is, of course, in the famous *Federalist* 10 that the strongest theoretical case for allowing partisanship to flourish in the polity is made. Despite Sheldon Wolin's criticism of James Madison as expressing "the fear of being overwhelmed by differences" and describing it as "Madison's transformation of difference so that certain forms of it became privileged" (Wolin 1989, 126), Madison does not eliminate the role of factions or difference in the political community, but rather turns to the constitutional structure that accepts and works with the differences that emerge from an epistemological rejection of a Platonic Truth and an acknowledgment of the differences in skill that mark the human race.

Madison agrees that factions built upon these inherent differences and upon the absence of certain truths are a vice and incur the "mortal diseases under which popular governments have everywhere perished." He does not deny that factions lead to "unsteadiness" and to "injustice," to the disregard of the "public good," but maintains that these factions are grounded in human nature and in the limits of human intelligence. "The latent causes of faction are thus sown in the nature of man," Madison asserts and unlike Hobbes, Socrates, or Rousseau, he does not try to root those causes out of man or restructure a state so that they are effaced. The "latent causes," as he calls them, cannot be excised for fear of losing that for which the government is instituted—liberty. Unlike Rousseau, for example, whose response to the powerful pull of the particular will and the consequent threat of slavery is to try to change human nature, Madison asks for no such changes, only the opportunity to mitigate "the effects," to protect against slavery institutionally rather than through the transformation of human psychology.

Whereas Rousseau can turn to civil religion for a unifying dogma (*On the Social Contract* 4.8) or the banning of theaters in Geneva to preserve the unity of the state (*Letter to M. D'Alembert on the Theater*), Madison abhors the creation of states where all have "the same opinions." Whereas the Socrates of the *Republic* can turn to the philosopher kings to rule a unified city, Madison responds that it is "in vain to say that enlightened statesmen will be able to adjust these clashing interests and render them all subservient to the public good." Whereas Hobbes could unify the commonwealth by urging that all acknowledge that to survive they must yield the never ending pursuit of power after power and allow one to represent them, that they themselves must withdraw from political engagement, give up the claims to knowledge of the truth, and enjoy the private life, Madison never assumes that reason in the form of laws of nature could so guide human passions to seek such a peace nor that the requisite withdrawal from public engagement on the part of citizens would ensure the preservation of the liberty or stability at the base of his political system. Thus, institutional structures such as representative bodies and the expansion "of the sphere" will moderate the effects of faction.

For Madison, then, partisan politics clearly has a theoretical grounding—in the very nature of the human being and in what we can claim to know; the question is not, for Madison, the legitimacy or illegitimacy of faction within the political community, but how we adjust the political regime so as to mitigate the harmful consequences of this basic fact of human nature. The other authors considered in this section, in contrast to Madison, see a positive role for differences among humans in the political regime. The perspective that Madison takes with his focus on liberty as the goal rather than human virtue or glory perhaps suggests some of the reasons that partisanship has acquired negative connotations in modern political discourse and for political theorists. For Madison it is an evil, theoretically grounded in who and what we are, ambitious and self-serving, a nature that cannot be erased nor understood as motivation for positive growth.

CONCLUSION

It is Madison who most powerfully still controls the language of the American political landscape and it is Madison who leaves us with the recognition that since men are not angels, we need the countervailing forces of ambition against ambition. Under these conditions, differences are controlled but not employed to aid in a noble endeavor as in Arendt or Aristotle. Madison gives us neither virtue nor a common good—only constitutional mechanisms in the pursuit of the liberty that allows for differences. In this, most modern political scientists appear his heirs, accepting partisanship as a necessary evil because men are not angels, rather than recognizing the potential benefits that might accrue to individuals themselves and to cities from the very clashing of the interests of the individual citizens. Unlike the authors considered in the first section, Madison cannot dismiss the partisan, but unlike the others considered in the second section, neither does he extol him.

We political theorists viewing the contemporary political world tend to view partisanship as a necessary evil.[8] Partisanship is necessary because human nature does not appear susceptible to the sort of transformations that Rousseau romantically envisaged as possible, if only his god-like legislator would appear (*On the Social Contract* 2.7), necessary because we have not had access (yet) to a Platonic Truth, and necessary because we are unwilling to take seriously Hobbes's advice that we must give up rule over ourselves. Arendt and Aristotle teach us that the theoretical grounding of the partisan need not reveal only the inefficacy of reason. For them, the uncertainty of a political Truth does not diminish the potential for human virtue and nobility through partisan engagement in the political world. Currently, the most powerful source for understanding the nature of partisanship in the American political world comes from *Federalist* 10 which sees no virtue in partisanship as such, but only an evil to be controlled, since it cannot be eliminated, through political institutions. The political scientists, who view partisanship as necessary for democratic institutions because of their concern for liberty, might, in turn, benefit from a consideration of how Arendt and Aristotle point to a theoretical support for partisanship that goes beyond the particularities of specific regimes. Both Arendt and Aristotle identify participation in the political regime as the source of our humanity, what raises us above the animals with whom we share proclivities to self-preservation and reproduction. Participation engages the mind, forces us to make judgments, sets us as actors before others, defending and defining our positions, and immerses us, as Arendt argues, in the competition for immortality. The Aristotelian and Arendtian lessons point to the positive role of conflict deriving from partisanship. Madison and his heirs leave us weakly enduring the partisan tamed by constitutional safeguards. It is Arendt and Aristotle who celebrate what partisanship may mean for human dignity.

NOTES

1. Hardly an issue of any major contemporary political science journal fails to include at least one article with "partisanship" in its title.

2. Although the current convention is to include the phrase "he or she" in our writing about politics, it is clear that for the authors under consideration in this section "he" is the appropriate pronoun. My use of the male pronoun here is not to condone the exclusionary language, but only to be faithful to the texts that I am considering.

3. Page numbers refer to Edwin Curely's edition of *Leviathan*. I also follow his punctuation and spelling.

4. For a fuller discussion of how Socrates achieves this translation see Saxonhouse, *Fear of Diversity*, 1992: chap. 6.

5. For an argument that Aristotle is not serious in his proposals for kingship, see Nichols, *Citizens and Statesmen*, 1992: 73–81.

6. For a fuller discussion of Aristotle's treatment of divisions within the city see Saxonhouse, *Fear Diversity*, 1992: chap. 9.

7. On the importance of recognizing Aristotle's acknowledgment that politics is the engagement of citizens in conflict see Yack, "Community and Conflict," 1985.

8. I have in this discussion tended to conflate the individual and the group. This may not be legitimate, but what is important about the question under consideration is whether communities can accept the existence of differences among their citizens, whether or not those differences are aggregated. The partisan as individual or as part of a faction forces the polity to address difference. This is the issue that the authors discussed above help us to address.

REFERENCES

Arendt, Hannah. 1958. *The Human Condition*. Chicago, IL: University of Chicago Press.

Eldersveld, Samuel. 1995. *Party Conflict and Community Development: Postwar Politics in Ann Arbor*. Ann Arbor, MI: University of Michigan Press.

Hobbes, Thomas. 1994. *Leviathan*. Edited by Edwin Curely. Indianapolis, IN: Hackett Publishing Company, Inc.

Nichols, Mary. 1992. *Citizens and Statesmen: A Study of Aristotle's Politics*. Savage, MD: Rowman and Littlefield.

Rousseau, Jean-Jacques. 1978. *On the Social Contract*. Edited by Roger Masters. Translated by Judith R. Masters. New York, NY: St. Martin's Press.

Saxonhouse, Arlene. 1992. *Fear of Diversity: The Birth of Political Science in Ancient Greek Thought*. Chicago, IL: University of Chicago Press.

Wolin, Sheldon. 1989. "*E Pluribus Unum*: The Representation of Difference and the Reconstruction of Collectivity." In *The Presence of the Past: Essays on the State and the Constitution*. Edited by Sheldon Wolin. Baltimore, MD: Johns Hopkins University Press.

Yack, Barnard. 1985. "Community and Conflict in Aristotle's Political Philosophy." *Review of Politics* 47:92–112.

CHAPTER 2

Political Theory and Constitutional Construction

Donald S. Lutz

INTRODUCTION

Those who engage in political theory have a paradoxical relationship with those who engage in practical politics. On the one hand political theory, if it is to be successful, must rise above partisanship. On the other hand, since from its birth political theory has aimed at marrying justice with the exercise of power, it must be politically engaged and in some way speak to those in power. Teaching future leaders and citizens in the classroom is one non-trivial means of approaching the paradox, but it is too indirect to constitute the kind of genuine conversation that is the focus of this volume. The position argued here is that the most direct and effective way for political theorists, qua theorists, to have a meaningful dialogue with politicians is to focus on questions of constitutional construction. Although there are many factors that inhibit the dialogue in general, and constitutional discussions in particular, the most important, it will be argued, are those that disincline and disable theorists from participating in a dialogue. The most decisive of these factors is the impoverished understanding political theorists have of their own enterprise. To meaningfully engage in constitutional dialogue we have to do more than articulate and justify political ideals; we must also seriously address the problems of approximating these ideals generally and in particular contexts. As we will see, this requires that we return to a more robust Aristotelian view of political theory, and that we rescue the notion of critical theory from those who practice it as a form of partisanship.

What reasons do politicians have to engage us in constitutional dialogue? As it turns out they wish to hear what we have to say, especially if we have prepared ourselves to speak with them, because they need answers to recurring questions of institutional design and operation which they readily admit they are not prepared to address. They seek our advice because questions of institutional design, or constitutionalism, are never really resolved once and for all. Moreover, such questions almost always raise fears of unintended consequences, and relative partisan advantage is rarely easy to see and therefore an uncertain guide. Since partisanship is inevitably diminished when the stakes are obscure, and when all feel as threatened by the unknown as by each other, most politicians are ready to search for a secure, common ground that can be addressed by people knowledgeable about politics but outside of the partisan struggle. Obviously the same condition occurs with respect to some policy issues, and when it does a theoretically conscious political science can expect to play a meaningful role. Yet the fear of unintended consequences is strongest when it comes to the "rules of the game," and on these matters questions of basic political ideals are more likely to be considered of direct relevance.

Let me illustrate both the interest of political actors and the nature of the problem with a few examples. For the better part of two decades I have repeatedly had the humbling experience of "advising" people engaged in the construction or reconstruction of their constitutions in countries on three continents. Several years ago an American professor whose name is familiar to every political theorist, and who teaches at a law school, which we regard as one of the two or three best in the country, addressed an assemblage of Czech and Slovak politicians engaged in writing a new national constitution. He argued that there was no particular reason to "privilege" liberal values in a constitution, and wondered aloud if there was any need to even have a written constitution since such documents tended to be "straightjackets" that got in the way of change. He then suggested a specific set of rights as defining constitutionalism in its best form, waving aside any questions of institutional design, even though these rights were merely "constructs" and "had no real truth value." The Czechs and Slovaks looked at him first in amazement, then in anger. This law professor, oblivious to his reception, then proceeded to Hungary to deliver the same advice under official State Department auspices.[1]

On another occasion a group of Europeans, working on adjusting several national constitutions to the emerging constitution of the European Union, organized a conference on Federalism. The readings, at their insistence, included papers written by Federalists and Antifederalists during the ratification of the U.S. Constitution. Two American political scientists argued vociferously that these papers were "irrelevant" and "misguided," and left it to the Canadian and British theorists present to argue for their critical, continued relevance. The irony that representatives from the two nations peopled by those who were on the losing side of the American Revolution argued so strongly for the relevance of American post-revolutionary documents was compounded by the surprising lack of familiarity with *The Federalist* on the part of the two Americans who were obviously uninterested in any form of federal structure on ideological grounds. The partisanship of the Americans was in stark contrast with the theoretical orientation of the others.

Finally, the chief justice of the Brazilian Supreme Court, accompanied by another member of the Court, toured the United States a few years ago asking academics at various major institutions how the Brazilian Supreme Court could go about interpreting and implementing the articles in the Brazilian Constitution that provide for Federalism and for judicial review. Toward the end of his trip, he confided that American academics seemed puzzled that he should care about Federalism as well as at a loss when it came to suggesting what was needed to make the judicial review actually work. Since he held a Ph.D. in political science and had studied the political philosophers from Aristotle to Constance who argue for constitutionalism, he was especially distressed by the general inability or unwillingness of American political scientists to provide practical advice on how to make constitutions function or to take constitutionalism seriously.

We can draw any number of conclusions from these examples, but the clearest one is that the discussion between academics and politicians is not prospering. Any number of reasons suggest themselves. Many political theorists have an anti-politics temperament, resulting from a lifetime spent contemplating the ideal compared to which all politics look corrupt and inadequate. Politicians have come to distrust the tendency for political theorists to favor global political engineering divorced from reality, and to sometimes produce theories that, when followed, become ideologies for totalitarianism if not elitist authoritarianism. Political scientists engaged in the empirical study of actual systems too often focus on matters that do not provide useful results for the design and improved operation of political systems. Politicians lack the time and incentive to seek advice from those not directly involved in their day-to-day travails. Political theorists too often come across as crabby critics bent on establishing their moral superiority. All of these may be true, and we can think of other reasons as well, but those of us serious about the constitutional project, who are correctly or incorrectly swept up into these discussions, have to report from the trenches of constitutional design that political theorists do have something useful to contribute, but that what we have to contribute is distressingly limited by a tendency for intellectuals to disparage not only politics and political actors, but also to dismiss the entire project of constitutionalism. The question thus becomes why we should want such a dialogue—why it is even needed.

The position argued here is that to the extent such a discussion between political theorists and politicians does not take place we damage the prospects for marrying justice with power. Since the hope of uniting justice with power was the reason for creating political philosophy in the first place, political theorists need to pursue the dialogue as part of what justifies their intellectual project. Politics is the realm of power. More specifically it is the realm where force and violence are replaced by debates and discussion about how to implement power. Without the meaningful injection of considerations of justice, politics tends to become discourse by the most powerful about how to implement their preferred regime. Although constitutionalism tends to be disparaged by contemporary political science, a constitution is the very place where justice and power are married.

Aristotle first taught us that a constitution must be matched to the realities of the political system—the character, hopes, fears, needs and environment of the people—which requires that constitutionalism be addressed by men and women practiced in the art of the possible.[2] Aristotle also taught us that a constitution (the *politeia,* or plan for a way of life) should address the improvement of people toward the best life possible, which requires that constitutionalism be addressed by political theorists who can hold out a vision of justice and the means for advancing toward it. The conversation between politician and political theorist stands at the center of their respective callings, and a constitution, even though it reflects only a part of the reality of a political system, has a special status in this central conversation.

Although the focus of this chapter is on a direct conversation between theorist and politician, there is an important, indirect aspect of the conversation that should not be overlooked—classroom teaching. Too often the conversation between politician and political theorist is described in terms of a direct one between philosophers and those holding power. Overlooked is the central need to educate as many young people as possible. Since it is difficult to predict who will, in fact, hold power, and because the various peoples who take seriously the marriage of justice with power are overwhelmingly committed to a non-elitist, broad involvement of the population, we should not overlook or minimize our importance as teachers of the many. Political leaders drawn from a people who do not understand what is at stake are neither inclined nor equipped to join the conversation. As we teach, we converse with future leaders. Perhaps not everyone who teaches political theory has had the same experience, but of the more than eight thousand students I have taught, I know of at least forty-nine who later held a major elective office, and at least eighty more who have become important political activists. This comes down to about five students per teaching year, and I could not have predicted which five it would be. The indeterminate future of any given student is one argument against directing our efforts at civic education toward the few, best students. A constitutional perspective suggests not only that those in power rely upon support and direction from a broad segment of the public, but also that reliance upon the successful civic education of the elite is not very effective, by itself for marrying justice with power in the long run.

One sometimes hears the argument that the truth about justice and the realities of power can be entrusted to only the few, since the many will not know how to handle this knowledge. The best that political theorists can expect to do is educate the few capable of using the knowledge and hope they end up as the rulers. The difficulty with such a position is not only the implicit elitism it embodies, but the more serious one that history shows how infrequently the "better sort" manage to gain power; or if they do, the strong tendency for them to be corrupted by power and forget their lessons. Political systems that are truly constitutional, that attempt to marry justice with power and not simply use a constitution as window dressing, tend overwhelmingly to include the broader population in collective decision making. This empirical reality may or may not negate the elitism assumption of such a position, but at the very least it points to one critical function for political theorists—to educate the many. In the end, even though this volume focuses on the conversation between theorist and politician, our proper audience includes students, politicians, and the citizens that comprise the polity Our main focus, however, is on the direct conversation between theorist and politician, and since a major point in the position argued here is that the most important factor impeding the conversation is the impoverished understanding of political theory from which we tend to work, it is to the recovery of a more robust understanding that we now turn.

THE RECONSTRUCTION OF POLITICAL THEORY

If we are to engage in a fruitful discussion with politicians, it is necessary to disentangle several types of activity covered by the term "political theory," since each activity rests upon a somewhat different sense of rationality, and each opens up to a conversation with politicians conditioned by a different rhetorical stance and a different set of limits. The distinctions about to be drawn are largely analytic ones since political theory includes them all. However, these different activities are distinguishable, and the nuanced explanation of what we are actually doing when we engage in political theory is helpful for understanding the variety of ways in which political theory can relate to political discourse. Part of the problem, it turns out, is not that politics and political theory pursue a different logic, but that political theory does not utilize a single logic.

The use of pure logic, of unbounded rationality, is often viewed as the source of political theory's pathology vis-à-vis the polis. Failure to ground logic—in the limits imposed by human nature, in the inevitable "friction" of institutional operation, and in the hopes, fears, and natural inclinations of real people—is usually termed rationalism. Rationalism is viewed as resulting in the death of political philosophers who "go public," or the radicalization of politics by ideologies that destroy politics, and therefore for the inability of political theorists and politicians to have useful and meaningful discourse. The image is one of theorists who choose to live rather than die, and who therefore limit themselves to the role of gadfly, sniping obliquely from a distance at politicians who resolutely ignore them, when not cutting university budgets, while engaging in corrupt, nefarious politics. If this sounds like a caricature it may be because the position has never been more successfully and effectively stated than in the Sunday comics. The vision is, in the end, comic, if not comedic.

To lay all of my cards on the table, I am one of those who view Plato's *Republic* as deeply ironic, as a cautionary tale against the dangers of fanaticism when engaging in political philosophy, while at the same time showing us how to proceed philosophically.[3] That is, I see Plato as laying out what an ideal political system would require, and, by showing us the nature of the inhuman decisions it would require us to make, indicating the limits to a merely rationalist approach to politics. Plato's method of philosophizing can indeed be dangerous in the hands of the less than careful reader, for failure to understand the implications of carefully wrought irony may lead the unwary to take the conclusions too literally and pursue the fanatical ends that are being rejected, or else to destroy the philosopher who has created a theoretical monstrosity. Plato's kind of political philosophy, although exemplary of philosophy at its deepest level, is indeed best done in private, or at least outside of explicitly political discourse. Plato's later work, *The Laws*, and then Aristotle's *Ethics/Politics*, become the exemplars for how to engage in political theorizing in public. It is no accident, I think, that constitutionalism begins with these works.

Aristotle notes in the *Politics* that political theory simultaneously proceeds at three levels—discourse about the ideal, about the best possible in the real world, and about existing political systems.[4] Put another way, comprehensive political theory must ask several different kinds of questions that are linked, yet distinguishable. In order to understand the interlocking set of questions that political theory can ask, imagine a continuum stretching from left to right. At the end, to the right, is an ideal form of government, a perfectly wrought construct produced by the imagination. At the other end is the perfect dystopia, the most perfectly wretched system that the human imagination can produce. Stretching between these two extremes is an infinite set of possibilities, merging into one another, that describe the logical possibilities created by the characteristics defining the end points. For example, a political system defined primarily by equality would have a perfectly inegalitarian system described at the other end, and the possible states of being between them would vary primarily in the extent to which they embodied equality. An ideal defined primarily by liberty would create a different set of possibilities between the extremes. Of course, visions of the ideal often are inevitably more complex than these single-value examples indicate, but it is also true that in order to imagine an ideal state of affairs a kind of simplification is almost always required since normal states of affairs invariably present themselves to human consciousness as complicated, opaque, and to a significant extent indeterminate.

A non-ironic reading of Plato's *Republic* leads one to conclude that the creation of these visions of the ideal characterizes political philosophy. This is not the case. Any person can generate a vision of the ideal. One job of political philosophy is to ask the question "Is this ideal worth pursuing?" Before the question can be pursued, however, the ideal state of affairs must be clarified, especially with respect to conceptual precision and the logical relationship between the propositions that describe the ideal. This pre-theoretical analysis raises the vision of the ideal from the mundane to a level where true philosophical analysis, and the careful comparison with existing systems can proceed fruitfully. The process of pre-theoretical analysis, probably because it works on clarifying ideas that most capture the human imagination, too often looks to some like the entire enterprise of political philosophy.[5] However, the value of Jean-Jacques Rousseau's concept of the General Will, for example, lies not in its formal logical implications, nor in its compelling hold on the imagination, but on the power and clarity it lends to an analysis and comparison of actual political systems. Among other things it allows him to show that anyone who wishes to pursue a state of affairs closer to that summed up in the concept of the General Will must successfully develop a civil religion. To the extent politicians believe theorists who tell them that pre-theoretical clarification of language describing an ideal is the essence and sum total of political philosophy, to that extent they will properly conclude that political philosophers have little to tell them, since politics is the realm of the possible not the realm of logical clarity.

However, once the ideal is clarified, the political philosopher will begin to articulate and assess the reasons why we might want to pursue such an ideal. At this point, analysis leaves the realm of pure logic and enters the realm of the logic of human longing, aspiration, and anxiety. The analysis is now limited by the interior parameters of the human heart (more properly the human psyche) to which the theorist must appeal. Unlike the clarification stage where anything that is logical is possible, there are now definite limits on where logic can take us. Appeals to self-destruction, less happiness rather than more, psychic isolation, enslavement, loss of identity, a preference for the lives of mollusks over that of humans, to name just a few possibilities, are doomed to failure. The theorist cannot appeal to such values if she or he is to attract an audience of politicians. Much political theory involves the careful, competitive analysis of what a given ideal state of affairs entails, and as Plato shows in his dialogues the discussion between the philosopher and the politician will quickly terminate if he or she cannot convincingly demonstrate the connection between the political ideal being developed and natural human passions. In this way, the politician can be educated by the possibilities that the political theorist can articulate, just as the political theorist can be educated by the relative success the normative analysis has in "setting the hook" of interest among nonpolitical theorists. This realm of discourse, dominated by the logic of humanly worthwhile goals, requires that the theorist carefully observe the responses of others in order not to be seduced by what is merely logical as opposed to what is humanly rational. Moral discourse conditioned by the ideal, if it is to be successful, requires the political theorist to be fearless in pursuing normative logic, but it also requires the theorist to have enough humility to remember that, if a non-theorist cannot be led toward an ideal, the fault may well lie in the theory, not in the moral vision of the non-theorist.

The second question a political theorist needs to ask is the extent to which an ideal can be approximated in the world of ordinary humans. The successful pursuit of this level of discourse requires what Aristotle termed *phronesis*, or practical wisdom. At this level of discourse the politician may have more to say to the theorist than vice versa. It is not so much a matter of accepting a politician's word that something is impractical, as much as it is of coming to understand the nature of the limits imposed by the world of politics as perceived by the politician. In the past, political theorists have relied on a careful study of political history to develop *phronesis*, and this is not a bad habit to preserve; but, because the limits faced by a particular political system will vary by time and location, experience in that particular setting is an important part of the platform on which political theory is erected, and politicians have a lot to say about the particularities of a given setting on the basis of their experience. Again, this does not amount to simply accepting a politician's word, or else things will tend to remain the same. Instead it requires a careful attention to the deeper structure of what political experience tells us. The role of the political theorist is similar to that of a therapist who says to the politician the equivalent of, "What I hear you saying is . . . " Theoretical analysis here consists in identifying and articulating the underlying patterns and the deeper problems contained in the words of politicians. What a political theorist has to say to a politician at this level amounts to an analysis of apparently contradictory and opaque experience. At this level, the discourse is limited not so much by the imperatives of the human psyche but by the logic of limits and conflicting values and goals. The conversation is still informed by the ideal, and motivated by a vision of the best, but it is now proceeding under the assumption that the ideal can only be approximated in politics, not achieved; as well as the assumption that the best possible is identifiable through an analysis of limits, at least in principle.

The next question to be asked is, "What are the facts of the situation we face?" Another way of putting the question is, "Given the continuum we have thus far described, where is this actual political system situated with respect to the best possible regime?" Aristotle collected well over a hundred "constitutions," and used these descriptions of actual regimes as the empirical grounding for his analysis. Political theorists since Machiavelli often include in their analyses an empirical, descriptive component. However, contemporary political science has often joined politicians in attacking the perceived lack of a systematic empirical component to political theory. Sometimes these political scientists speak as if the only theoretical questions worth asking have to do with empirical relationships. The attack on the enterprise of political philosophy in general was sometimes met with a counter-attack by political theorists on the poverty of empirical science. This well-remembered dispute, at least in its more extreme form, seems now to be largely history. Empirical theory is part of the total project, and advances in this component have enhanced our concern for the other questions.

We now understand that empirical description is always the first step in the discovery of empirical regularities. As such regularities are uncovered they hold out the possibility of answering at a more advanced level the next question posed by political theory: "How do we arrange things so that we can move closer to the ideal." That is, it makes little sense to seek empirical knowledge if it is not to be used. If it is to be used, how is it to be used—that is, toward what ends? If some institutional behavior can be reduced to a set of regression equations that describe empirical tendencies, and this allows us to manipulate institutional variables so as to enhance certain outcomes, which outcomes do we choose to enhance? The so-called new institutionalism is essentially predicated on the marriage of empirical and theoretical approaches that are nested in the broader philosophical framework just outlined. Empirical political theory is limited by the logic of empirical evidence, as well as by the logic of effectiveness (an ends/means logic), but it is ultimately justified by the logic of human hopes and aspirations as well as by the logic of the possible. If it were not, then an empirical political science focused on the preservation of the status quo, the manipulation of the masses for the benefit of the few, or the pursuit of humanly degrading states of affairs might well be our legacy.

In recent years we have witnessed an increasingly loud set of voices that has leveled just this charge against empirical political science, from the right as well as the left. I would like to term this disparate set of thinkers as engaging in "critical theory." Although the term "critical theory" has been used in a narrow sense to describe those associated with or intellectually descended from the Frankfurt School, I use it here in a broader linguistic and philosophical sense to identify those who have engaged in either sustained critiques of modern political and social problems or in pointed, determined, and responsible critiques of the extent to which social and political reality can be studied empirically. I would include among responsible critical theorists, for example, Hannah Arendt, Michael Oakshott, Jürgen Habermas, Leo Strauss, Max Horkheimer, and Sheldon Wolin. I have listed these exemplary scholars, and the list is not anywhere complete, to illustrate that the praise and cautions to follow are not aimed at any particular school, ideology, or theoretical orientation within the very diverse group described as engaging in critical theory. But not everyone working in the shadow of one or more of these thinkers has been free of the intellectual "pathologies" to be outlined below. Any version of critical theory can degenerate into a pathology. Still, one must remember that the *absence* of critical theory in the overall project of political inquiry is a fundamental problem addressed in this chapter.

To the extent that critical theorists have attacked empiricism per se, to that extent it is an attack on all of political theory, since the questions asked by empirical political science are an important and necessary part of the entire enterprise. To the extent critical political theory has attacked a free-floating empiricism isolated from the broader enterprise, it has sought to reintegrate the enterprise. Critical political theory works from the logic of deficiency. It attacks the actual state of affairs in the name of human aspiration for that which is in some sense better. To denounce something as deficient is to compare that reality with an ideal, or else there is no grounding to the critique. In this way, critical theory returns us to the total logic of the continuum. A critical stance is natural for political theory, and expresses the inevitable conflict between political theory and politics as practiced. It is a healthy, necessary antidote to politics as usual inside the cave, and practiced well serves as a means of motivating politicians to enter into a discussion with political theorists. Practiced badly, critical theory is only the contemporary manifestation of the age-old pathology to seek the creation of the ideal in an actual world that will not bear the weight of the enterprise without seriously harming the human aspirations that political theory exists to serve. This is the kind of political theory that gets political theorists banished, killed, or reduced to ineffectual sniping. Practiced badly, critical theory also needlessly undermines respect for all institutions, including those that are in fact basically healthy and helpful. The hallmark of the latter pathology is the sophistic stance that there are no discoverable truths transcending culture and ideology upon which we can rest institutional design. This stance, ostensibly in the service of the downtrodden and marginalized, leaves us with no arguments with which to contest the assaults of power and the powerful, and in the long run quietly justifies the rule of the stronger and demoralizes those who would oppose and tame raw power with enduring principles of justice, now reduced to mere expressions of competing ideologies.

To the extent politicians do listen to political theorists who fail to practice the entire project of political philosophy, to that extent we stand in danger of contributing to one of the natural pathologies inherent in raw politics. Failure to inform politics with discourse about ideals enhances the pathology of pursuing mere power indifferent to justice. At best politics remains reactive and without purpose, and at worst it pursues only the ends imposed by the most powerful among us. Authoritarianism is the child of this pathology. Failure to inform politics with discourse about the best possible contributes to the pathology of fanaticism by leaving politics open to the pursuit of fanatical ends, of which communism and fascism are the most recent exemplars. Totalitarianism is the child of this pathology. Failure to address the current empirical realities or the means of improving on them contributes to the pathology of political alienation. Not knowing where we are at the moment, and therefore what needs improvement, or not knowing what effective means are available for achieving such improvement, leads to policies and institutions that are increasingly viewed as irrelevant to human needs and aspirations. The child of this pathology is political instability. Critical theory provides the impetus to use empirical analysis for improving institutions and for moving us from the status quo, but practiced badly it merely undercuts belief in any institutions and contributes to the political alienation that enhances instability. Ironically, critical theory in this guise also contributes to the loss of linkage between ends and means, which undermines the hope for movement toward any ideal, and thereby aids those who would provide at least stability whether justice is part of the result or not. On the other hand, a political theory that serves the integrated questions just outlined is comprehensible to politicians, if not always welcomed by them, and leaves open the possibility that political theorists may contribute to the marriage of justice with power by providing arguments, grounded in human aspiration as well as in empirically supported analysis and philosophically sound logic, that can be used by constitutionally oriented political actors to address the needs and aspirations of the poorer, less powerful, more marginal parts of society as well as the rest of society. Either we accept the possibility of such politicians coming to the fore, and the efficacy of constitutional politics, or abandon the project of political theory entirely and resign ourselves, at best, to a mutual yet sterile stance of rhetorical moral superiority.

WILL THEY LISTEN?: PROSPECTS FOR THE CONVERSATION

The way into the conversation may not always be straightforward. One natural opening is that politicians are quite willing to listen to suggestions from political scientists concerning the construction of public policy. Public policy is always predicated on the assumption that the current state of affairs can be improved upon in some manner. When working on problems in public policy political scientists, at least implicitly, must work from some normative stance that places potential policies in the context of human aspirations and the possibility of moving closer to some state of affairs defined by the best possible. It is no accident, in my opinion, that as the public policy paradigm has moved closer to the center of the discipline, political theory has lost its temporary status as a pariah in political science. Many politicians may, in fact, be focused on improving their competitive political status rather than on pursuing the good, but public policy discourse between politicians and political scientists is a natural and effective means of drawing politicians into a broader framework of normative and theoretical concerns. The effect would be greatly enhanced if public policy analysis operated more explicitly in an environment where institutional analysis of the sort exemplified by the "new institutionalism" where the empirical tendencies of institutions were better understood.

Another avenue for drawing politicians into such a discussion centers around the design of institutions. A political institution is defined by a set of rules describing some process of decision-making that is agreed to and followed by the relevant actors. An integrated set of political institutions, whether defined in a written document or simply followed without such formal guidance, is the definition of a constitution. A written constitution, as it is often pointed out, does not describe all of the important political processes, but it does end up confining and conditioning even those political processes that are not directly addressed in the constitution.[6] Politicians are more than willing to listen to political scientists about matters of institutional design, and the special virtue of constitutional discourse is that it raises the discussion to the level where the entire set of questions addressed by political theory end up being considered.

The recent proposal for term limits is a case in point. Without considering here the merit of the idea, this seemingly simple proposal for one institutional change has led to a discussion of its possible effects on the entire interlocking set of institutions defined by the Constitution. Before they know what they are doing, politicians and political scientists alike find themselves discussing propositions about the interlocking effects of different institutions, the probable empirical effects of the proposed change on one political variable or another, the probable direction in which the political system will be moved, and the desirability of moving in that direction. It is precisely in constitutional discourse that the entire set of questions asked by political theory are addressed, and this for the simple reason that constitutions encode answers to all of these questions. Preambles and bills of rights lay out the ideals which animate the design of the institutions. The institutions themselves rest on implicit empirical propositions to the effect that if we follow such and such a set of rules the kind of behavior that will result will have certain predictable characteristics, not in the sense of specific outcomes but in the sense of predictable tendencies. The proposed change rests on an assumption of moving us toward the ideal, as well as on a critique of the current state of affairs that finds it deficient with respect to these ideals.

The surprising fact is not that politicians tend to ransack anything that political scientists might have said about a proposed constitutional change. The surprising fact is how little we have to tell them. Nor is this a minor problem. If we cannot tell them about the probable tendencies of a given institutional design, which is one of the easier tasks we face, why do we have any confidence that what we have to tell them about more ephemeral matters, such as the probable outcome of a particular election, is grounded any more securely? Let me put the matter a little more directly by proposing that our *ability* as political scientists to speak to constitutional/institutional matters is the very litmus test of our ability to speak usefully to politicians, and our *willingness* to speak of constitutional/institutional matters is the litmus test of our willingness to speak to politicians at all. Those political scientists unable and unwilling to engage in such discourse have opted out entirely from any possible discourse with elected political actors, political activists, and interested citizens. There is nothing inherently wrong with opting out of the direct conversation, but it is futile to pretend that discourse with political actors could proceed in splendid isolation from constitutional/institutional matters. Therefore, any political scientist interested in such discourse will need to ask herself/himself if their research is aimed at contributing to an understanding of constitutional/institutional possibilities, probabilities, and actualities. In sum, if the discourse between political theorists and political actors is not going well, we need to examine our contribution to the problem that may lie in our own unwillingness and/or inability to address matters of mutual concern.

Perhaps one way of conceptualizing the problem is to use the physical sciences as a comparative enterprise. Much of what we do in contemporary political science looks like an attempt to imitate theoretical physics and basic scientific research—to seek new, fundamental knowledge through research that is unfettered with respect to agenda or immediate utility. If this scientific model is worth anything at all, then it is instructive to remember that without applied research designed to link fundamental knowledge with real-world problems we would still be lighting our streets with gas lamps, or perhaps stumbling about in a world of shadows. That is, the possible application of knowledge has been the strongest spur to theoretical knowledge. For those who reject such a model altogether, I need to say that I am not enamored of, nor are political actors interested in, discourse about how many rational voters can dance on the head of an ideal, or discourse about how all political institutions are merely and inevitably the instruments of oppression of those in power. In these latter instances, the issue is not one of merely methodological irrelevance but moral irrelevance. Our problem is not as simple as choosing between science and morality, but rather the more stark one of choosing between trying to integrate the entire enterprise of political theory or not trying at all.

Constitutionalism, like the rule of law upon which it is built, requires some level of consensus among the people, elite and common, who would use these constructs as more than window dressing. At the beginning, the level of consensus may be low in terms of breadth or weak in terms of depth, but without a certain level of consensus we can have neither political institutions nor constitutional principles to guide these institutions. Consensus cannot be produced constitutionally, but must result from politics—literally the decision to replace force and violence with some *modus vivendi* of discourse about how to proceed collectively. Such discourse in turn requires guiding principles and rules that will serve to undergird and safeguard the continued use of speech and persuasion rather than force and violence. The institutional/constitutional construct, if it is successful over time, will enhance consensus, but along with an increased depth in consensus may come an enhanced breadth in the range of problems and issues that are subject to such disciplined speech. That is, success in some vital areas of political conflict is likely to lead to the desire to bring all conflict under these successful, accepted rules. The temptation is to increasingly constitutionalize political conflict, and the danger here is one of overconstitutionalizing politics. Part of the institutional/constitutional perspective is an emphasis on *phronesis*, or practical wisdom.

There is wisdom in knowing the limits of the constitutionalism. In the face of the natural tendency to overemphasize the importance and beneficial consequences of what we happen to do, humility requires that we admit limits to what political theory can accomplish. Too much constitutionalism, and too much focus on only institutions, is as much a pathology as too little.

Overconstitutionalizing manifests itself in a tendency toward including all policy matters in the constitution in an attempt to rationalize and settle these conflicts. Because change is inevitable, and change brings the need to alter public policy, overconstitutionalizing politics leads to the constitution becoming a tightening straightjacket of rules that must be constantly addressed, which in turn makes the constitution, and the basic rules of political discourse it encodes, increasingly the source of conflict. The constitution, and constitutionalism itself, becomes increasingly controversial, and is progressively discredited. Political instability and public demoralization follow in the wake of this tendency. The decline of constitutionalism benefits only the powerful.

As political theorists we need to ask ourselves if we are helping to effectively encode justice, or undercutting the "marriage" which we take so much for granted that we heedlessly ignore its importance and contribute to its decline. To the extent we function as a cognitive elite of mandarins who refuse to engage in the discussion with political actors, and give aid to those among them who might preserve the marriage, to that extent we must plead guilty. In the end, if we do not face the possibility of guilt, the day of reckoning will judge us guilty anyway, and political theory will, in fact, be, despite all our protestations to the contrary, not dead, but sublimely irrelevant to the people it was designed to serve.

NOTES

1. Performances such as these led Vaclav Havel to write "The Responsibility of Intellectuals," criticizing the "betrayal of the intellectual." This essay was first delivered as a speech in Wellington, New Zealand on March 31, 1995; and then reproduced in *The New York Review of Books*, 22 June 1995.

2. To the extent constitutions need to address common, unchanging human hopes, fears, and needs—what is usually termed human nature—to that extent these constitutions will converge toward a set of institutions that address these commonalities. To the extent constitutions need to address the particularities of a people and their environment, they will tend to contain divergent, even unique institutions.

3. By "fanaticism" I mean the serious attempt to impose a vision of an ideal or perfect political system on actual political systems.

4. The distinction between the three levels of analysis informs all of Aristotle's *Politics*, but he explicitly discuses these differing levels in Book IV, chap. 1.

5. I could cite a number of exemplary theorists, but as a group they tend to be found practicing what used to be known as "analytic philosophy." The hallmark of these thinkers is the statement: "The job of philosophy (and therefore of political philosophy) is to clear up confusion. Since confusion usually is linguistically rooted, philosophy comes down to clarifying the meaning and usage of words." Typically, once word meaning and usage is cleared up, inferences are logically straightforward and not subject to further theoretical investigation. Although the analytic and ordinary language approaches are part of what we must do in the total project of political theory, the cramped style of analysis that tends to "privilege" formal logic often impoverishes political thought. This tendency is also present in certain offshoots of analytic philosophy, such as game-theoretic and rational choice theories, and must be guarded against here as well.

6. The most frequently cited example of an institution not addressed in our constitution is the party system. Although many contemporary constitutions do address a party system, there is no inherent need to do so. In the case of our Constitution, for example, since political parties seek to gain control of political offices defined in our national Constitution, our political parties inevitably develop structures and processes that are heavily conditioned by the Constitution. As a consequence, Federalism and the separation of powers virtually define the fragmented nature of our party structures, as well as the internal processes that create state and national party systems. Political parties in America are not extraconstitutional, but profoundly constitutional, and as such really need no further constitutional specification. Indeed, such specification might well produce a party system that is too inflexible in the face of demographic, economic, and historical change and thus contribute to constitutional instability. In this regard as in others, I would argue that the U.S. Constitution continues to be a model for the balance between the need for architectonic direction in line with political theory and the dangers of overdetermination in the face of the inevitable changeability and open-endedness of politics.

CHAPTER 3

Constitutional Doctrine and Political Theory

Edward Bryan Portis

Like everyone else, political theorists tend to believe that what they do is important, that it potentially has far-reaching implications. For this reason, they are inclined to think that ideas matter and, therefore, that consensus on fundamental principles is an important requisite of public order. To say essentially the same thing in a different or at least a more focused way, political theorists are inclined to believe that there must be a theoretical basis for constitutional legitimacy. Such an assumption does not necessarily presume anything about either the intent or philosophical sophistication of the historical actors responsible for any particular constitutional system. It does presume, however, that the viability of their efforts depends upon compatibility with generally accepted theoretical propositions. To what extent constitutionalism might require either theoretical consciousness or consensus to permeate various strata of the population is an empirical question most theorists are ill-equipped to answer. At a minimum, however, an operative "public philosophy" among the politically cognizant would seem to be essential if constitutional legitimacy indeed rests upon some sort of theoretical consensus.[1]

This is not a self-evident assumption. In recent years, some have argued that social complexity and its resulting interdependence have made popular support more dependent upon the effective provision of social services than compatibility with widely held notions of political freedom or other social ideals (see especially Zolo 1992; Luhmann 1990. Also relevant are Offe 1984; Bobbio 1987). If the functional is more relevant than the ideal, effective administration may be far more important in sustaining public order than some sort of normative legitimacy.

Indeed, some proponents of this thesis suggest that the increasingly complex nature of society necessarily renders normative aspirations of political authority futile, and therefore a potential source of social frustration and instability rather than public order (see in this connection Zolo 1992, 105–109).

Such a hypothesis, of course, assumes that reasoned normative aspiration is not a precondition of constitutional legitimacy, which is the primary point at issue. In the last analysis, whether a public philosophy is essential for constitutional government is as much an empirical as a theoretical proposition. Nonetheless, I believe there is good reason to doubt the resiliency of what might be called a purely "utilitarian" constitutional order. I will argue that long-term political viability not only requires a constitutional creed, but also that this creed be given a significant degree of theoretical articulation. Consequently, I affirm the potential political significance of theoretical discourse.

My primary concern, however, is not with this issue, but rather with the political role of political theorists. For it is easy to conclude, and may even seem self-evident, that the need for a constitutional creed of some theoretical sophistication ipso facto establishes a political role for academic political theorists which transcends partisan politics. Obviously, if a constitutional creed must be articulated there must be articulators, and there are certainly good grounds to doubt that the creed will serve its function if it is defined largely by partisan politicians. Meaningful constitutionalism requires, I will argue, a relatively non-partisan "constitutional elite." Yet my primary conclusion is that political theorists cannot be part of this elite. Both the nature of political theory as an intellectual enterprise and the functional requisites of a viable constitutional creed preclude political theorists from assuming responsibility for its articulation and propagation. Although I readily grant that a thriving community of political theorists probably contributes to the vitality of constitutional norms, this contribution must be largely incidental.

THE NEED FOR CONSTITUTIONAL THEORY

All constitutions probably arise out of factional accommodation, and it would be foolish to claim that they ever are primarily the result of an intellectual consensus on the best way to maximize collective ideals. This is not to say that popular mores are necessarily irrelevant, or that politically influential elites are never idealistic [compare McDonald's recent work (1985) with McDonald 1965]. Just as the methods we adopt to pursue our individual interests are constrained by our habits and moral priorities, so too are those adopted, either by design or practice, to make possible authoritative collective decisions. But immediate interests rarely have more than a tenuous relationship with moral priorities, and while the range of methods employed to pursue these interests may be limited by considerations of right and wrong, practical considerations and ingenuity ultimately determine both the options and the selection.[2]

Irrespective of whatever practical considerations that may have led to its birth, however, each constitution requires a logically coherent constitutional theory in order to function as a constitution. To support this assertion, I will first argue that the imperatives of judicial administration necessitate normative priorities that go beyond the text of a written document. I will then argue that the very complexity of modern nation states, which leads some contemporary observers to deny the relevance of constitutional theory, actually mandates that the normative priorities necessary for any constitutional system be given theoretical expression.

A constitution without normative priorities could be no more than a coherent (in the sense of noncontradictory) collection of explicit, largely self-evident stipulations. And for it to exist those charged with ensuring the compatibility of the legal code with these explicit edicts would have to practice a strategy of constitutional interpretation even more strict than what is known popularly as "strict constructionism." This approach to constitutional interpretation, elements of which can be found in Robert Bork's writing and some of Justice Hugo L. Black's occasional statements (see Bork 1971; Black 1968, 14), should not be confused with an attempt to find guidance in the supposed intentions of those who drafted, ratified, or amended the constitutional document.[3] This sort of strict constructionist might refer to the historical record to help fix the meaning of the terms actually employed in a written constitution, but he or she could not privilege anyone's notion of what the constitution *should* say. Instead, the explicit language of a written constitution would have to discipline those entrusted with its application, and to provide meaningful guidance this language must be narrowly construed. If founders fail to adequately express their intentions, too bad for the founders. Otherwise, the constitution would be more that a set of stipulations.

In fact, a constitution must be more than this, and the interpretive practice of strict constructionism, strictly understood, is impossible. A number of reasons dictate this conclusion. Technically, the belief that words can be "narrowly" construed only makes sense if one can assume a "core" consensus on their meaning and this, in the absence of theoretical consensus, is at least questionable. More fundamentally, the very idea of constitutional law rests upon the assumption that some stipulations take precedence over others. Because by definition constitutional law is superior law, its very existence implies some basis for its claim of superiority.[4] Some stipulations ought to enjoy constitutional status and others should not. Indeed, it is the function of those entrusted with administering constitutional law to adjudicate claims of precedence in the context of a highly complex, diverse, and fluid legal system. Their task cannot be a simple matter of language analysis because no written text, or a collection of texts, can contain unambiguous instructions for evaluating claims that particular cases, statues or executive actions are or are not covered by the constitutional stipulations in question. As a practical matter, those who apply constitutional stipulations in a judicial context must have some understanding of *why* they are constitutional in order to judge among competing claims.

To affirm, however, that a constitution must be more than a set of explicit stipulations is not yet to establish that it must entail a constitutional theory. It is still conceivable that the controlling standards of judicial administration could be almost purely utilitarian and pragmatic. As indicated previously, all constitutions probably incorporate historic accommodations among political elites which have resolved or at least mollified deep-seated tensions among persisting segments of the population. To the extent this is the case, constitutions can draw their moral support from the same source as Hobbes' sovereign, the fear of social conflict, perhaps even of civil war.

But even if a constitution were originally no more than a practically coherent collection of modus operandi, it still would require a logically coherent and articulated constitutional theory if it were to contribute to social and political stability. For neither the fear of conflict nor any other practical benefit of constitutional rules is sufficient in itself to maintain its effectiveness. The primary reason for this is social complexity. Far from making normative criteria irrelevant to modern society, social complexity and interdependence accentuate their importance.

Complexity may typically be accompanied by centralization of authority, but it also means specialization, expertise, and diffusion of decision-making. Modern mass societies necessitate massive delegation of decision-making; this, in turn, requires explicit codification of general guidelines. Administrative discretion is an inevitable fact of life in these societies, and if the rule of law is to mean anything relatively explicit standards are essential. But in a complex society an exhaustive catalogue of do's and don'ts is simply impossible. The various techniques of curbing capricious and arbitrary exercise of administrative power, such as professional training and judicial review, presuppose a codification of relevant standards.

With administrative discretion comes considerable opportunity for personal graft, and it is difficult to see how corruption could be contained with a largely utilitarian code based upon a generalized fear of disorder. Once the historic accommodations have become historic, fear of instability is not likely to be a very effective imperative. Indeed, without further moral support, it is difficult to see how the accommodations themselves can be maintained. For once the terrors of social strife subside, the inconveniences of accommodation remain. The pressure to minimize the costs of compromise through petty but steady encroachment would seem to be almost irresistible, and, if social order depended solely upon fear, Hobbes' sovereign would be a more effective political expedient than constitutional accommodation.

It is nothing new to suggest that the logic of personal advantage is an insufficient foundation for public order, and that the vast majority of citizens must believe that the collectivity is sanctioned by higher ends. Even Hobbes presumed that the masses were unlikely to appreciate his logic, and that tradition and religion were essential supports for political legitimacy (there are exceptions; see Rogowski 1974). To these nonrational sources of moral support we might add national identity. But I want to argue not just that political legitimacy has a moral component but that a viable constitutional system requires an articulated constitutional theory. For the existence of a "public philosophy" is not a matter of popular credulity, but of elite consensus.

Actually, in the complex, and relatively literate societies of the present, a sharp distinction cannot be drawn between elite and the masses. There are many gradations of mid-level elites in all areas of social life that require a high level of organization, and in a mass society almost all areas do. Certainly, in the administration of public policy, a significant percentage of the population with varying degrees of responsibility and political sophistication must be involved. Cultural maxims may suffice for those serving relatively menial functions, but, as the level of responsibility and discretion increases, organizational personnel must have an ever greater grasp of the code defining the purpose of public authority. Moreover, those with the greatest discretion must be increasingly committed to this code if it is actually to govern their behavior. And just because we cannot make a sharp distinction between mass and elite or even between mid-level and "real" elites in a highly complex administrative society, we cannot presume a certain threshold will be reached where this commitment will be based on utilitarian rather than normative considerations.

There is little reason to think, then, that complexity renders social ideals irrelevant. Instead, it is likely to increase the need for their articulation, for civic education.[5] To the extent that this need is not met, for whatever reason, there is the possibility of a "legitimation crisis." In fact, however, those societies considered relatively complex appear to be least susceptible to serious constitutional crises, and I suspect that the reason is that some degree of consensus is likely to be a condition for the development of a high degree of administrative complexity. Politically, it is at least plausible that the end of the cold war has consolidated a liberal consensus which began to take shape after World War II in the kind of political systems we call "complex."[6] In any case, those societies generally acknowledged to be among the most complex, such as the United States, Japan and the major European nations, have been the most constitutionally stable and the least corrupt. This is not to say they have not experienced a good deal of political turmoil, nor even to take issue with those who maintain that these societies are increasingly ungovernable because of increased demands and expectations. This would seem, however, to be more of a problem for political leaders attempting to maintain public confidence than for the constitutional system as a whole (see Lehman 1992, 140; Beetham 1991, 168).[7]

THE NEED FOR A CONSTITUTIONAL ELITE

We cannot, however, ignore the problems of politicians. The defining characteristic of constitutional law is that its stipulations are aimed at public authority and apply only indirectly to individual citizens. If the preceding observations are valid, constitutional government requires a constitutional creed, yet there is the possibility, even the probability, that the creed will not be taken very seriously by those with the greatest responsibility for the conduct of public affairs. Cynicism is hardly unknown among the politically ambitious, and perhaps should be expected from politicians required to manipulate collective symbols in order to build popular constituencies in a highly competitive environment.

Be this as it may, it is difficult to imagine that the politically ambitious will be constrained in the long run by inconvenient constitutional mores, or that they typically will acknowledge even to themselves, let alone others, contravening them. They must cope with a competitive environment where an exaggerated sense of personal honor may be a handicap, and in light of the importance of some of the issues might even be construed as a form of irresponsible self-indulgence. Given the potential enormity of the social and personal stakes in partisan conflict, as well as the abstractness if not ambiguity of constitutional principles, the only effective way to preserve the integrity of constitutional limitations from the transgressions of political leaders in a democracy is to make it politically costly to ignore or distort constitutional principles. Two mechanisms are often put forth as means to ensure that constitutional infidelity will be transformed into political vulnerability—institutional division of power and public scrutiny. Although I suspect that both are to some degree necessary, it is my purpose to explicate and accentuate the importance of a third, more important mechanism; namely, the existence of what I will call a "constitutional elite." The other two mechanisms, however necessary, cannot be effective in the absence of such a stratum of citizens.

This is especially the case with institutional arrangements intended to insure a division of power, such as the famed "checks and balances" of the American Constitution. These devices might slow the erosion of constitutional limitations, but to expect to contain their decline by institutional tinkering alone would be naive. The general idea, of course, is to pit "ambition against ambition," supposedly resulting in mutual monitoring by rival political factions. This may under the right circumstances prevent a concentration of power, but political pluralism cannot in itself guarantee constitutional integrity. To the extent that it works, a division of power can do no more than increase the likelihood that politicians will have to compromise with one another; indeed, if political paralysis is to be avoided, they must. But the issue of constitutional integrity has little to do with whether politicians have to compromise, but rather with whether their compromises will conform to constitutional norms (compare Dahl 1956, 83). Given the priorities of the ambitious and the pressures of partisan politics, the mere fact that politicians might jealously oversee one another provides small comfort.

Since professional politicians, left to themselves, are particularly prone to infringe upon inexpedient constitutional guidelines irrespective of institutional safeguards, we must look to their fellow citizens to keep them constitutionally honest. The second mechanism to make constitutional infidelity politically costly is simply public scrutiny. A number of obvious conditions must be fulfilled for this mechanism to be effective. The first is that there must be a sufficient degree of constitutional piety among the citizenry. The second is credible sources of political information sufficiently independent of both government and party organizations. However difficult it may be to meet these conditions in many countries, a third condition is a far greater obstacle, and this is the ability of the citizenry to recognize encroachments upon constitutional boundaries. This presumes not just a certain level of knowledge and awareness, but also independence from their political leaders. Yet this is a contradiction in terms. People have leaders because they think or feel they need them. To some significant degree they must trust them, and must assume that they share their constitutional piety; otherwise, they do not have leaders. Citizens with partisan leaders are themselves partisan, and while they may readily accept accusations of constitutional duplicity by opposing politicians, they will not be quick to question the constitutional integrity of those they consider leaders. In a partisan environment, constitutional piety among the general populace may effect the rhetoric of politics, but it is not likely by itself to make constitutional encroachment politically costly.

What is needed to maintain constitutional integrity is a sufficient number of individuals who are both relatively well informed and relatively influential, and who have the personal incentive to place the protection of constitutional norms above their own partisan predilections. This may appear to be a tall order, but I will argue that it is reasonable to suppose that many such individuals exist. Obviously, however, we are dealing here with a conceptual construct rather than with a clear and distinct demographic group. The extent to which individuals embody its characteristics is a matter of degree, and whether those who do so to a high degree are sufficiently numerous to make a difference is not something that I can demonstrate here, but only infer from the fact of constitutional stability. I call this segment of the population a "constitutional elite," rather than some sort of "attentive public" (compare Key 1961, 265, 282–84, 546–47; and Almond, 1950, 233), because the latter notion, being based on relative political sophistication and interest, is much too broad, incorporating the highly partisan as well as the relatively detached. I use the word "elite" not to indicate some sort of superiority, for I will argue that its members must be both politically and theoretically naive, but rather a degree of social privilege.

Such an elite must have three distinct characteristics if it is to exist and serve to maintain the viability of constitutional norms. The first is obvious—these individuals must be able to recognize infractions of constitutional norms. This means they must have a fairly sound understanding of the constitutional creed and be able to effectively articulate at least its broad outline and its major elements. This certainly does not mean that the study of constitutional theory must be their business, but only that they be the recipients of a fairly good education, and be of sufficient intellect to have taken advantage of such an education.

The second characteristic is not so obvious, and is more difficult to depict. By definition, the members of a constitutional elite must be "high-minded," but if their willingness to subordinate partisan commitments to constitutional principle were simply the result of selflessness, one might reasonably question whether such an elite could ever be so large as to make a difference. However, the willingness to sacrifice partisan advantage does not require saintliness, and the high-minded need not be selfless.[8] The constitutional order must be meaningful to members of a constitutional elite, and it will be so if they identify with it. Their personal status and their sense of self-esteem must in some way be connected with the history and institutions of their country.

To some extent this might be the result of education, but a more certain source of this kind of identity is likely to be family history, as it connects with the evolution of national political institutions. Relatively few, of course, can claim lineage from historically important political figures; but this is not necessary. A considerable percentage of families plausibly claim connections to the political history of their country. Among the cherished historical artifacts of my own thoroughly plebeian family, for example, are letters from soldiers serving in the Civil War and World War II, and my middle name derives from the decision of a great-grandfather, a Nebraska farmer, to name one of his sons in honor of William Jennings Bryan. Most families are likely to have and be aware of significant connections with the political history of the larger community. Ellis Island is as much a part of our historical consciousness as Plymouth Colony, and involvement in such recent events as those associated with the Civil Rights movement or even the Vietnam War serve to integrate family and national history.

The decisive factor, however, is not the extent of the historical connections, but rather what is made of them. The salience of these connections to a person's personal identity probably is significantly related to that person's estimate of the social importance of his or her family. Put differently, it is the perceived social status of one's family that is likely to make it important to a person's sense of self-esteem, and to incline the individual to assume a special responsibility for what are taken to be venerable principles of public identity. Perhaps mere consciousness of being a member of one of the "better families," and therefore part of a social elite with special responsibilities supposedly justifying its status claims, will suffice to encourage identification with the conventional morality and constitutional norms of a society.[9] Be this as it may, it seems reasonable to assume that an appreciable proportion of the population is susceptible to this kind of identification.

Not only does higher social and economic status encourage the second characteristic of a constitutional elite, but it is probably essential for manifestation of the third as well. For while the constitutional elite must be politically influential, its influence cannot be due primarily to its members' partisan commitments. They must be influential without having to secure the support of significant political constituencies. Otherwise, their influence would be too closely bound with partisan appeal to allow for them to rise above it. More generally, they cannot be political leaders in the broader sense of having primary responsibility for making public policy or setting policy priorities; they cannot be players in the game, irrespective of whether they would consider themselves politicos or statesmen. For they cannot be expected to monitor the behavior of ambitious politicians if they have political ambitions of their own. They need to be influential, but they cannot wield political power.

This requirement raises two questions: First, how can a constitutional elite be influential without wielding political power and, second, how can they get to be influential without seeking power? Neither question presents difficulties. As every political scientist knows, in modern societies all chief executives, and especially political leaders, have great difficulty in setting priorities for the organizations they supposedly lead (the classic work, of course, is Neustadt 1960). The influence of high-level functionaries is a fact of life, and a constitutional elite can be influential if its members occupy significant management positions in sufficient numbers in such key social organizations as governmental agencies,[10] major business corporations, religious organizations, the mass media, the military, and perhaps even higher education. It would be difficult to discern with any precision the political cost of earning the distrust or provoking the enmity of large numbers of such people, but I think it safe to say that all but the most obtuse of politicians would consider it politically risky.

Very few positions in key social organizations are sinecures, most being open in varying degrees to almost all with the requisite credentials or experience. However great its imperfections, we live in a meritocracy. But a meritocracy, especially an imperfect one, is no threat to social stratification, and there is ample evidence that social and economic elites are quite adept at giving their off-spring enhanced opportunities for acquiring especially advantageous credentials.[11] Although the socially privileged may not produce sufficient numbers of qualified fledglings to dominate the upper echelons of major organizations, they are almost always represented far beyond their proportion of the population. Consequently, there need be no worry for their lack of collective influence.

CONSTITUTIONAL THEORY AND THEORETICAL DISCOURSE

Such is the nature of a constitutional elite. Obviously its members need a degree of theoretical awareness, but I do not think they can be political theorists any more than they can be political leaders. As discussed in the first section of this chapter, every constitutional creed entails a public philosophy involving distinct theoretical presuppositions. For a constitutional elite to perform its function, a sophisticated understanding of these presuppositions, as well as of their distinctiveness, is certainly advantageous even if not absolutely necessary. But the important point in the present context is that if the constitutional creed is to be a creed, it cannot be seen as problematic. If the defenders are to be reliable, they cannot be too inclined to question.[12]

Consider, then, how members of the constitutional elite would have to view their subject matter if they were political theorists. Although they undoubtedly could defend and articulate the constitutional theory much better than other citizens, they could not seriously question the culturally dominant consensus they must share with them. Consequently, they would have to see political thought as a "tradition," as a progressive series of past efforts to formulate a rational and humane basis for political authority. In this progressive tradition, civilization has learned from its mistakes as well as from its more notable philosophic dissidents. The latter, of course, would be seen as successfully surmounted challenges to the increasing consensus on the nature of rational legitimacy and the proper ends of public authority.

Just as instructive as what these political theorists would have to believe about political theory is what they could not believe. They could not believe that all claims of legitimacy are no more than rationalizations of arbitrary privilege, any more than they could believe that there are no grounds on which to assess theoretical validity. Nor could they believe that theoretical truth is assessable only to a philosophical elite, and that the masses must be fed an intellectual diet of useful myths. To the contrary, they must think not only that the citizenry can be educated in constitutional principles, but also that it is vitally important that they be so. There must be no esoteric teaching for these guardians of the constitutional order. Critical theorists, postmodernists and even orthodox Strausseans, if such exist anymore, would seem to be disqualified from the role.

The point is not that these proscribed positions happen to be affirmed by a significant number of political theorists (I happen to reject all of them), but rather that political theorists take them seriously and argue about them. However controversial these positions may be, they are not and, to the extent that political theory is a meaningful form of scholarly discourse, cannot be proscribed. But the real problem comes not from the positions that would have to be proscribed, but rather from that which would be prescribed.

Although one might possibly find a political theorist who maintains that the history of political thought displays a progressive unveiling of the true principles of political right, culminating with the conventional wisdom of the age, anyone who thinks this an obvious truth has little incentive to engage in theoretical discourse.[13] From this perspective, theoretical debate has already done its work, and only the application of established moral truths to the ever changing details of practical politics and public policy remains to occupy the energies of those with a theoretical bent. A concern for alternative views of the nature of political community and the purpose of public authority could be no more than an antiquarian interest for this sort of political theorist. And only a certain voyeurism, pugnaciousness, or missionary zeal could account for such an individual's willingness to engage in intellectual dispute with the advocates of supposedly obsolete or bizarre theoretical alternatives.

Even though members of a constitutional elite must be interested and to some extent involved in public affairs, and they must be more theoretically articulate than most citizens, they are unlikely to qualify by any serious test as either politicians or political theorists. In fact, politicians are likely to be rather contemptuous of these "good government types" because of their political naiveté. However important they may be in the administration of public policy or providing leadership to nonpublic organizations, they must typically be politically passive. In politics, consistent high-mindedness is likely to require a degree of obliviousness.

Political theorists are more likely to be patronizing than contemptuous, but they also will find these essential guardians of constitutional integrity naive. They must be theoretically naive because they must accept as self-evident things which are actually problematic. In the present context the important point is that their theoretically naiveté is a condition of their political function. Because constitutional government requires a public philosophy, the things over which political theorists argue are politically important. But the mere fact they argue about these things renders political theorists radically unfit to be the guardians even of constitutional principles they affirm. For, to put it simply, theoretical discourse itself is inherently subversive of constitutional consensus.

POLITICAL THEORY AS USEFUL SUBVERSION

Since political theory as an intellectual endeavor is subversive of an important dimension of political order, it is something to be either repressed or tolerated. No reader is likely to be surprised that I, as a political theorist, think it deserves toleration. I have two reasons for this assessment, beyond blatant self-interest, both concerning the impact of theoretical discourse during the education of potential members of the constitutional elite. On the one hand, exposure to theoretical alternatives is probably essential for meaningful commitment to the constitutional creed. On the other, dissident political theorists will undermine the constitutional faith of only a small percentage of their students, and their loss is not going to affect the ability of a constitutional elite to serve its function. In sum, a robust community of political theorists is likely to do some good, and for the most part is usually going to be quite harmless.

The utility of theoretical debate is to be found first in the highlighting of the distinctive features of the public philosophy. When things are so self-evident that they can be taken for granted, they usually are invisible. One does not have to be a Hegelian to recognize that we understand things in terms of what they are not at least as much as by familiarity with what they are. Moreover, if an observer has access to only one interpretative scheme, then he or she will interpret everything in its terms and will lack the ability to quickly spot the anomalous (compare Anderson 1993, 108–109). Since it is important that members of the constitutional elite be able to react negatively to constitutional transgressions before they become part of their country's history, it is also important that they understand what is not, as well as what is, part of their creed.

There is another reason they must not take the constitutional creed for granted, and this is that they must take it seriously. Awareness of theoretical dissent is a precondition for theoretical commitment. As John Stuart Mill effectively pointed out, it is very difficult to take conventional beliefs seriously unless somebody questions them. For conventional beliefs are always in danger of being reduced to a set of proper answers to questions that no longer need to be asked. When the answers need no defense, not only are the reasons they are good answers likely to be forgotten, but even that they are answers to serious questions (Mill 1859, chap. 2). If members of a constitutional elite are to be ready to defend the constitutional creed, they must see it both as something worth defending and something that might need defending.

A noticeable degree of theoretical dissent, then, is likely to be functional to the vitality and, in the long run, the endurance of a collective creed. Yet like many antidotes, dissent can be toxic in large doses.[14] It is easy to imagine a lurid scenario in which the enemies of received truths achieve hegemony in selected academic disciplines and systematically destroy the constitutional faith of new generations of influentials, planting the seeds of alien doctrine and cultural alienation. With an active imagination, it is easy to imagine anything. This particular scenario rests upon a couple of extremely unlikely assumptions. The first is the notion that viewpoints incompatible with cultural predilections (other than the ubiquitous skepticism of all genuine scholarship) could establish some sort of meaningful hegemony in an academic discipline. Individual departments may indeed be susceptible, and intellectual fads may temporarily attract a great deal of professional attention. But in any discipline of significance the number of true adherents to culturally alien approaches to its subject matter is likely to be limited, and once they achieve distinction counterrevolution is inevitable.[15] Moreover, as discussed in the previous section of this essay the very nature of theoretical discourse will prevent political theorists from displaying a significant degree of theoretical unity—at least as long as they remain true to their craft.

The second unlikely assumption is a ludicrous estimate of the potential influence of scholarship and higher education on the cultural sentiments of students. In actual fact, I think, even when free from administrative pressures academicians must accommodate themselves more to their students than their students to them. If they stray too far from cultural expectations, they will have few voluntary students. For most of our students, even the bright ones, critique only provokes the reaffirmation of cultural verities, and about the best for which we can hope is that they do so at a somewhat higher level of sophistication.

The few we deflect from the straight and narrow are not only unlikely to be functioning members of the constitutional elite, they also will be handicapped by their unconventional views from attaining those positions of influence in which the constitutional elite needs to be significantly ensconced. But they are among the talented ones, and in a relatively open society they can find opportunity enough to meaningfully employ their talents, and at least we have saved them from theoretical naiveté. For that they will be thankful, and we need not worry for their sake. Nor need we assume the responsibility for training a constitutional elite. Because cultural convention can take of itself, we can refuse with a clear conscience to be priests. And whatever our potential to be politically efficacious,[16] we need not strive to transcend our partisan predilections, but only to be resolute in our efforts to ensure they are not blind.

NOTES

1. Walter Lippman (1955, 104) defined this term as a "code of civility," which implies a consensus that can be intellectually articulated. William M. Sullivan (1982, 10, and 208) disagrees, defining the concept in terms of mutuality and personal identity. Obviously, my use of the term is much closer to Lippman's than Sullivan's.

2. "Very frequently the 'world images' that have been created by 'ideas' have, like switchmen, determined the tracks along which action has been pushed by the dynamics of interest" (Weber 1958, 280).

3. Robert Bork does recommend founders' intentions as a guide to constitutional interpretation, which seems to me to be incompatible with his majoritarianism. For an uncompromising advocate of "original intent," see Berger, *Government by Judiciary*, 1977: 363-396.

4. In this connection, see the much more sophisticated arguments in Barber, *On What the Constitution Means*, 1984, and Arkes, *Beyond the Constitution*, 1990.

5. Émile Durkheim based much of his social thought upon this point. See Durkheim, *The Division of Labor in Society*, 1933, especially 52, and Durkheim, "Society and Its Scientific Field," 1964, especially 384.

6. This would seem to be the premise of Francis Fukiyama's widely read book, *The End of History and the Last Man*; also see Huntington, *The Third Wave*, 1991: 46-72.

7. It is not surprising that many of the politicians interviewed by Karl A. Lamb, *The Guardians* (1982, 14-27), equated lack of confidence in government with a crisis of the system. They would, wouldn't they?

8. Compare Robert A. Manzer's, "Hume on Pride and Love of Fame," (1996, 333-355), cogent analysis of Hume's constitutional psychology.

9. It is conceivable that professional identity, especially when combined with an ethos of public responsibility and service, could support the inclination to defend constitutional norms. Yet according to Brint's, *In an Age of Experts* (1994), analysis of the public role of the professions, "social trustee professionalism" has largely been displaced by "expertism" in the service of clients.

10. From a much more normative perspective, Rohr, *To Run a Constitution* (1986, 185), argues that, in order for constitutional principles to be reconciled with the fact of the administrative state, a professional ethos for public administrators based on their oath to the constitution is needed. Such an ethos implies

a degree of independence from political authority, requiring administrators to monitor the constitutional integrity of constitutional masters: "In a regime of separation of powers, administrators must do the work of statesmen."

11. Three decades ago Hacker, "The Elected and the Anointed" (1961, 539–549), found that members of the Senate were significantly less likely to have attended an Ivy League institution than presidents of major corporations, despite the fact that they differed far less in their relative social backgrounds than might be expected. More significant in the present context is that an extremely high percentage (70 percent as opposed to 27 percent for senators) of corporation presidents sent their offspring to such institutions. According to data collected by Thomas R. Dye, *Who's Running America* (1983, 196–198), 73 percent of institutional leaders in the United States have degrees from relatively expensive private colleges and universities, most from the twelve most prestigious of such institutions. No doubt a number of students earned scholarships that allowed them to attend these institutions, but the percentage having attended the handful of exclusive prep schools would seem to support the assumption that these institutions continue to provide opportunities primarily for the offspring of the socially privileged.

12. Wolin, *The Presence of the Past* (1989, 141), has called "for a citizen who can become an interpretive being, one who can interpret the present experience of the collectivity, reconnect it to past symbols, and carry it forward." This call is based upon the obviously correct observation that the nature of one's national birthright is contestable, and that it is the right and perhaps the duty of citizens to ascertain what it will mean. When the mass of citizens become political theorists, they will then be able to dispense with both political leaders and a constitutional elite. But as long as they need one, I think they need the other.

13. Actually, such diverse critics of the historical approach to political theory as David Easton and Allan Bloom agree that it leads to (or rests upon) normative relativism rather than an affirmation of prevailing standards. See Easton, *The Political System*, 1953: 233–254, and Bloom, "The Study of Tacts," 1980: 126–127.

14. Foley, *The Silence of Constitutions* (1989), argues that a significant degree of theoretical ambiguity is crucial to the vitality of any constitution. This may be so, but Graham Walker, "The Constitutional Good" (1993, 102), it seems to me, adds an essential qualifier. "A successfully constituted polity probably enjoys a benign amnesia, going for long stretches without having recourse to its reasons. But the reasons must exist. . . . When the limit case arrives, when many people are asking threshold questions in public, toying with alternative constitutions or with chaos, these reasons will have to be recovered."

15. Gunnell's, *The Descent of Political Theory* (1993, chap. 10), argument that the "behavioral revolution" was in part a reaction to the theoretical influence of the academic refugees from Germany before and during World War II, is in this context suggestive.

16. I personally think it is very low. See Portis, *Max Weber anbd Political Commitment*, 1986.

REFERENCES

Almond, Gabriel A. 1950. *The American People and Foreign Policy*. New York, NY: Harcourt, Brace and Company, Inc.

Anderson, Charles W. 1993. *Prescribing the Life of the Mind: An Essay on the Purpose of the University, the Aims of Liberal Education, the Competence of Citizens, and the Cultivation of Practical Reason*. Madison, WI: University of Wisconsin Press.

Arkes, Hadley. 1990. *Beyond the Constitution*. Princeton, NJ: Princeton University Press.

Barber, Sotirios A. 1984. *On What the Constitution Means*. Baltimore, MD: The John Hopkins University Press.

Beetham, David. 1991. *The Legitimation of Power*. Atlantic Highlands, NJ: Humanities Press International, Inc.

Berger, Raoul. 1977. *Government by Judiciary: The Transformation of the Fourteenth Amendment*. Cambridge, MA: Harvard University Press.

Black, Hugo L. 1968. *A Constitutional Faith*. New York, NY: Alfred A. Knopf.

Bloom, Allan. 1980. "The Study of Texts." In *Political Theory and Political Education*. Edited by Melvin Richter. Princeton, NJ: Princeton University Press.

Bobbio, Norberto. 1987. *The Future of Democracy*. Minneapolis, MN: University of Minnesota Press.

Bork, Robert. 1971. "Neutral Principles and Some First Amendment Problems." *Indiana Law Review* 47.

Brint, Steven. 1994. *In an Age of Experts: The Changing Role of Professionals in Politics and Public Life*. Princeton, NJ: Princeton University Press.

Dahl, Robert A. 1956. *A Preface to Democratic Theory*. Chicago, IL: University of Chicago Press.

Durkheim, Émile. 1933. *The Division of Labor in Society*. New York, NY: The Free Press.

———. 1964. "Sociology and Its Scientific Field." In *Essays on Sociology and Philosophy*. Edited by Kurt H. Wolff. New York, NY: Harper and Row, Publishers.

Dye, Thomas R. 1983. *Who's Running America? The Reagan Years*. 3rd ed. Englewood Cliffs, NJ: Prentice-Hall, Inc.

Easton, David. 1953. *The Political System: An Inquiry into the State of Political Science*. New York, NY: Alfred A. Knopf.

Foley, Michael. 1989. *The Silence of Constitutions: Gaps, 'Abeyances' and Political Temperament in the Maintenance of Government*. London: Routledge and Kegan Paul.

Fukiyama, Francis. 1992. *The End of History and the Last Man*. New York, NY: The Free Press.

Gunnell, John G. 1993. *The Descent of Political Theory: The Genealogy of an American Vocation*. Chicago, IL: University of Chicago Press.

Hacker, Andrew. 1961. "The Elected and the Anointed: Two American Elites." *American Political Science Review* 55:539–549.

Huntington, Samuel P. 1991. *The Third Wave: Democratization in the Late Twentieth Century*. Norman, OK: University of Oklahoma Press.

Key, V. O., Jr. 1961. *Public Opinion and American Democracy*. New York, NY: Alfred A. Knopf.

Lamb, Karl A. 1982. *The Guardians: Leadership Values and the American Tradition*. New York, NY: W. W. Norton and Company.

Lippman, Walter. 1955. *The Public Philosophy*. Boston, MA: Little, Brown and Co.

Lehman, Edward W. 1992. *The Viable Polity*. Philadelphia, PA: Temple University Press.

Luhmann, Niklas. 1990. *Political Theory in the Welfare State*. New York, NY: Walter de Gruyter.

Manzer, Robert A. 1996. "Hume on Pride and Love of Fame." *Polity* 28:333–355.

McDonald, Forest. 1965. *E Pluribus Unum: The Formation of the American Republic, 1776–1790*. Boston, MA: Houghton Mifflin Company.

McDonald, Forest. 1985. *Novus Ordo Seclorum: The Intellectual Origins of the Constitution*. Lawrence, KS: University Press of Kansas.

Mill, John Stuart. 1859. *On Liberty*. London: John W. Parker and Son.

Neustadt, Richard E. 1960. *Presidential Power*. New York, NY: John Wiley.

Offe, Claus. 1984. *Contradictions of the Welfare State*. Cambridge, MA: MIT Press

Portis, Edward Bryan. 1986. *Max Weber and Political Commitment: Science, Politics, and Personality*. Philadelphia, PA: Temple University Press.

Rogowski, Ronald. 1974. *Rational Legitimacy*. Princeton, NJ: Princeton University Press.

Rohr, John A. 1986. *To Run a Constitution: The Legitimacy of the Administrative State*. Lawrence, KS: University Press of Kansas.

Sullivan, William M. 1982. *Reconstructing Public Philosophy*. Berkeley, CA: University of California Press.

Walker, Graham. 1993. "The Constitutional Good: Constitutionalism's Equivocal Moral Imperative." *Polity* 26:102.

Weber, Max. 1958. *From Max Weber: Essays in Sociology*. Edited by H. H. Gerth and C. Wright Mills. New York, NY: Oxford University Press.

Wolin, Sheldon S. 1989. *The Presence of the Past: Essays on the State and the Constitution*. Baltimore, MD: The Johns Hopkins University Press.

Zolo, Danilo. 1992. *Democracy and Complexity: A Realist Approach*. University Park, PA: The Pennsylvania State University Press.

PART II

*Theoretical Deliberation
and Partisan Politics*

CHAPTER 4

Rationality in Liberal Politics

Thomas A. Spragens, Jr.

The topic we are addressing is, in its generic form, one of the oldest and one of the most continuous issues of political theory and political practice: What is the role of reason in politics? Is politics, rightly understood and rightly practiced, an activity in which the cognitive powers play an important role? Or is it an arena in which the participants deploy only their will, unconstrained by rationality in any way or form? The answers given have ranged from one extreme to the other—from those who see the only legitimate form of society as one in which reason reigns supreme to those who deny reason any possible or legitimate political function at all. My purposes here are twofold: first, to play the role of Lockean "underlaborer," adding some clarity to the issues at stake by clearing away some of the conceptual underbrush; and second, to stake out what I regard to be the most salutary and defensible answer to the question within the context of liberal democracy.

First, the underbrush. In order to get a clear fix on the issues and on what is at stake, it is important to pay some careful attention to the definition(s) of the two key terms of the equation: reason and politics. Each of these concepts has been assigned a multiplicity of meanings. Many of these definitions are conceptually and normatively tendentious, sometimes intentionally so. As a consequence, what is offered as an answer to the question about the proper role of reason in politics may sometimes be little more than exercise in tautology, masking itself as an empirical claim.

My first suggestion in my capacity as underlaborer is that we should try to dispense as much as possible with substantively loaded definitions of the term "politics." If politics be defined either by reference to claims about ordinary usage or by stipulation as "a form of conflict," a conceptual value-slope is created that works—without necessity of argumentation—against those who believe that political life is/can be/should be seen and conducted as a cooperative enterprise. Thus, a lot of perspectives, and not simply those of rationalist philosophers, become labeled as "anti-political." On the other hand, Christian Bay (1965) once wrote an article that contrasted politics and "pseudo-politics." On his account, "politics" was defined as a form of public association in which people worked together on behalf of a principled conception of the common good. And a form of interaction that was a matter of purely self-interested haggling or conflict he proposed to style as "pseudo-political," hence a mere pretender to the real thing. Here the conceptual value-slope runs the other direction. My suggestion is that we accept neither one of these stipulative definitions—which tend to, and are often intended to, prejudice our view of the role that reason may or may not play in public life—and try to get back to more level ground, conceptually speaking. I propose that we ask about the role of reason in our "political association," with "political" here referring simply to the space (I started to say arena or forum, but note how these metaphors themselves are conceptually prejudicial) in which we create our public institutions and formulate our public policies. The extent to which the mode of association is cooperative or conflictual, deliberative or willful, is left open.

It is also important not to predetermine the outcome of our inquiry by adopting uncritically a particular conception of "rationality." We must keep clearly in mind that both philosophers and people on the street use the terms reason and rationality in a variety of ways. Whether "reason" has any possible and desirable role to play in politics, therefore, may depend upon exactly what form or conception of rationality one has in mind. And, correlatively, either a positive or negative answer to the question may be entirely misconceived by someone who does not understand or has a different understanding of what concrete form of intellectual operation is being denoted. To take one specific example, it would be a mistake to conclude from Michael Oakeshott's (1962) strictures against "rationalism in politics" that he is commending to us a conception or practice of politics as an unadorned clash of wills-to-power or as sheer inertial torpor. Instead, he is seeking in a Burkean vein to discourage us from thinking that a fully explicit and theoretical form of reasoning should guide our political actions.

THE MODALITIES OF POLITICAL ASSOCIATION

If we look first at the various modalities of political association, real and potential, it becomes apparent that they cover a wide spectrum ranging all the way from total cooperation to violent conflict, from love to war. Each point along this spectrum has been designated by some political analyst or another as either (1) an empirical model of what politics in its essence really is, or (2) a normative model of what it should be.

At one extreme, politics may be conceived as essentially a form of barely sublimated warfare. The Clausewitzian maxim that war is "politics by other means" in effect is taken to hold in both directions: the equation is taken not only to signal the political character of the conduct of war but also the warlike character of the conduct of politics. People relate to each other as enemies and antagonists, seeking to assert mastery over the other, and deploying whatever weapons may be available to do so. The weapons of choice may be military, but they may also be rhetorical (broadsides) or legal (attacks). The game is the same in either case: control or be controlled. Be master or be a slave. Normatively speaking, then, "good" politics means recognizing the brutal game for what it is and playing it hard and well. In their different ways, Machiavelli and Carl Schmitt could be said to conceive politics in this way and to draw what seem to them to be the appropriate lessons.

Another way to conceive politics is to see it as a form of bargaining. Here the parties remain self-interest maximizers and hence, in a world of scarce resources and some zero-sum encounters, competitors. But it is here assumed that some form of police power umpires and manages the conflict to make it a fair fight—with "fair" in this context referring not to substantive principles of justice but to procedural restraints to prevent violence and cheating. This is Clausewitz plus the Marquis of Queensbury: politics is still basically a fight, but there are rules to ban gouging and brass knuckles. And in the private domain, of course, people may be governed by higher and gentler motives. This is politics as a market, as it were. And in their somewhat different ways, rational choice theorists, pluralists, and libertarians have championed the conception as an empirical representation of politics or a normative model or both. There are also hybrids between the market and the warfare model. One thinks here of "offers you can't refuse" or Lyndon Johnson's alleged habit of convincing fellow pols by telling them that, if they didn't go along with him, he would retaliate in Lorena Bobbitt's fashion.

At a somewhat higher (morally speaking) level still, one not only can conceive politics as basically an individualistic or group-oriented quest to maximize one's own welfare, but also conceive the proceedings as regulated by substantive principles that set the parameters of acceptable distribution of the goods desired. This conception presumes both that human beings are self-interested and that they are also moral creatures who will inhibit their avarice by adopting and adhering to substantive criteria of social justice. Adherents of this conception also tend to assume, more negatively, that some combination of psychological and sociological forces makes it unrealistic to expect any closer forms of political identification among citizens or any deeper forms of cooperation on behalf of a common good. This perspective has, of course, been given a sophisticated and influential embodiment in the work of recent deontological liberals such as John Rawls (1971, 1993) and Bruce Ackerman (1980).

The self-understanding of the classical polity set out most memorably perhaps by Aristotle conceived of political association in yet another way—as a public form of friendship generated by common devotion to the city's welfare and values. Civic friendship was also generated in part, as exemplified in Pericles' funeral oration, by a sense of common identity and common patrimony. It exemplified its transcendence of self-interest by its capacity to inspire a willingness to sacrifice one's individual welfare—sometimes even one's life—to the benefit of the commonwealth. It also received expression in the Athenian case by fulfilling public duties and participating in public deliberation (Pericles: "[We] regard him who takes no part in these duties not as unambitious but as useless . . . and instead of looking on discussion as a stumbling-block in the way of action, we think it an indispensable preliminary to any wise action at all"),[1] or in the Spartan case by more military forms of solidarity. This conception of political association is given contemporary expression by those who draw upon the tradition of civic republicanism (Bellah et al. 1991; Sullivan 1986) by neo-Aristotelian liberals like William Galston (1991), by pragmatists like Charles W. Anderson (1990), and Philip Selznick (1992) who draw upon the Deweyan and Peircean account of collective prudence, and by participatory democrats like Ben Barber (1984).

At the other extreme from the politics as warfare model stands the ideal conception of politics as a perfectly harmonious association of the unselfish and altruistic. For the most part, this is simply a limit-case rather than a seriously entertained empirical possibility. Those who pursue it as the only truly worthwhile mode of human affiliation generally recognize that they must seek it in quasi-monastic enclaves rather than in large-scale geographically hegemonic polities. But perhaps some hopeful anarchists, millenarians, or flower children could be seen as committed to a more ambitious agenda along these lines.

THE MODALITIES OF REASON

Turning from the spectrum formed by the analytically distinguishable modes of political association to the concept of rationality, we need likewise to distinguish among different and sometimes competing conceptions. All sorts of important distinctions among various forms of politically relevant intellection could be drawn. But, for my purposes here, I want to sketch a topology based upon two criteria: first, whether the subject of political rationality be the few or the many; and second, whether the object be the useful, the fair, or the good. Combining these two criteria yields six categories of the political deployment of rationality, each of which has had its adherents.

The paradigm case of the rational few who know the useful is Bentham's Legislator, who shapes his legislation in conformity with the felicific calculus. It is more difficult to find explicit avowals of the rational few who rationally ascertain what is just. However, some interpretations and appropriations of John Rawls and Ronald Dworkin at times seem to come perilously close. On this account, those who may be deemed "justice experts" (judges, law professors, and professors of moral philosophy) should deploy their wisdom to determine what is just and then give these norms statutory and constitutional embodiment through windows of opportunity provided by the process of adjudication and legal interpretation. The few who know the good were championed long ago as philosopher-kings by Plato. And although a democratic culture provides very little leverage or legitimacy for such "elitist" conceptions, a culture that canonizes scientific expertise has produced some contenders for that role. Examples in the literature would include Harold Lasswell's flirtation with psychiatric technocracy and Lester Frank Ward's visions of a coming "sociocracy" (See Spragens 1981, pp 161ff). These models of rational authority regarding the good life have had relatively little impact on our public life; but, at least if Philip Rieff (1966) and Alasdair MacIntyre (1981, especially chapter 3) are right, the therapeutic mentality has played a significant role in shaping the surrounding culture.

Political models that rely upon instrumental rationality by the many have been and continue to be influential both in the academic and the larger political worlds. The libertarian ideal of the polis as a vast marketplace for the expression of the rational (i.e. calculative, self-interested) choices of individual participants is one leading example. The pluralist conception of democracy as a political marketplace where an equilibrium is generated through interest group competition is another. The category of knowledge of the right that is open to or generated by the many presumably includes Immanuel Kant's account of pure practical reason. (Kant saw himself as vindicating the moral intuitions of average everyday people, inspired in this respect by Rousseau.) And it is given a contemporary hermeneutic rendering in Rawls's conception of the "overlapping consensus" about fairness that he claims to find in the liberal democratic society (see Rawls 1993, introduction and chap. 4). Finally, the idea that the many can "reason together" about their common good is given expression in Jürgen Habermas's perfect market of deliberative rationality, the "ideal speech situation," in Ben Barber's depiction of "strong talk" as the center-piece of a democratic polity, and in James S. Fishkin's account of demo-cratic dialogue and deliberation (see Jürgen Habermas 1979, chap. 1; Barber 1984, 173 ff; James S. Fishkin 1992, 1991).

REASON'S ROLE IN POLITICS

Once we recognize the great variety of modes of political association, and once we also acknowledge the different types and alleged reposi-tories of rationality, it should become apparent that no simple and straightforward answer can be given to queries about reason's role in politics. It all depends upon which modes of reason and politics one has in mind. Even then we may give different answers, but at least we can know what we are talking about.

The laundry list of types of reason and types of politics can be narrowed considerably, and the issue given a sharper focus, if we exclude from consideration those types of each that fail to meet the basic criteria of liberal democratic legitimacy and if we also exclude categories that fail the test of empirical plausibility. Disagreement can ensue, of course, over the specific criteria and their application; but for the sake of argument I shall set aside on these grounds half of the modes of both reason and politics that I canvassed. We can set aside, first, those modes of politics that are based simply on power. The grounds for exclusion here were succinctly put by Jean-Jacques Rousseau (*Social Contract* 1.3): "force does not create right." Politics as warfare and as offers that can't be refused, then, can be ignored. Those models may, indeed they do, account descriptively for some public actions; but they cannot be part of an account of a legitimate democ-racy. At the other end of the spectrum, I propose to ignore the "politics as love" model as empirically unrealistic. I don't know many, or any, small-scale private associations that live up to this model, and it is hard to imagine any larger political society doing so.

Regarding the conceptions of political rationality I surveyed, I propose setting aside all of those that presume some small subset of the citizenry to be the privileged epistemological subjects of what is useful, right, or good. To do that, it need not be denied that moral philosophers, lawyers, and social scientists have thought more fully than most about these matters. It only needs to be insisted that their insights must, in a democracy, receive the endorsement of popular consent before they can be the basis for legitimate policy.

These exclusions leave us with three plausible and legitimate modes of political association in a liberal democracy: (1) bargaining among competitive individuals or groups within a framework of rules to prevent fraud and violence; (2) living side by side in accordance with neutral canons of justice; (3) joining together in civic friendship to seek a common good. We are also left with three plausible and legitimate modes of political rationality: (1) instrumental rationality, that discerns interests and the most efficient means to achieve them; (2) deontological rationality, that apprehends morally compelling criteria for the allocation of rights and duties; and (3) practical rationality, that ascertains what is humanly good by discursive and deliberative procedures. As it turns out, moreover, each of the forms of rational conduct serves as the most important type—although not necessarily the only one—in the context of one of the modes of political association. The question of reason's place in politics, therefore, becomes the issue of the relative worth and the proper role of these three modes: bargaining/instrumental reason, justice/deontological reason, and common good/deliberative reason.

My normative thesis, then, consists of the answer that I would endorse in response to that question. My contention is that all three of these modes of association/rationality have a legitimate and important part to play in the organization and conduct of a well-ordered liberal democracy. All three forms of rational behavior are morally defensible—at least within the proper contexts—and all of them have practical value in a democratic polity. This may sound like a cop-out, an answer designed to avoid hard choices and please everyone. But if we elaborate and defend this thesis by examining some of its logical corollaries, we find that not to be the case. For this is an answer that would seem not altogether welcome to some very influential participants in this debate.

For example, it follows from this thesis that some of the more lofty expectations and moral demands of Habermasian idealists and participatory democrats cannot be sustained. The short answer to the question "can practical deliberation replace political struggle as the process through which collective policy priorities are established?" is "certainly not." It is neither reasonable nor appropriate, then, to disparage as morally illegitimate a democratic process that falls short of the model of a full rational consensus and/or an ideal speech situation.

There are two main reasons for this impossibility, one of them anthropological, the other moral and epistemological. Politics can never be purely deliberative, first, because as James Madison (*Federalist Papers* 10) put it succinctly, "men are not angels." (And, if transported to our gender- conscious age, Madison would no doubt hasten to affirm that his affirmation is not gender-specific.) We are not angels in two senses, both of them relevant here: we are not incorporeal, and we are not morally pure. Not being incorporeal, we all have legitimate interests—in food, shelter, and the like—that press upon us and bias our actions and judgments unavoidably. This is a fact of life that needs to be accommodated rather than deplored. As someone once said in defense of the British practice of "interested MP's": "somewhere perhaps there are people without interests, but not, happily, here." We also, and relatedly, are not angels in the sense that we are not morally pure and/or capable of utter neutrality/objectivity in our practical judgments. Even were we "angelic," moreover, serious limitations would still militate against the full competence of deliberative rationality in making public policy. The issues addressed by practical reasoning do not, as Aristotle pointed out long ago, admit of determinative answers. They only allow contestable and ambiguous determinations of better and worse, discrimination among shades of grey. This indeterminacy problem afflicts both the empirical judgments about future cause/consequence relations that are inseparable from most policy choices and also the trade-offs among competing goods that are another necessity in most instances.

On the other hand, it also follows from my basic thesis that the bargaining/instrumental rationality mode of politics is not in itself adequate to sustain a well-ordered society. That suggests that modus vivendi theories, or libertarian theories, or pluralist theories of democracy should not receive our endorsement. The reasons here are both moral and pragmatic. The moral reason is, quite simply, that a human being whose associations with his or her fellow human beings are purely instrumental is not living much of a life. John Stuart Mill makes the point rather eloquently in chapter 3 of his *Considerations on Representative Government* (1962, 73):

> A neighbor, not being an ally or an associate, since he is never engaged in any common undertaking for the joint benefit, is therefore only a rival. Thus even private morality suffers, while public is actually extinct. Were this the universal and only possible state of things,

the utmost aspirations of the lawgiver or the moralist could only stretch to making the bulk of the community a flock of sheep innocently nibbling the grass side by side.

The pragmatic reservation about the modus vivendi/bargaining conception of liberal society concerns its long-term coherence and stability. Both the libertarian and the pluralist models embody a presumption, likely taken from classical economics, that the natural outcome of a bargaining process is an equilibrium. But this presumption is highly questionable. It takes for granted background conditions of widespread agreement to established rules of the game. That may be a defensible assumption when the market is purely an economic one, contained within sociological, political, and moral frameworks that buffer and sustain it. But when generalized to the social order as a whole, one may rightly wonder whether the sustaining context no longer exists and whether, therefore, political pluralism may not be guilty of making excessively sanguine empirical forecasts on the basis of a purely conceptual analogy. Social bonds keep economic competition from turning into outright warfare. The "dog eat dog" world of the marketplace is not literally that, because norms and institutions are in place to constrain it. But if all of society is a marketplace in which each is a rival to all others, this anomic condition can easily prove disintegrative. If we relate only as competitors, what begins as bargaining easily becomes offers you can't refuse, and those in turn may easily precipitate more violent conflicts and political disaggregation. The pluralist equilibrium may be, in short, an incipient war of all against all viewed through rose-tinted spectacles.

My thesis that all three layers/forms of political association are important in a well-ordered liberal democracy also implies the untenability of Rawls's argument that agreement regarding norms of social justice is a possible and sufficient way to overcome the deficiencies of the modus vivendi approach. In the first place, as I have argued in more detail elsewhere, the fundamental unfairness of life and the presence of gratuitous elements in the moral universe make it impossible to settle rationally upon a single set of distributive principles as demonstrably fair (See also, Spragens 1993). Simply put, the problem is that the contingencies of the world ineluctably allocate assets and sufferings quite unfairly. We can cope with and try to compensate for these "natural injustices," but only at the price of introducing other elements of unfairness or compromising other moral values. The other major problem in this context is that real world human beings are not deontologists: their moral intuitions about distributive justice are permeated and influenced by their moral intuitions about the good. The empirical consequence of these two difficulties is the falsification of Rawls's hermeneutic claims about an overlapping consensus. Rational people of good will with a liberal democratic persuasion will be able to agree that some possible distributive criteria are morally unacceptable. But, as both experience and the literature attest, hopes for a convergence of opinion on definitive principles of distributive justice are chimerical.

Rawls—too sanguine about the possibility of convergence by a democratic citizenry on determinate principles of justice—is also arguably too pessimistic regarding the possibilities of at least some degree of convergence on at least some aspects of a common good. As Rawls and others have insisted, the "fact of pluralism" vis-à-vis morality and religion make the attainment of consensus on some comprehensive vision of the common good highly problematic. But we have both logic and evidence to suggest that we need not abandon all efforts along these lines and assume a populace locked into a panoply of incompatible and incommensurable paradigms of the good life. The human good is not a fully coherent encapsulated conceptual lump. There are, to borrow Michael Walzer's phrase, "spheres" of goodness as well as spheres of justice. So whether we agree or not about whether the good life ultimately consists in a Nietzschean quest or in Christian fidelity or in bourgeois prudence, we might nonetheless be able to agree on what a good foreign policy or a good municipal services system looks like. Maybe not. Maybe the moral/religious presuppositions are all pervasive. But that remains to be demonstrated, not simply asserted. And much evidence leads me to doubt it.

THREE LAYERS OF A WELL-ORDERED LIBERAL DEMOCRACY

It follows from this argument regarding the several forms of rationality and their political functions that a healthy liberal democracy that faces up to the fact of pluralism and that accords due regard to the possibilities and the limitations of human propensities and capacities will be an association composed of three layers. Each of these layers will be characterized by its own distinctive mode of interaction, its own practices, its own skills, its own ethic. These different layers will be identifiable and distinguishable. But they will not function entirely separately, and each will be shaped by the contextual presence of the others.

The first of these modalities of political association will be essentially contractual. This is a mode of association that governs the economy and a significant part of political interaction. This is the realm in which bargaining, horse trading, wheeling and dealing, brokering, compromising, and vote-swapping occupy center stage. This realm encompasses much of everyday political life, and it is a perfectly legitimate component of a democratic society.

This is the realm in which instrumental rationality reigns supreme, the arena in which straightforward "rational choice" explanations are proper and effective. It is a thoroughly partisan realm because it is grounded in the pursuit of self-interest, and interests in a free society always are in conflict. Interests, of course, may also coincide in important ways, as, for example, when Ben Franklin admonished his colleagues that they would either all hang together or hang separately. This phenomenon is what sustains the logic of collective action and what makes it important for a society to develop ways to facilitate cooperative behavior when that is clearly in everyone's interest to have that happen. This cooperation could be deemed an expression of what Aristotle deemed to be the lowest form of friendship, friendship based upon mutual usefulness one to another (Aristotle *Nicomachean Ethics*, 8.3).

Even this self-interested, instrumental rationality mode of political association, it should be noted, has its own ethic. This ethic is essentially what is sometimes depicted as that of good business practice. It encompasses honesty, fair dealing, the avoidance of fraud or misrepresentation, and living up to one's promises. What is important to observe here, moreover, is that this fair dealing business ethos is made possible in part because the contractual realm is situated in the context of the other layers and modalities of democratic association. Those we bargain with are also people who share with us a commitment to justice and people with whom we seek the good life. Without that shaping and constraining context, the bargaining mode of social interaction tends to slide almost ineluctably toward mutual predation.

The second layer or associational mode of a healthy democratic society is centered about the quest for justice, the human commitment to "doing the right thing." Here the important human capacity is the sense of fairness, the relevant rationality deontological. Here citizens deploy their reason to try to ascertain what each is "due" to assess what constitutes a fair allocation of social benefits and burdens and to decide what punishment is fitting for various crimes.

The ethic of this mode of association is basically juridical. Fairness requires, for example, some of the most central constitutional constraints on collective behavior *vis à vis* individual citizens: no *ex post facto* laws, equal protection of the laws, no cruel and unusual punishment, guarantees of a fair trial, and so on. The commitment to justice leads beyond the requirements of sound legal practice, moreover, into those considerations that shape a democratic society's distributive policies: its tax codes, its welfare provisions, its fair employment requirements, and so on.

The sense of justice and the quest to achieve it both depend upon and help to reinforce respect for one's fellow citizens. It forces people to consider others not merely as possible means to satisfy their own wants and needs but as ends in themselves. It infuses society with a moral dimension and creates at least an abstract form of civic friendship (Rawls 1971, 106). It is also true, however, that the sense of justice does not expunge partisanship. What one conceives as just is mediated by one's own experiences and interests. As someone in a congressional office once said to me with a laugh: "Nobody ever comes in here looking for a favor. All they want is a fair advantage." Moreover, our world is so constituted that some moral tragedy is unavoidable, and the expectation that the world can be made totally fair for everyone is as a result delusionary. Against this background, the consequence is contention among conceptions of justice that converge in some respects but compete in others. The sense of justice in tandem with deontological rationality can lead to mutual respect among citizens and infuse society with a moral dimension that chastens and constrains the lust for wealth and power. But it may in some cases actually sharpen conflicts when, as sometimes happens, contending parties believe that their cause is not merely in their interest but is also predicated upon the terms of justice.

The final layer of a good liberal democracy embodies what Aristotle considered to be the highest form of friendship. This is the form of association reflected—no doubt in somewhat idealized fashion—in documents such as the Mayflower Compact, wherein the citizenry avows its common devotion to some conception of the human good and pledges cooperative and even possibly self-sacrificing efforts on behalf of its attainment. Some of the finest pieces of political rhetoric, moreover, such as Lincoln's Gettysburg Address and Second Inaugural or Franklin D. Roosevelt's Four Freedoms Speech, seek to draw the attentive *demos* into such a vision of and allegiance to a good or goods in common. In a pluralist society, these conceptions of the good are not likely to be "comprehensive," to borrow Rawls's designation. But they are nonetheless arguably more robust conceptions than he or other steadfastly deontological liberals tend to recognize (Rawls 1993, xvi ff, and 58 ff, inter alia).

This is the mode of political association in which something resembling Aristotle's *phronesis* is the relevant form of rationality. It is a realm governed by the human capacity to deliberate about and discern what is good for human beings—or at least what is good and fulfilling for the human beings who compose the society in question. So long as the notion of "self-interest" is understood, not as a primitive form of immediate gratification but instead as "utility in the largest sense, grounded on the permanent interests of man as a progressive being" (Mill 1956, 14), it is not too much of a reach to see this form of practical reason as formed by a combination of technical and deontological reason, situated within a political community that has some sense of common identity and common purposes. The object is enlightened self-interest, but, mediated by deontology's "moral point of view," that notion must here point toward refer to a general rather than a particular good.

TRANSCENDING PARTISANSHIP

To sustain the contention that this "higher" form of civic friendship and practical reason represents a plausible model of political association in the context of a modern liberal democracy, it is necessary to confront and challenge a central claim of old-fashioned Machiavellianism and trendy postmodernist cynicism. That claim is best summarized in the recent insistence by Stanley Fish (1994, 18–20, 38, 39, inter alia) that you "can't transcend politics." What Fish and others mean to convey by this insistence is that partisanship is fundamental and pervasive in all human interaction and no deployment of our rational powers can rise above it. Moreover, the claim to have done so is itself ideological and corrupt, because it falsely presents one set of human interests as something more than that—as something impartial and deserving of a higher legitimacy.

"You can't transcend politics" means that we cannot escape bias, partisanship, partiality. This is so in two respects. First, we cannot escape the pull, the influence, the bias of our own (partial, particular, partisan) interests over the ends we seek. Second, our perception of the political situation cannot escape the angle of vision dictated by our own particular location in time and space. Our perspective, as well as our goals, is always highly partial. When we claim otherwise, we are in error. When we claim authority and legitimacy for our goals and our views on the grounds that they are "objective" or "rational," we are always unjustified.

The problem with this argument is that it is exceptionally unnuanced. To assess it, we must first distinguish between a strong and a weak form that it might take. The weak form of the thesis is: we cannot ever completely rise above the partisanship of self-interest or the partiality of our viewpoint. Except perhaps for a few genuine saints, none of us ever attains Kierkegaard's "purity of heart." And not even a saint can inhabit the mind of Laplace's God or attain a Cartesian archimedean point. So far, so good. This weak version of the pan-partisanship thesis seems to be unexceptionable, albeit these days philosophically jejune. Are there any serious thinkers out there who contend otherwise? Surely not. Perhaps, however, it is still salutary to make this point vis-a-vis the philosophically untutored or deliberately arrogant ideologues who claim for themselves, their cause, and their ideas a degree of moral and/or cognitive purchase that in fact is delusionary.

The strong form of the thesis is more interesting but also more problematic. Indeed, I would argue that it is patently false. That thesis, often more implied than directly stated, is that we cannot rise to any extent at all above self-interest or attain a somewhat broader and larger perspective on politics than the partial viewpoint with which we unavoidably begin. It is only this strong form of the thesis, however, that leads to the cynical conclusion that collective prudence and moral deliberation have no genuine and important role to play in political life. In the cynic's view, we are so utterly mired within an attachment to our narrow interests and so hopelessly blinkered by our particular perspective that we should cut the hypocritical moralistic malarkey and get on with an honest and unadorned version of our agonism. The counsel becomes that of blatant partisanship unconstrained by principle or inhibition. Thus, Fish's (1994, 114) counsel on free speech issues:

> so long as so-called free-speech principles have been fashioned by your enemy (so long as it is his hoops you have to jump through), contest their relevance to the issue at hand; but if you manage to refashion them in line with your purposes, urge them with a vengeance.

Thus, a sophistic form of argumentation (i.e. claim to have sustained a strong thesis with arguments that bear only upon a weak thesis) leads to the sophistic admonition to pursue partisan ends without scruple.

Whatever the merits of the realist's insistence that no one can legitimately claim to have self-evident truths in practical matters or claim to be utterly non-partisan, the cynical claim that we cannot soften, mitigate, and partly rise above narrow partisanship and idiosyncratic perspectives in our political pursuits is both wrong and pernicious.

We falsify this claim every day in our associations with family, friends, and the larger public. We don't achieve utter dispassion, complete impartiality, philosophical or scientific veridicality. But we rise above our narrowest interests and perceptions to understand others' viewpoints and desires (Mansbridge 1990). And we understand that political legitimacy requires taking these viewpoints and desires into account. If only saints could transcend partisanship entirely, only sociopaths fail to do so at all. Were we incapable of this feat of mind and will, Madison (*Federalist* 55) is right in that case: "Nothing less than the chains of despotism [could] restrain [us] from destroying and devouring one another."

There are two principal cognitive resources available for this feat of partial transcendence of narrow self-interestedness and narrow perceptions that I am claiming to be both possible and important. Each of these cognitive resources, in turn, is effectual in practical terms only to the extent that it is linked with and fueled by the relevant moral passions in each case. With Hobbes (*Leviathan* 1.13), then, I would contend that the "possibility to come out of [the war of all against all] consists partly in the passions, partly in reason." But my account would suggest that Hobbes's conception of the range of both the passions and reason is too limited and that is why he is left with the logic of absolutism. His reason is purely calculative, his passions purely preservative and acquisitive. Hence, the Sovereign awaits with his necessarily swift sword.

In parallel but in contrast, I would argue that the first cognitive resource that sustains the upper layers of democratic association, hence providing a way of escaping a predatory politics, is the sympathetic imagination. Human beings have—to a considerably varying degree, to be sure—an imaginative capability of indwelling the situation, the feelings, and the responses of others. Possessing this capability to some degree is necessary not only to function successfully in everyday human interaction, but also is arguably essential to providing historical or sociological explanations of behavior (Collingwood 1956). When this cognitive ability is conjoined with compassion, it becomes one way of rising above the destructive dynamics of all against all. Various accounts have been offered of this process and its socially beneficent effects—accounts that diverge in some respects but nonetheless overlap in essentials. The Scottish moralists, including Adam Smith in his *Theory of the Moral Sentiments*, gave it a central place in their account of human sociability and morality. In a similar vein, James Q. Wilson begins his etiology of the moral sense with sympathy. Jean-Jacques Rousseau places considerable emphasis on the social functions of "natural pity." And it seems fairly clear that some element of sympathetic imagination is a necessary part of the movement from resentment to generosity in a post-Nietzschean morality (Wilson 1993; Rousseau *A Discourse on the Origin of Inequality*; and Connolly 1991).

The second cognitive resource of the partial transcendence of narrow partisanship/partiality is what I have elsewhere termed "the discipline of reason." Deploying the term "discipline" in a favorable sense in these times of acute Foucauldian sensitivity to any form of social control may be imprudently unfashionable. But the reference in this case is to the manner in which the logic and dynamics of practical/ moral discourse force the participants to adopt what Kurt Baier has termed a "moral point of view." And the moral point of view is one that necessarily departs from and steps outside of the particular standpoint and interests of any individual or group. David Hume actually captured the dynamics of this forced departure from egoism and the adoption of a more impartial and general perspective in his *Principles of Morals*:

> The more we converse with mankind . . . the more shall we be familiarized to those general preferences and distinctions, without which our conversation and discourse could scarcely be rendered intelligible to each other. Every man's interest is peculiar to himself, and the aversions and desires which result from it, cannot be supposed to affect others in a like degree. General language, therefore, being formed for general use, must be molded on some more general views, and must affix the epithets of praise or blame, in conformity to sentiments which arise from the general interests of the community. (Hume, *An Enquiry Concerning the Principles of Morals* 5.2)

The consequence is that a consistent egoist is communicatively incompetent, to borrow a Habermasian notion, when it comes to moral discourse. The egoist either must remain mute, or must surrender his egoism—in his speech, even if not in his motivations.[2] John Rawls (1971, 130–136) has thematized the same point in what he terms "the formal constraints of the principle of right." The logic of moral discourse, he argues, systematically winnows out as rationally unjustifiable any moral principles that are not general, universal, and capable of public acknowledgment.

These morally rationalizing dynamics of practical discourse are most effective, no doubt, when they are informed and sustained by what Rawls has termed the "two moral powers" or what we could equally well characterize as the "core moral passions": the passion for justice and the desire to attain the human good. Interestingly, however, even where these passions are weak, a strongly institutionalized pattern of authoritative public discourse centered on public policies and the normative justifications for them works to control and limit unfettered partisanship in the citizenry. A purely partisan group or politician is, like the consistent egoist, pushed into a corner, as it were, by the demands of moral and practical rationality. Either pure partisans must abstain from the dialogue and suffer therefore a loss of legitimacy, or else they must adopt a more general and impartial viewpoint, however hypocritically, and provide for their preferred polities an accounting centered around a conception of justice or what Madison termed "the permanent and aggregate interests of the community." Thus, even those who are disinclined to transcend their partisan interests and/or are deficient in the cognitive resources and abilities to accomplish that feat are dragged into at least a partial transcendence of their partisanship/partiality by the structure of public dialogue and the force of its inherent logic.

In the heyday of the Enlightenment, this constraint upon our spontaneous immersion in our own selfish desires and biased perceptions would have been referred to as being hauled before the bar of reason. Part of the Enlightenment's faith in the power of reason to effectuate impartiality and moral objectivity was a product of a widespread belief that objective and even self-evident moral truth was transparent to the rational mind. That moral Cartesianism is now quite properly considered to be an unwarranted hope grounded in a delusionary epistemology. But if the focus is placed not on the alleged substantive luminosity of moral reason and instead is placed upon the procedural dynamics of dialogic practical reasoning, there remains something of genuine validity and importance in the Enlightenment intuition that reason has a significant and beneficent role to play in politics. This function of reason is particularly valuable in the politics of liberal democracies, where traditional sources of authority lose their claim to legitimacy and therewith their ability to provide some counterweight to the centrifugal forces of self-interest that are always present in political society and that are given additional potency by liberal individualism and the democratic insistence on the consent of the governed.

CONCLUSION: REASON, DEMOCRATIC PRACTICE, AND THE VOCATION OF POLITICAL THEORY

I have argued here that a well-ordered democratic society comprises three layers or modes of association among its citizenry. The first is the political marketplace of free exchange and contractual agreements among individuals on the basis of mutual interest. The second is the juridical mode of association in which the democratic citizenry seeks to establish norms of social justice and to allocate the benefits and burdens of their common life in accord with them. And the last mode of association is that of civic friendship, in which the democratic citizenry seeks to know and to attain together a humanly good life of its members. Each of these modes of association, I have argued, deploys a distinctive mode of rationality: instrumental, deontological, and practical respectively. And in the case of the last two of these, the logic of moral discourse functions to compel a focus on transsubjective principles and norms of behavior, thereby simultaneously compelling the various participants in the public dialogue to transcend their idiosyncratic interests, identities, and viewpoints. Absent this feat of partial and imperfect transcendence of unadorned and unmediated partisanship, I have suggested, a democratic society will begin to succumb to the logic of mutual predation limned for us so memorably by Thomas Hobbes.

This argument carries with it, it seems to me, implications both for democratic practice and for the vocation of political theory. A democratic society, it suggests, needs to nurture what John Rawls has called the "moral powers" and their attendant passions: the devotion to justice and the desire to pursue a humanly good life. It should nurture as well the intellectual virtues that are necessary to render these passions effectual: the powers of the sympathetic imagination and the capacity to consider and assess public policy in a dialogic and rationally disciplined fashion. And it should bolster wherever and however possible those practices and institutions that foster the most broad based public dialogue possible and that force political partisans to perform those feats of partial transcendence which are required of all those who would participate in this form of discourse.

Such an understanding of the structure of a democratic society—and the role that reason in its various modes plays within it—also carries implications for understanding the vocation of political theory and its political role. Political theory, on this account, by the very nature of what it does—namely, inquire into the lineaments of the good society and subject both existing and possible regimes to rational critique—is a form of "political" action, and this in two significant senses. First, it shapes and constrains political behavior and political choice. Second, it is not politically neutral in the strong sense of that term. On the other hand, it is not a partisan activity in the usual sense of that designation. It is not a politically neutral occupation, because it is committed *de facto* to bringing all political regimes and practices before the bar of reason. Hence, political theory as a vocation stands in serious tension with any political regime based upon a denial of the authority of reason. Thus, political theory as a vocation has no logical or legitimate role to play in a regime such as Nazism in which will is accorded explicit dominance over the claims of reason. And it accords equally ill with the assumptions behind theocratic regimes. Likewise, political theory has no logical space to operate in the context of a regime whose legitimacy myth presumes that reason's work is already finished in politics—that the political world has already been definitively understood and that it remains only to change it. In all these instances, political theory as a vocation is either enchained or extirpated. It is not neutral *vis à vis* reason's reach and hence it is anomalous to irrationalist, anti-rationalist, and post-rationalist regimes. Political theory cannot be practiced in polities that insist upon supplanting critique and dialectic with catechism.

Although it is not, then, politically neutral—and therefore not compatible with or welcome within some forms of political life—political theory is not politically partisan in the sense of operating pursuant to particular interests or predetermined outcomes. This is not to say that political theorists cannot be themselves partisans in that sense. Indeed, we all are that to some extent or other. It is to say that no competent or honorable political theorist seeks to circumvent the rational and critical scrutiny of those to whom he or she speaks, either in print or in the classroom. Those who seek to evade the discipline of reason in this manner become partisans *simpliciter* and theorists *manqué*. In this respect, Plato was right. Philosophers may be rhetoricians, but those who are merely rhetoricians are not philosophers.

In another equally important respect, however, Plato was, as a consequence of his philosophical positivism and attendant political authoritarianism, quite wrong. So long as we are fallibilist but not pyrrhonist in our moral epistemology, we should recognize that liberal democratic regimes are the natural homes of political theory and the places where the functions of political theory are most integral to the premises and practices of political life and legitimacy. For it is these regimes that make legitimacy consist in the consent of a citizenry presumed to be both rational and possessed of the moral powers. In that context, rational discourse about what is to be done seems an essential component of legitimate politics, since that form of contestation is essential to the creation of a popular will that can pass muster—that is, to the formation of a popular will that can claim to be rational consent rather than aggregate whimsy.

To say that liberal democratic regimes are the natural homes of political theory is not to say that tensions do not characterize the relationship between them. In its deployment of critical reason, political theory must seem somewhat subversive to all regimes, liberal democracies included. Political theoretical critique casts a skeptical eye on all legitimacy myths, and it must puncture claims to political certitude and hegemony. It also will be subject to critical and potentially corrosive scrutiny the justifications set forth on their own behalf by powerful interests in democratic societies, including perhaps those enshrined by a democratic majority. This constant critique is socially useful but often not politically welcome.

This critical function of political theory is one that even moral cynics and epistemological skeptics can appreciate and accredit. But political theory also plays a more constructive role in liberal democracies, one that the cynic fails to appreciate and one that a thoroughgoing and unqualified cynicism would ultimately undermine. Relying upon the moral powers and their attendant passions for its energy and relying upon the logical and linguistic constraints of moral discourse for its direction, political theoretical dialogue assists the movement toward the more complex form of objectivity in political and practical affairs envisioned by Karl Mannheim, someone who was as aware as anyone of the ways that our sociological particularities and partisan interests produce competing perspectives. Mannheim explained:

> The problem, he wrote, is not how we might arrive at a nonperspectivistic picture but how, by juxtaposing the various points of view, each perspective may be recognized as such and thereby a new level of objectivity attained. Thus we come to the point where the false ideal of a detached, impersonal point of view must be replaced by the ideal of an essentially human point of view which is within the limits of a human perspective, constantly trying to enlarge itself. (Mannheim 1936, 296–297)

Political theory at its best, I would argue, functions constructively in precisely this fashion. It admits into its conversation conflicting perspectives and arguments that ineluctably are grounded in our sociological particularities and our partisan political interests. These perspectives are then set against each other and subjected to critical scrutiny in the context of those logical and linguistic constraints that constitute the discipline of reason. From that agonistic dialectic, narrowly partisan perspectives tend to lose credence and get winnowed out. Or they become broadened, amended, and complexified into new, more capacious and synthetic normative conceptions of the political world. These syntheses are neither final nor complete but continue to undergo continual change and revision under the impact of further challenge.

What results from this process of critical moral dialogue between competing perspectives is, then, not some final Hegelian scientific super-synthesis, much less some Cartesian perfect transcendence. But what does result, I would argue, is a greater tendency among all participants to be self-critical about their naive attachments and premises and a great and salutary pressure toward inducing in them a more enlarged, more comprehensive, and more impartial viewpoint regarding their society, their fellow citizens, and the issues of public policy they must address. From the kind of robust and rationally disciplined political dialogue embodied in political theory, one learns, as John Stuart Mill (1962, 168) put it, "to feel for and with his fellow citizens and becomes consciously a member of a great community." This is a form of discourse and discipline that pushes toward those "more comprehensive and distant views" (Mill 1962, 138) that are the cognitive base of the public spiritedness that Mill, Tocqueville, the civic republicans, and even James Madison thought essential to the health of a democratic body politic. It is a form of discourse, moreover, that sharpens the habits and skills necessary for serious democratic deliberation. And this, I would insist, is no small contribution to the democratic enterprise of self-governance.

NOTES

1. Pericles, "Funeral Oration," in Thucydides 1982 (110).
2. See Baier, *The Moral Point of View,* 1968: 189: "Moral talk is impossible for consistent egoists."

REFERENCES

Ackerman, Bruce. 1980. *Social Justice and the Liberal State.* New Haven, CT: Yale University Press.

Anderson, Charles W. 1990. *Pragmatic Liberalism.* Chicago, IL: University of Chicago Press.

Baier, Kurt. 1958. *The Moral Point of View.* Ithaca, NY: Cornell University Press.

Barber, Benjamin. 1984. *Strong Democracy.* Berkeley, CA: University of California Press.

Bay, Christian. 1965. "Politics and Pseudopolitics." *American Political Science Review* 59: 39–51.

Bellah, Robert, et al. 1991. *The Good Society*. New York, NY: Random House.

Collingwood, R. G. 1956. *The Idea of History*. New York, NY: Oxford University Press.

Connolly, William. 1991. *Identity/Difference*. Ithaca, NY: Cornell University Press.

Dworkin, Ronald. 1977. *Taking Rights Seriously*. Cambridge, MA: Harvard University Press.

Fish, Stanley. 1994. *There's No Such Thing as Free Speech, and It's a Good Thing, Too*. New York, NY: Oxford University Press.

Fishkin, James S. 1991. *Democracy and Deliberation*. New Haven, CT: Yale University Press.

———. 1992. *The Dialogue of Justice*. New Haven, CT: Yale University Press.

Galston, William. 1991. *Liberal Purposes*. Cambridge: Cambridge University Press.

Habermas, Jürgen. 1979. *Communication and the Evolution of Society*. Translated by Thomas McCarthy. Boston, MA: Beacon Press.

MacIntyre, Alasdair. 1981. *After Virtue*. South Bend, IN: University of Notre Dame Press.

Mannheim, Karl. 1936. *Ideology and Utopia*. Translated by Louis Wirth and Edward Shils. New York, NY: Harcourt, Brace, and World.

Mansbridge, Jane, ed. 1990. *Beyond Self-Interest*. Chicago, IL: University of Chicago Press.

Mill, John Stuart. 1956. *On Liberty*. Indianapolis, IN: Bobbs-Merrill.

———. 1962. *Considerations on Representative Government*. Chicago, IL: Henry Regnery.

Oakeshott, Michael. 1962. *Rationalism in Politics*. New York, NY: Basic Books.

Rawls, John. 1971. *A Theory of Justice*. Cambridge, MA: Harvard University Press.

———. 1993. *Political Liberalism*. New York, NY: Columbia University Press

Rieff, Philip. 1966. *The Triumph of the Therapeutic*. New York, NY: Harper and Row.

Selznick, Philip. 1992. *The Moral Commonwealth*. Berkeley, CA: University of California Press.

Spragens, Thomas A. 1981. *The Irony of Liberal Reason*. Chicago, IL: University of Chicago Press.

————. 1993. "The Antinomies of Social Justice." *The Review of Politics* 55(2):193–216.

Sullivan, William M. 1986. *Reconstructing Political Philosophy*. Berkeley, CA: University of California Press.

Thucydides. 1982. *The Peloponnesian War*. Translated by Richard Crawley. New York, NY: Modern Library.

Wilson, James Q. 1993. *The Moral Sense*. New York, NY: The Free Press.

CHAPTER 5

Deliberative Democracy and the Limits of Partisan Politics: Between Athens and Philadelphia

Adolf G. Gundersen

In contrast to "deliberation," which means "the thoughtful consideration of alternative courses of action,"[1] we might think of "partisanship" as "struggle to enact a fixed course of action." So defined, the differences between deliberation and partisanship are as obvious as they are profound: deliberation requires openness and the cooperative exercise of the intellect; partisanship presumes closure and involves the factional exercise of rhetorical manipulation or raw power. As a general rule, it also follows that deliberative democracy will flourish in inverse proportion to partisanship. For this reason deliberative democrats need a strategy for eliminating (or at least containing) partisanship. This paper advances such a strategy, a strategy which I recommend based on a critique of the two alternatives that have for some time dominated thinking in this area. The first of these alternatives is advanced by a wide-range of participatory democrats. On their view, partisanship can not only be contained, but also perhaps eliminated altogether, by having would-be partisans confront one another in public decision-making bodies. The participatory strategy ultimately rests on the belief that all partisan conflict is susceptible to transformation as long as partisanship is confronted directly. Indeed, the participatory strategy for dealing with partisanship enjoins two sorts of confrontation: confrontation *among citizens* and confrontation *with an actual decision*. The second alternative strategy for dealing with partisanship that I examine here, no less well known, is Madisonian. Its strategy for limiting partisanship is in many ways the mirror image of that proposed by participatory democrats. Where the participatory strategy puts its faith in confrontation, the Madisonian strategy puts its faith in separation—again of two sorts. For the Madisonian, the worst effects of partisanship can be contained by first separating citizens from the actual task of decision-making and then by institutionalizing separate sources of decision-making power.

Although I believe there is something to be learned from both the participatory and the Madisonian strategies for dealing with partisanship, I end up rejecting both of them in favor of an alternative which weds Madisonian institutional insights to participatory democrats' concern with the individual citizen. I argue that the best way to limit the unavoidable influence of partisanship is to confine partisan maneuvering to the latter stages of decision making and policy formation. I conclude that *both* distance and proximity can be made to serve the ends of deliberative democracy, that, indeed, distance and proximity must be combined in any effective strategy for limiting partisanship.

DELIBERATION AND PARTISANSHIP:
MUTUALLY EXCLUSIVE, MUTUALLY DELIMITING

That deliberation and partisanship are mutually exclusive does not seem particularly controversial. Deliberation is a process of weighing alternative courses of action. Partisanship is the exercise of power on behalf of a chosen course of action. Especially when viewed in the context of democratic politics, deliberation and partisanship thus seem irreconcilable. First, and most obviously, deliberation involves weighing alternatives; partisanship involves coercion, negotiation, or, in its most discursive form, rhetorical manipulation. Second, deliberation requires balancing or adjudicating between a plurality of views; partisanship presupposes that one view has been judged superior (or advantageous). Third, deliberation requires only an opposing viewpoint; partisanship requires an opponent.

But it hardly follows from any of these differences that the aim of deliberative democracy should be the wholesale elimination of partisanship. On the contrary, deliberation and partisanship are also mutually delimiting. Assuming we value deliberation, we ought to limit partisanship. But I believe that the value we place on deliberation itself also requires that deliberative democrats acknowledge the necessity—and therefore value—of partisanship.

Deliberation, however closely tied to action, is not the same thing as acting. However we construe the relationship between thought and action, most of us would agree that there is an essential difference between thinking through a course of action and *deciding upon* or *choosing* one. Deliberation requires the consideration of alternatives; choice requires the elimination of all but one alternative. Hence, collective action—the *raison d'être* of deliberation—paradoxically requires that deliberation give way to partisanship. Except in the abstract world of an ideal speech situation, deliberation is limited by partisanship. Choice, in other words, is always partial, always partisan. Without deliberation, action is a mere exercise of will; but without action, deliberation is reduced to mere contemplation.

The distinction between deliberation and contemplation is often missed or glossed over by deliberative democrats in their zeal to drive home the distinction between raw power (or partisanship) and deliberation. However distinct deliberation and partisanship might be, we also need to recognize that eliminating partisanship is not only impossible, it is undesirable—for to do so would be to abolish deliberation in the process. Indeed, the very existence of political deliberation requires, even entails, partisanship. This seeming paradox is really no paradox at all: deliberation is thought that is directed at action, thought whose *telos* is a decision. Take away all prospect of action, take away the need to decide or choose, and deliberation does not simply wilt, it ceases to exist altogether. When we also remember that political choice is by definition collective, we can see why political deliberation depends on partisanship: deliberation requires action, which requires choice, which in political life is collective, which (in a democracy) requires moving from "the many as individuals" to "the many as one."[2]

From the standpoint of deliberative democracy, then, eliminating partisanship would be self-defeating. Partisanship is, rather, to be accepted as a necessary component of democratic governance. At the same time, however, democratic deliberation requires that partisanship be kept within strict limits because, all other things being equal, limiting partisanship is likely to open up more space for deliberation. Limiting partisanship, in other words, amounts to an indirect way of promoting deliberation. As obvious as that may seem, few defenders of deliberative democracy have paid much attention to the problem of limiting partisanship. Most advocates of deliberation end up falling back on tried and presumably true recipes, endorsing either a Madisonian strategy directed at containing partisanship or a participatory strategy aimed at transcending partisanship. My complaint here is not that these strategies have somehow outlived their usefulness, but that they are *themselves* limited. Neither containment through separation nor transcendence through confrontation is alone a sufficient strategy for blunting partisanship. On the contrary, both have a role to play in minimizing the inevitable force of partisanship in democratic politics.

THE PARTICIPATORY AND MADISONIAN STRATEGIES

With roots that extend at least as far back as Pericles' funeral oration,[3] the participatory alternative is certainly the most venerable of the two dominant strategies for containing partisanship. It is also the more ambitious of the two, aiming as it does not simply at the diffusion or containment of partisanship but rather at its transcendence. The formula is as well known as it is simple: Participation in democratic decision-making turns self-interest into civic virtue.

Notice that the emphasis here is on participation in the act of making public decisions. Even when participatory democrats underline the deliberative nature of public decision making, they are assuming that citizens are deliberating *at the point of decision*, that deliberation will issue in proximate action. For example, Benjamin Barber's "strong talk" (1984) and John S. Dryzek's "discursive democracy" (1990) are both decision-making procedures as much as they are modes of deliberating.

Given what I said earlier about the inescapable necessity of partisanship, it will come as no surprise that I find this strategy hopelessly naive. More specifically, it is the immediacy of the link between deliberation and decision-making or action that I believe is problematic in the participatory strategy for countering partisanship. Participatory democrats are right to suppose that public discussion *does* encourage civic virtue, and does allow at least a partial transcendence of partisanship. But deliberation's chances of blunting partisanship are hindered, not helped, by wedding it to participation. By binding deliberation directly to decision-making, the participatory strategy renders deliberation itself partisan.

Deliberation is only complete when it issues in decision, and decisions are inherently partisan. No form of deliberation is exempt from the requirement to move from thought to action, from a consideration of plural options to a decision that this or that particular option is best. Hence, no form of deliberation can do away with partisanship altogether. Collective choice is always a matter of moving from plural wills to the unity of decision. As soon as the demand for unity, required by action itself, is imposed, deliberation *must* come to an end. The closer the choice point comes, the greater the pressure will be to cease deliberating. Participatory arrangements thus tend to exaggerate existing partisan biases.

The participatory strategy for dealing with partisanship envisions citizens deliberating about public affairs over which they have some immediate control. Partisanship, in other words, is to be controlled (or transcended) by engaging citizens directly in public decision making. The participatory strategy thus views partisanship as a kind of disease that can be cured homeopathically: inject partisanship into the political process early on, and the body politic will fight it. On the face of it, this prescription seems promising. Direct action in the public sphere might conceivably transform partisanship by heightening citizen interest in public affairs, by discouraging the narrow consideration of self-interest, and/or by promoting an exploration of shared interests. But notice what the metaphor assumes: that the body politic really does have the equivalent of an autoimmune system that need only be triggered so as to kick into high gear. Unfortunately, we cannot simply presume that such an immune system exists. As a result, partisanship cannot be expected to give way automatically before the beneficent dynamics of public participation. On the contrary, the closer citizens get to the point of decision, the more likely partisanship is to become contagious. Inserting partisanship into politics before deliberation has had a chance to develop any immunity to it in the form of public mindedness will render politics more, not less, partisan.

Aristotle and Rousseau, who occupy lofty positions in the participatory democratic pantheon, understood the problem well. Ruling and being ruled in turn requires a certain kind of citizen. For Aristotle, this meant that the *polis* had to take special care in educating its young and in attending to the formative influence of its laws. And Rousseau admitted that, absent the intervention of a civil religion or civic savior, such citizens were likely to be hard to come by. Both thinkers were sensitive, in a way their contemporary disciples are not, to the fact that fashioning publicly minded citizens on the potter's wheel of participation *presupposes* a certain kind of clay. Both were aware that participation will transform partisanship *only* if participants are *already* ready to participate *as citizens*. Likewise, Pericles knew full well that he was preaching to the converted.

The Madisonian strategy, by contrast, does not pretend to remake partisans into public- spirited or even deliberative citizens. Its aspirations are only to contain the partisanship that is an inevitable component of "government by men, not angels." The Madisonian approach to partisanship is nothing if not ironic: limit the effects of partisanship by providing systematic institutional support for a variety of factions. Madison's very aversion to factions led him to design a system which protects them even as it constrains them. Both Federalism and the separation of powers force compromises among partisans and thereby create a space for deliberation in the decision-making process. But divided government secures partisans' positions even as it forces them to abandon partisan purity. Representative government, meanwhile, frees up further space for non-partisan politics by severing the close link between citizens and decision making[4]—but it does nothing to counter partisanship at the level of the average citizen.

Designed partly with the failings of the participatory strategy in mind, the Madisonian strategy attempts to overcome the problems created by fusing public discussion and action by interposing representatives between the two and then by dividing the power wielded by partisan decision makers. The problems with this strategy are two. First, it wholly ignores the question of limiting partisanship among ordinary citizens. Where the participatory strategy was flawed, the Madisonian strategy is simply silent. It offers us no means to ensure that the interests that partisan representatives are representing are themselves anything but partisan. Hence, the Madisonian strategy may succeed in blunting partisanship at the point of action, but not at the point of discussion. And even that is questionable. Indeed, I believe that the Madisonian strategy's great claim to fame, that divided power will encourage deliberation, is greatly exaggerated. The Madisonian strategy deals with partisanship by forcing one partisan to confront another at the point of decision. But, as I argued above, the point of decision is an inherently partisan moment. Divided government produces some deliberation, yes. But more often it produces bargaining, negotiation, and maneuvering for power. Government is occasionally deliberative. But it is always authoritative and, hence, partisan.

Although the participatory and Madisonian strategies for dealing with partisanship are usually cast as polar opposites, each in its own way rests ultimately on a shared faith in the power of decision-making procedures. While it is true that the participatory democrat stresses face-to-face confrontation where the Madisonian stresses separation and division, both strategies ultimately attempt to counter partisanship *at the point of decision*. That, in the end, is a mistake. It dooms the participatory strategy to failure and the Madisonian strategy to impotence, if not irrelevance. The participatory strategy cannot successfully explain how deliberation is to arise out of partisan confrontation; the Madisonian strategy can do so, but remains mute about how partisan confrontation might be limited in the first place.

Neither Madisonians nor participatory democrats have much to say about limiting partisanship among citizens prior to their entry into a decision-making arena. Participatory democrats assume the problem away, convinced that partisanship will melt away in the cauldron of public assemblies. Madisonians, realistic to the point of cynicism, assume that partisanship is simply part of the political landscape and seek only to filter it. On the one hand we are told that partisanship is there to be transcended, on the other that it must simply be accepted. Deliberative democrats have for some time sensed that this is a false dichotomy. We neither have to hope for a world of pure consensus nor acquiesce to a world of irremediable antagonisms. In the remainder of this essay, I outline a third option, one that combines the participatory democrats' appreciation for the role of ordinary citizens with Madison's matter-of-fact appreciation of the dynamics of political choice. From the participatory democrat, the strategy I defend here borrows the goal of dealing with partisanship in a fundamentally democratic way. At the same time, however, this strategy imitates the Madisonian perspective's emphasis on the importance of detachment and shared responsibility. Such a strategy would, in short, attempt to limit the role of partisanship *at the grass roots* through procedures and processes that acted at a distance from actual decision-making processes and which simultaneously encouraged partisans to recognize their interdependence. Such a strategy would cast citizens in the role of neither mere voters nor all-powerful legislators. Instead, it would seek to enable all citizens to participate as equal members of society's ongoing platform committee: the all-important body that frames the debate that representatives are called upon to periodically adjudicate and codify.

A VIA MEDIA: SEPARATION AND CONFRONTATION

The middle path I want to recommend between the participatory and Madisonian strategies for countering partisanship results from marrying the better half of each of them. If we subtract the idea of direct decision-making from the participatory strategy, we are left with the idea of citizens confronting one another directly. If we then wed that notion to the Madisonian idea of encouraging interdependence, we arrive at the basic outline of an alternative approach to the problem of partisanship, an approach that, because it incorporates elements of *both* separation *and* confrontation, lies somewhere between the participatory and Madisonian strategies, somewhere "between Athens and Philadelphia." Such an approach would stress sustained political engagement outside of formal decision-making bodies. It would view the problem of containing partisanship as an ongoing task, involving all citizens and depending to a great extent on the degree to which citizens see themselves as interdependent actors with overlapping values and interests. Finally, such an approach would see partisanship not as an unfortunate residue of the darker side of human nature or an evil to be banished from a secular Eden, but as the inevitable concomitant of democratic decision-making. Let us look a bit more closely at each of these four elements.

Indirect political engagement is perhaps the single most important element of the strategy I am recommending here. It is also the most emblematic, as it results from a fusion of confrontation and separation. But what kind of political engagement might conceivably qualify as being both confrontational *and* separated from actual political decision-making? There is only one type, so far as I can see, and that is deliberation. Political deliberation is by definition a form of engagement with the collectivity of which one is a member. This is all the more true when two or more citizens deliberate together. Yet deliberation is also a form of political action that precedes the actual taking and implementation of decisions. It is thus simultaneously connected and disconnected, confrontational and separate. It is, in other words, a form of indirect political engagement.

This conclusion, namely, that we ought to call upon deliberation to counter partisanship and thus clear the way for deliberation, looks rather circular at first glance. And, semantically at least, it certainly is. Yet this ought not to concern us very much. Politics, after all, is not a matter of avoiding semantic inconveniences, but of doing the right thing and getting desirable results. In political theory, therefore, the real concern is always whether a circular argument translates into a self-defeating prescription. And here that is plainly not the case, for what I am suggesting is that deliberation can diminish partisanship, which will in turn contribute to conditions amenable to continued or extended deliberation. That "deliberation promotes deliberation" is surely a circular claim, but it is just as surely an accurate description of the real world of lived politics, as observers as far back as Thucydides have documented.

It may well be that deliberation rests on certain preconditions. I am not arguing that there is no such thing as a deliberative "first cause." Indeed, it seems obvious to me both that deliberators require something to deliberate *about* and that deliberation presumes certain institutional structures and shared values. Clearly something must get the deliberative ball rolling and, to keep it rolling, the cultural terrain must be free of deep chasms and sinkholes. Nevertheless, however extensive and demanding deliberation's preconditions might be, we ought not to lose sight of the fact that, once begun, deliberation tends to be self-sustaining. Just as partisanship begets partisanship, deliberation begets deliberation. If that is so, the question of limiting partisanship and stimulating deliberation are to an important extent the same question.

Fortunately, we now have innovative recommendations aplenty for stimulating deliberation,[5] covering virtually every institution in American society, including, of course, government itself. The problem at the moment is choosing from among them in such a way as to achieve the widest and longest lasting impact. Although prioritizing deliberative reforms is a far more complex task than it might appear to be at first glance,[6] each element of the *via media* I am recommending here establishes a separate criterion that reform proposals ought to meet. These four criteria helps us sort through the plethora of proposals now being discussed by academics and policymakers. This is as true of this first element as it is of the other three, for it calls not for expanding deliberation *tout court* but, rather, for expanding deliberation *outside the context of public decision-making bodies*. Hence, it calls on us to resist plans for stimulating deliberation through the radical decentralization of society. It likewise recommends that we demand more of deliberative reform than that it shore up existing deliberative institutions, however valuable that might be. Instead, the premium this strategy places on indirect political engagement asks us to look for deliberative opportunities precisely in those places we are least accustomed to looking for them: families, churches, civic organizations, professions, public spaces, and the like.

To encourage indirect political engagement by encouraging political deliberation is, in one sense, quite radical, for although it is not at all the same thing as adopting the view that "everything is political," it is tantamount to claiming that "everything can be a site for political deliberation." Conversely, from another perspective this view hardly represents much of a challenge at all, for it simply asks us to recognize the obvious fact that, ever since Athenian citizens carried the business of the assembly and courts into the *agora*, politics has always seeped out through the cracks of formal institutions. And it is to recognize that, at least within certain limits, this is not only proper, but desirable—desirable because decisions that are discussed are likely to be wiser than those that are not, wherever they happen to be discussed.

In general terms, then, aiming somewhere between Athens and Philadelphia means spurring deliberation. But we can locate our target more precisely than that. We saw earlier that the second element of this strategy is to *counter partisanship not only at the institutional treetops, but at the grass roots as well*. This second criteria narrows our search to reforms that might stimulate deliberation there—where it is insulated from the inherently partisan pressure to adjudicate disputes and issue policy. But just what does stimulating grass-roots deliberation mean? It means encouraging citizens to actively deliberate outside of formal decision-making institutions at what is normally thought of as the "pre-political" level. It means stimulating political discourse in places that are not normally thought of as "political." It means working to promote thoughtful exchanges among those who are political, but not yet partisan. It means cultivating a public both willing and able to engage one another in political discussion. Finally, and most centrally, it means finding creative ways to support the civic fabric of society, of strengthening those institutions which, while not charged with the responsibility for making political decisions, are potential sites for political deliberation.

The argument for countering partisanship at the grass roots by supporting political deliberation there is pretty simple: If deliberation is a good thing in "deliberative bodies" like congress, isn't a good thing among average citizens, too? To suppose otherwise is to hold either that the average citizen is *in*capable of deliberation or that the average citizen is *less* capable of deliberation than the average representative. Both positions collapse upon even the most glancing scrutiny. To hold that the average citizen is *in*capable of deliberation is both patently antidemocratic and empirically questionable, to say the very least. To hold that the average citizen is *less* capable of deliberation than the average representatives is perhaps slightly less antidemocratic and empirically dubious, but achieves this very modest gain in credibility only at the cost of landing in the out-and-out contradiction of valorizing deliberation in one place while denigrating it in another.

If deliberation contains moments of both confrontation and engagement, democratizing deliberation by making it the province of the citizenry rather than leaving it in the hands of representatives has the potential of greatly expanding the degree to which confrontation and engagement become society-wide traits, traits which work on an ongoing basis to blunt the worst effects of partisanship. At least as important, such a democratization of deliberation is likely to enhance the deliberativeness of the polity since it will encourage deliberation at one remove from the locus of decision making—precisely the place it is most likely to succeed.

I began this section by arguing that political deliberation at some remove from decision- making structures is a form of both separation and engagement. I have also just argued that political deliberation might be made essentially democratic, so that it works at the grassroots, among ordinary citizens, rather than solely in the chambers of government. Now it is time to ask whether such citizen deliberation is capable of *heightening citizens' appreciation of their own interdependence.* Can deliberation be counted upon to supply this, the third element of the *via media* sketched above? Yes, it can—and for reasons that will be familiar to all students of Western political thought.

The Madisonian strategy seeks to encourage interdependence among decision makers by dividing power among them. But that is not an option if we are considering citizens rather than their representatives, since in the case of citizens there is no (institutional) power to divide. (Alternatively, we might say that "divided power" is already to a large extent a reality among citizens. But the result is the same.) How then might we proceed? To answer this question we need only look at the Madisonian strategy as a dynamic process rather than as a one-time solution. Madison envisioned the separation of powers and Federalism as means to combat factions in the name of a larger public interest. In one of the greatest ironies in political theory, it was precisely *division* that was to produce *unity*.

As remarkable as the Madisonian solution to partisanship might be, or perhaps because it is so remarkable, we have tended to focus on the outcomes it produces, without fully appreciating the intermediate term in this equation: deliberation. Although divided power makes deliberation possible by opposing interest to interest, it is ultimately deliberation that makes possible the definition of shared values and interests, and the formulation of plans to implement them. Under the U.S. Constitution, divided power creates the reality of interdependent representatives. On the Madisonian theory, interdependence ideally produces deliberation, which in turn defines its terms and contours. *Even on the Madisonian view,* then, deliberation is not simply a pious wish, but is instead the means by which the formal, institutional interdependence of the Constitution is translated into the substantive interdependence of law and policy. On the Madisonian view, in short, deliberation defines or articulates a preexisting interdependence. Even on this rather hardheaded view, in other words, deliberation is not simply a by-product of interdependence, but is required if interdependence is to be expressed in actual decisions.

Will deliberation work the same way among ordinary citizens? Yes and no. Yes, deliberation will tend to heighten citizens appreciation of their interdependence. At the same time, the results are likely to be analogous rather than identical to those in formal governmental bodies, since citizen deliberation must of course function in the absence of the institutional interdependence established by the US constitution, with its clear specification of joint responsibilities. The theoretical mutuality of interests assumed by the Constitution exists among ordinary citizens, too. The difference is that they have only their interests, not the impetus of divided power, to encourage them to discover and articulate them. Granted. But once they begin to do so, they are every bit as likely to succeed as the average representative. Citizen deliberation, in other words, will intensify citizens' appreciation of interdependence.

Although I cannot prove the point, there are compelling reasons to think that citizen deliberation yields an awareness of overlapping interests. I have already alluded to the first, and perhaps most telling of these: if governors in a system of divided government such as our own succeed in deliberating their way to the public interest (however imperfectly or irregularly), surely ordinary citizens can be counted upon to do the same thing. Indeed, if my initial argument that decision-making spells the end of deliberation is on the mark, then we have good reason to expect citizens to deliberate *better* than their representatives. One can add to these theoretical considerations a lengthening list of empirical findings which suggest not only that citizens are willing and able to engage in political deliberation, but also that they are quite able to do so—able, that is, precisely in the sense of coming to a deeper appreciation of the collective nature of the problems they face (Dale et al. 1995; Gundersen 1995; Dryzek 1990; see also Gundersen *n.d.*, chapter 4).

In the end, the claim that deliberation enhances interdependence is hardly a radical one. After all, if deliberation will of itself diminish partisanship, as I started out by saying, it must at the same time enhance interdependence.

To aim between Athens and Philadelphia requires, perhaps more than anything else, a changed way of thinking about partisanship. Institutions and ways of thinking tend to change together; hence if the institutional reorientation suggested here is to take root, it must be accompanied by a new way of thinking about partisanship. *Shifting our appraisal of partisanship* will amount to a nothing less than a new attitude toward politics. It will require that we aspire to something new, something that is at once less lofty (and less threatening) than the unity to which direct democracy is supposed to lead, but more democratic (and more deliberative) than encouraging political deliberation among a selected group of representatives. As I argued above, it will require that we seek to stimulate deliberation among all citizens.

With Madison, we need to view partisanship as inevitable. Collective choice, indeed choice itself, is a partisan affair. But we also need to resist the equation of politics and partisanship. If politics is seen as nothing more than a clash of partisan interests, it is likely to stay at that level. Conversely, for deliberation to work, it must be seen as reasonable, if not all-illuminating—as efficacious, if not all-powerful. At the same time, of course, citizens must borrow a page from the participatory democrat's book by coming to view deliberation as their responsibility rather than something that is done only by others in city hall, the state capitol, or Congress—others who are, after all, under direct and constant pressure to act rather than deliberate. Politics, in other words, must be resuscitated as an allegiance to democratic deliberation.

SOME PRACTICAL ILLUSTRATIONS

How might the four elements of the strategy I have outlined be put into practice? In the space that remains I want to point out a number of practical reforms consistent with what has been said so far. Before I do, though, I should point out that they are meant primarily as illustrations of the sort of policies and processes that are consistent with my intermediate strategy, not as a full platform, much less as an exhaustive catalogue. Even were space to permit a more elaborate discussion, the practical implications of the position I am advocating resist any final or complete codification for the simple reason that deliberation and democracy are both inherently open-ended processes. One cannot predict where deliberation will take us, especially if deliberation is taken seriously by ordinary citizens. And that applies as much to the question of how and where deliberation is to take place as to anything else. That having been said, it is still worthwhile to ask what sorts of things might bring us closer to a society "between Athens and Philadelphia."

Encouraging political deliberation is both easier and more difficult than we commonly believe. It is easier to stimulate deliberation than is commonly believed, because the opportunities for doing so are much wider than the Madisonian strategy leads us to believe. Indeed, they are far wider than even the participatory strategy admits. Conversely, it is more difficult to stimulate deliberation than is usually appreciated because deliberation requires more than the right setting. It also requires motivation, skill, and no small measure of dedication.

Nevertheless, however reformers may have simplified the problem of encouraging deliberation, they have been right to insist that it is indeed possible. More to the point here, they have been unusually creative and systematic in advancing concrete proposals for deliberative policy reform. Although we may view some of these proposals as alternately naive and timid, there is no shortage of promising options. Perhaps as important, many of the deliberative reforms that have been advanced in recent years are likely to be mutually reinforcing. To illustrate this, consider the following, much abbreviated, list of reform proposals.

1. Reinterpret the First Amendment so as to prioritize the value of public discourse over private expression (Sunstein 1995; Fiss 1988, 185–186).

2. Permit so-called fusion voting (cross-endorsement) so as to stimulate challenges to the dominant political parties (see Argersinger 1990, 288–89).

3. Improve the quality of publicly provided goods and services so as to encourage an appreciation for civic values and, indirectly, public discourse (Spragens 1990).

4. Use public schools to teach deliberative skills and encourage respect for public deliberation (Gundersen *n.d.*, 267; Bean and Apple 1995; Steiner 1994).

5. Limit corporate access to broadcasting time (Lindblom 1990, 297–98) while expanding public-access broadcasting (Max M. Kampelman in Fishkin 1991, 99–100).

6. Redistribute income in the name of "equal deliberative opportunity" (see Gundersen 1995, 195–98; Spragens 1990, 221).

7. Institute a system of "interest group vouchers" to equalize access to information resources (see Fishkin 1991, 99–100).

8. Reorient journalistic norms away from "objectivity" toward discursive truth (Linksy 1990).

9. Promote programming on television and radio based on the deliberative participation of viewers and listeners as an alternative to the "bulletin-board" style of much of today's current talk radio and television (Gundersen 1995, 206).

10. Expand the use of "deliberative opinion polls" (Fishkin 1991);

11. Use advocacy groups to spur deliberation among the larger public rather than simply "informing" or "educating" nonmembers (Gundersen 1995, 205–206);

12. Make voluntary organizations more deliberative internally (Habermas 1989; Sciulli 1992; Wuthnow 1991);

13. Encourage deliberation among spouses (Gundersen *n.d.*, 272–76).

As even this condensed catalogue makes plain, the problem for the deliberative reformer is not in finding ways to enhance public deliberation, but in choosing where to start. Fortunately, as I noted before, the other three elements of the middle path provide us with some guidance there.

According to the particular deliberative approach to combating partisanship I argued for above, our first priority must be to stimulate deliberation among the citizenry as a whole. It is there where the Madisonian approach is weakest; it is there where we must work most strenuously. This means focusing our efforts on broadening citizen opportunities for public deliberation outside the "corridors of power." It means expanding public deliberation in places we are not used to thinking of as public.

As strenuously as we ought to pursue this goal, approximating it should not prove overly difficult. Our Madisonian reflexes, well-ingrained and reinforced in recent decades by heavy doses of democratic elitism and rational choice theory, ought not to prevent us from taking advantage of the opportunities for expanding and deepening citizen deliberation that exist all around us. Consider again the reforms just listed. Taken as a whole they are a potent reminder that deliberation can flourish—and be nurtured—virtually anywhere. And only the first few items on the list depend on wholly formal changes in the way politics is conducted; most of the rest depend upon a mix of formal and informal action. A few can even be pursued by entirely "private" or "voluntary" means. And virtually all of them can contribute to enhanced deliberation among the population as a whole.

As wide open as the possibilities for deliberative reform might be, some of the items on the short list need to be given special attention if citizen deliberation is to flourish in society as a whole. One of the reasons for aiming somewhere between Athens and Philadelphia, remember, was to use deliberation to promote a sense of interdependence among citizens. To the extent that a given reform encourages citizen deliberation at all, it will contribute to this end. But some reforms are probably going to be more effective in this respect than others. The last three items, which call for greater public deliberation among advocacy groups, voluntary associations, and marriages, respectively, are likely to be especially helpful in this regard for the simple reason that they address what are normally considered "private" organizations. If we not only recognize the public potential of such associations, but also actively support it as well, the dividends in heightened citizen appreciation of their mutual interdependence are likely to be very great, indeed.[7]

A new *via media* will also encourage a new attitude toward partisanship, one that recognizes its necessity, but believes in the possibility of confining it within clear limits. Citizens, like their representatives in Washington or the state capitol, will deliberate only if they see some value in doing so. Deliberation does not work very well in a world in which everyone behaves like the Athenian ambassadors in the Melian dialogue or in which everyone believes that, when all is said and done, Thomas Hobbes really *was* right. Here too, every single item on the above list can probably play some role. Deliberation begets deliberation, partly because it works—and people *see* that it works.

At the same time, I would argue that here we must take a long view. Reorienting how society thinks about politics (in this case, how it thinks about a *thinking* politics), is no small matter. It requires a solution with reach, from an institution that enjoys widespread public support, and in a way that is capable of dealing with the important cognitive component involved in all deliberation. Here I do not think there is an alternative to public schools—which, for starters, means strengthening them, not weakening them, as now seems fashionable. It also means changing curriculum to emphasize the inevitability of partisanship, struggle and manipulation, on the one hand, and the desirability and possibility of public deliberation, on the other. Schools should, of course, also teach deliberative skills. But my view is that the big change must come here: in the broad orientation to political life that they convey. Schools should be places where kids learn the lessons of Pericles and James Madison—and then learn to move beyond them.

CONCLUSION

Most of what I have had to say here stems from the view that partisanship is both the bane of deliberation and its natural outcome. Partisanship puts an end to deliberation—and in one sense that is all well and good, since deliberation is not an end in itself but is, rather, "thought-directed-at-*action*." Between thought and action, there will always be a place for partisanship in any democratic society worthy of the name. At the same time, partisanship that inordinately encroaches on the thoughtful activity of deliberation itself ought to be limited wherever possible. Here there is broad agreement among democratic theorists. But this agreement quickly breaks down over the issue of *how* to limit partisanship. The participatory strategy is to turn partisans against each other and to thus extinguish the flames of partisan rivalry. Less optimistic, the Madisonian strategy is to separate decision makers from the heat of partisan conflict, while forcing representatives to cooperate with each other. Having rejected both of these strategies, I argued for a *via media* between Athens and Philadelphia, one which borrows liberally from both of the older strategies. Its centerpiece is citizen deliberation, which I argued is capable of blunting partisanship. We cannot wish partisanship away. Nor can we force citizens to stop taking sides. All we can do is encourage its opposite. Fortunately, because deliberation begets deliberation, it is entirely reasonable to think that we can do so successfully. That place "between Athens and Philadelphia" is not so far off as we might think.

NOTES

1. I defend this definition at some length in Gundersen *n.d.* (chap. 3).

2. Even were partisanship not an ineliminable aspect of political choice, for a variety of reasons it is unlikely that deliberation could ever fully displace it. See Gundersen, *The Socratic Citizen, n.d.*: (Chapter 8).

3. In Thucydides' recreation of that speech, Pericles observes that "Instead of looking on discussion as a stumbling-block in the way of action, we [Athenians] think it an indispensable preliminary to any wise action at all" (1982, 110).

4. In the *Federalist 10*, Madison notes that the aim of representative government is to "refine and enlarge the public views by passing them through the medium of a chosen body of citizens." The result, he argued, would be "more consonant to the public good than if pronounced by the people themselves, convened for the purpose" (as quoted in Rossiter 1961, 82).

5. In recent years, theorists have advanced scores of proposals for stimulating deliberation directly. I refer to many of these and add some proposals of my own in Gundersen, *The Environmental Promise*, 1995: chap. 7 and in Gundersen, *The Socratic Citizen, n.d.*: chap. 9. Here my prescriptive discussion will necessarily be brief.

6. This is partly because doing so persuasively requires, among other things, that one invoke (and defend) a systematic theory of deliberative democracy. For one recent attempt to derive a deliberative reform menu in this way, see Gundersen, Ibid., *n.d.*: chap. 9.

7. For both empirical evidence that deliberation does in fact lead to a heightened appreciation of interdependence, as well as a theoretical explanation as to why we might expect this to be the case, see Gundersen, *The Environmental Promise*, 1995.

REFERENCES

Michael W. Apple and Bean, James A. 1995. "The Case for Democratic Schools." In *Democratic Schools*. Edited by Michael W. Apple. Alexandria, VA: Association for Supervision and Curriculum Development.

Argersinger, Peter H. 1990. "'A Place on the Ballot': Fusion Politics and Antifusion Laws." *American Historical Review* 85:287–306.

Barber, James. 1984. *Strong Democracy*. Berkeley, CA: University of California Press.

Dale, Duane, Amy Purvis, Terry Lockamy, and Steve Thompson. 1995. "Collaborative Problem Solving in Cameron County, Texas: The Coexistence Committee." Discussion Paper 95–8. Center for Biotechnology Policy and Ethics, Texas A & M University; College Station, Texas, 77843–4355.

Drysek, John S. 1990. *Discursive Democracy: Politics, Policy, and Political Science*. New York, NY: Cambridge University Press.

Fiss, Owen M. 1988. "Free Speech and Social Structure." In *Equal Opportunity*. Edited by Norman E. Bowie. Boulder, CO: Westview Press.

Fishkin, James S. 1991. *Democracy and Deliberation*. New Haven, CT: Yale University Press.

Gundersen, Adolf G. 1995. *The Environmental Promise of Deliberative Democracy*. Madison, WI: University of Wisconsin Press.

———. n.d. *The Socratic Citizen: A Deliberative Theory of Democracy*. Forthcoming.

Habermas, Jürgen. 1989. "Volkssourveränität als Verfahren." *Merkur* 6:465–477.

Lindblom, Charles. 1990. *Inquiry and Change*. New Haven, CT: Yale University Press.

Linsky, Martin. 1990. "The Media and Public Deliberation." In *The Power of Public Ideas*. Edited by Robert B. Reich. Cambridge, MA: Harvard University Press.

Majone, Giandomenico. 1990. "Policy Analysis and Public Deliberation." In *The Power of Public Ideas*. Edited by Robert B. Reich. Cambridge, MA: Harvard University Press.

Madison, James, Alexander Hamilton, and John Jay. 1961. *Federalist Papers*. Edited by Clinton Rossiter. New York, NY: New American Library.

Reich, Robert R. 1990. "Policy Making in a Democracy." In *The Power of Public Ideas*, ed. Robert R. Reich. Cambridge, MA: Harvard University Press.

Sciulli, David. 1992. *Theory of Societal Constitutionalism: Foundations of a Non-Marxist Critical Theory.* New York, NY: Cambridge University Press.

Spragens, Thomas. 1990. *Reason and Democracy.* Durham, NC: Duke University Press.

Steiner, David. 1994. *Rethinking Democratic Education.* Baltimore, MD: Johns Hopkins University Press.

Sunstein, Cass. 1995. *Democracy and the Problem of Free Speech.* New York, NY: Free Press.

Thucydides. 1982. *The Peloponnesian War.* Translated by Richard Crawley. New York, NY: The Modern Library.

Wuthnow, Robert. 1991. "The Voluntary Sector: Legacy of the Past, Hope for the Future?" In *Between States and Markets.* Edited by Robert Wuthnow. Princeton, N.J.: Princeton University Press.

CHAPTER 6

Working in Half-Truth: Some Premodern Reflections on Discourse Ethics in Politics

Mary G. Dietz

The international association of writers (PEN) held its 61st World Congress in Prague in 1991, five years to the month after the "revolution of the Magic Lantern" and the whirl of events that marked the beginning of the end of the Communist regime in Czechoslovakia, and a rebirth of politics (Ash 1995, 34).[1] The general political theme of the PEN congress posed a problem to politics, insofar as it raised questions about the role of the intellectual, and about the relationship of the intellectual to the professional politician. As Timothy Garton Ash reports, the problem was not merely a matter of academic debate but had itself become politicized in the Czech Republic "around the . . . magnetic polarity between the two Vaclavs, now better known as President Havel and Prime Minister Klaus" (Ash 1995, 34). Ash, who was himself an invited speaker at the congress, sought to clarify the problem by positing the following distinction:

> The intellectual's job is to seek the truth, and then to present it as fully and clearly and interestingly as possible. The politician's job is to work in half-truth. The very word party implies partial, one-sided. (The Czech word for party, *strana*, meaning literally "side," says it even more clearly). [1995, 35]

Ash's formulation put him at odds on one end of the polarity with Prime Minister Vaclav Klaus, who was also present at the congress and spoke in favor of the proposition that there is no clear dividing line, or special status, that the intellectual enjoys over the professional politician

(Ash 1995, 35). In fact, Klaus found Ash's notion that politicians work in half-truth "incredible," and he accused the author of *The Magic Lantern* (1990) of delivering a "political" speech against politicians, from the side of a partisan (and perhaps morally self-righteous) "intellectual" (1995, 35).[2] On the other end of the polarity, Ash's formulation was also at odds with President Vaclav Havel's view of politics as "work of a kind that requires especially pure people, because it is especially easy to become morally tainted" (37). "The way of a truly moral politics," Havel writes, "is neither simple nor easy" (38). With this in mind, Havel opened the PEN congress by acknowledging the distinctive position of the intellectuals and calling upon his "dear colleagues" to take responsibility and "have an impact on politics and its human perceptions in a spirit of solidarity" (34). Herein lies his hope that "a new spirituality" might come to politics (37).[3]

Klaus and Havel hold different views about the role and integrity of the intellectual in politics. Nevertheless, we might notice a shared, as spoken, conviction between them concerning the possibilities for *purity* in politics. Klaus registers the conviction on the side of the politician, and by adamantly resisting both Ash's uneasy metaphor of "half-truth," and Havel's investiture of the intellectual over the politician as the morally superior seeker-of-truth. Havel registers the same conviction on the side of the intellectual, by arguing (against both Ash and Klaus) that in a corrupted age politics can be transfigured by the moral commitments of those intellects and writers who refuse to be dissuaded by "the lie" that "politics is a dirty business" (Ash 1995, 37).[4] In this shared speech that commends itself to the purity of politics, the magnetic polarity between the two Vaclavs galvanizes into the form of a nearly Platonic political ideal. On this level, it matters not whether intellectuals are politicians or whether, by some dispensation of providence, politicians can become intellectuals. What matters is that both Vaclavs speak in the name of a politics that carries with it the imprimatur (if not the promise) of purity and truth.

Against this Vaclavian politics of truth, Ash deploys the alternative formulation of "working in half-truth" in order to distinguish "the professional party politician's job" from the intellectual's, especially as it is "reflected, crucially, in a different use of language" (1995, 35). Here he amplifies what it means to work in the language of half-truth:

> If a politician gives a partial, one-sided, indeed self-censored account of a particular issue, he is simply doing his job. And if he manages to "sell" the part as the whole then he is doing his job effectively. . . . If

an intellectual does that, he is not doing his job; he has failed in it. (1995, 36)

Ash is anxious to insist that he is not casting the intellectual as "the guardian or high priest of some metaphysical, ideological or pseudo-scientific Truth with a capital T" (1995, 36). Thus, the difference between the role of intellectual and the role of the politician is not equivalent in any easy way to the epistemological divide between absolute Truth and relativism, or the metaphysical divide between objective reality and subjective experience. Whatever else they are, Ash's intellectuals are not Platonic philosopher-kings; although from the perspective of Platonic philosophy his politicians are surely sophists and rogues. The divide between Ash's truth-seeking intellectual and his partisan politician has rather more to do with the linguistic and ethical terrain on which they work, and not the upper ether of epistemology and metaphysics. If this terrain is organized along lines of "responsibility," then we might understand the divide between the intellectual and the politician as a matter of assuming, as Ash puts it, "qualitatively different responsibilit[ies] for the *validity, intellectual coherence* and *truth*" of speech in each of these irreducible domains (Ash 1995, 36, italics mine).

SOME MACHIAVELLIAN PRESUPPOSITIONS

Ash's observations raise many interesting issues about the nature and the role of intellectual activity, in and outside of politics. But I want to appropriate the formulation of "working in half-truth" in a Machiavellian spirit, in order to suggest that it captures not only an "elementary fact" about the job of the partisan party politician, as Ash provocatively contends (1995, 35), but also something about the intrinsic impurity and partisanship of the peculiar domain of speech-action that we call "politics." As we shall see, the "intrinsic impurity" thesis embodies a substantial challenge to certain modern theoretical approaches to politics, insofar as it carries with it at least two Machiavellian presuppositions. First, the intrinsic impurity thesis implies that as a field of reality, politics cannot be adequately contained under the formal rubrics of a modern legal/juridical or a constitutional/democratic political philosophy alone. Second, it implies that political speech is not as open to the possibility of "redemption" under the normative claims of validity, coherence, and truth as some philosophical modernists and discourse ethicists appear to anticipate.

I am calling these presuppositions "Machiavellian" in less than a philosophical and more than a metaphorical sense. In the first instance, the limitations of a purely legal/juridical approach to politics are anticipated in Machiavelli's beastly advice in *The Prince* concerning the "two methods of fighting, the one by law, the other by force." The former, Machiavelli observes, "is often insufficient," hence one must "have recourse to the second." Then follow his famous remarks upon the lion and the fox (Machiavelli 1950, 64). In the second instance, Machiavelli anticipates the limitations of a concept of political speech as a practice of redeeming validity claims (especially with regard to sincerity), when he advises the prince that politics requires both the appearance of such qualities as sincerity, but also a "mind so disposed that when it is needful to be otherwise you may be able to change to the opposite qualities" (1950, 65). In short, a truly *virtu*ous prince-as-political-actor must not only be always ready to *intend to deceive* others, but also able to resist attempts by others to "redeem" the (sincere) intention behind the speech-act that deceives.

In light of these Machiavellian insights, we might also bear in mind Foucault's observation that even the "best" theories and philosophies do not constitute very effective protection against disastrous political choices. We should reckon with the fact that there is an extremely tenuous link between a philosophical conception of (political) language as communication, or a philosophically grounded account of political principles on the one hand, and the concrete speech dynamics of strategic political actors who appeal to such principles on the other.[5]

The intrinsic impurity of politics thesis that I am alluding to and the "political metaphysic without a philosophy"[6] that it represents, are not especially *en vogue* in political theory today. Theorists who are committed to leveling the "genre distinction" between politics and culture, or politics and society, or the personal and the political, or the "spheres" of public and private, will find suspect the effort to endow politics with a special kind of intrinsicality, although some may find the ambiguities embedded in the notion of "half-truth" appealing.[7] Theorists who are engaged in philosophical efforts to rationalize politics in terms of justice and equality, or "the basic intuitive ideas" of constitutional democracy, will find the moral implications of working in half-truth troubling, although they may appreciate the effort to distinguish politics as a form of action or a mode of procedure. At the highest political philosophical reaches of the latter group we can find John Rawls' theory of justice and political liberalism. In Rawls's view, the basic intuitive ideas of democratic politics include the notion that society is a fair system of cooperation (not conflict) between free and equal persons. Behind the idea of "person" are two moral powers that Rawls identifies: a capacity for a sense of justice, and a capacity for a conception of the good (Rawls, 1985, 233).

An even more important example of the philosophical effort to rationalize politics is Jürgen Habermas' influential discourse theory of deliberative democracy. Habermas conceives of the basic principles of the democratic constitutional state in relation to a normative conception of democratic deliberation among rational and reasonable agents who have themselves adopted the moral point of view (Habermas 1993, especially chapters 1,2). In both Rawls' and Habermas's philosophies, the normative structure of constitutional democracy is invested with a Kantian respect for individuals as free and equal persons, and for the impartiality of laws that all can agree to on that basis. Because I think that Habermas's political philosophy of discourse ethics provides the most powerful theoretical vindication of the practical attitude that I have been calling a "Vaclavian politics of truth," I will consider it more fully below, and in relation to the Machiavellian position on politics that I will proceed to defend.

HABERMASIAN DISCOURSE ETHICS

Jürgen Habermas has recently been developing a strong link between a philosophical conception of language (as communicative rationality) geared toward the redemption of validity claims; and the concrete dynamics of politics as speech-action. He unites the two in a discourse theory of politics as deliberative democracy, where the public use of reason is distinguished by the enactment of procedures (validity relations) through which participants (as free and equal citizens) achieve agreement through critical discussion, or at least engage in "action oriented toward reaching understanding" (Habermas 1993b, 133). Habermasian citizens are truth-seekers insofar as, in Habermas's words, "the sphere of validity relations is . . . internally differentiated in terms of the viewpoints proper to truth, normative rightness, and subjective truthfulness or authenticity" (Habermas 1990, 115).[8] In short, Habermas's defense of rationality and reasonableness, and his equally compelling conception of politics as democratic deliberation, are both directed toward identifying and rooting out of politics "distorted communicative" conditions. In clarifying the relation between speech and politics, Habermas notes that "discourse theory has the success of deliberative politics depend not on a collectively acting citizenry but on *the institutionalization of the corresponding procedures and conditions of communication*" (n.d. 12, italics mine). The "procedures and conditions" to which Habermas refers emerge out of a theory that (a) thematizes a "terrain of argumentation" in which validity claims are made; (b) assumes that all speech presupposes a "background consensus" among participants; and (c) anticipates that the validity claims inherent in the performing of a speech action can be "vindicated" or "redeemed" (*Einlosen*) when the background consensus among interlocutors breaks down or is challenged.[9]

Habermas links linguistic intersubjectivity as *practical discourse* to the vindication of validity-claims that all citizens make (either implicitly or explicitly) as speakers. Therefore, discourse theory reconstructs four claims that are potentially redeemable in every statement a speaker makes, and grounded in the very character (or the "universal pragmatics") of our linguistic intersubjectivity: (1) intelligibility (or comprehensibility); (2) truth (regarding the propositional content); (3) justifiability (or appropriateness, in terms of the norms invoked); and (4) truthfulness (or sincerity, in the sense that the speaker does not intend to deceive the listener). Undistorted communication (and hence the success of deliberative politics) is thus secured in procedures and conditions in which interlocutors can, if necessary, redeem the four validity-claims to intelligibility, truth, justifiability, and truthfulness that are themselves embedded in every speech-act.

The premise behind the highly specialized discussion that Habermas calls "practical discourse" is the desire *to reach agreement* on the basis of "rationally motivated approval of the substance of an utterance" (Habermas 1993b, 134). Thus, discourse ethics establishes what Habermas calls a "fundamental idea": interactions are *communicative* "when the participants coordinate their plans of action consensually, with the agreement reached at any point being evaluated in terms of the intersubjective recognition of validity claims" (Habermas 1993b, 58).[10] To clarify this point, Habermas draws his now well-known distinction between two types of social interaction—*communicative* and *strategic*:

> Whereas in strategic action one actor seeks to *influence* the behavior of another by means of the threat of sanctions or the prospect of gratification in order to *cause* the interaction to continue as the first actor desires, in communicative action one actor seeks *rationally* to *motivate* another by relying on the illocutionary binding/bonding effect (*Bindungseffekt*) of the offer contained in his speech act. (Habermas 1993b, 58)[11]

The normative and procedural implications of Habermas's analytic distinction are instructively sketched by Simone Chambers:

As opposed to strategic action, where participants are primarily interested in bringing about a desired behavioral response, in communicative action, participants are interested in bringing about a "change of
heart." For example, in strategic action participants often attempt to
sway each other by introducing influences unrelated to the merits of
an argument, for example, threats, bribes, or coercion. . . . Communicative actors are primarily interested in mutual understanding as opposed to external behavior. . . . Only the "force of the better argument"
should have the power to sway participants. (Chambers, 1996, 99)

Habermas's distinction between "pure" communicative action and
strategic action raises many difficulties, not the least of which is its
adherence to an idealized model of communication that, as Habermas
himself acknowledges, does not fit a great deal of everyday social
interaction (McCarthy 1991, 132). Machiavelli's famous riposte to those
thinkers who "have imagined republics and principalities which have
never been seen or known to exist in reality" (Machiavelli 1950, 56)
seems pertinent here, for the idealized model that Habermas imagines
and the distinction that supports it appear boldly to deny the Machiavellian insight that "how we live is so far removed from how we
ought to live, that he who abandons what is done for what ought to
be done, will rather learn to bring about his own ruin than his preservation" (56). I will return to this point as it relates to politics later.

For now, it is important to underscore that Habermas relies upon
the communicative-strategic distinction to do at least two things: first,
to show that on the level of linguistics, communicative action enjoys
an "originary" priority over strategic and all other modes of linguistic
usage, which are themselves "parasitic" (Rasmussen 1990, 38) or "derivative" (McCarthy 1991, 133) upon the former.[12] Second, on the level
of political theory, Habermas introduces the distinction in order to
limit the exercise of threats and coercion (or strategic action) by enu-
merating a formal-pragmatic system of discursive accountability (or
communicative action) that is geared toward human agreement and
mutuality. Despite its thoroughly modern accouterments, communicative action aims at something like the twentieth-century discourse-
equivalent of the chivalric codes of the late Middle Ages; as a normative
system it articulates the conventions of fair and honorable engagement between interlocutors. To be sure, Habermas's concept of communicative action is neither as refined nor as situationally embedded
as were the protocols that governed honorable combat across European cultural and territorial boundaries and between Christian knights;
but it is nonetheless a (cross-cultural) protocol for all that. The entire
framework that Habermas establishes is an attempt to limit human

violence by elaborating a code of communicative conduct that is designed to hold power in check by channeling it into persuasion, or the "unforced" force of the better argument (Habermas 1993b, 160).[13]

At its most abstract normative level, discourse theory formulates what Habermas calls an *"ideal speech situation."* This formulation has come in for its share of criticism, especially on the grounds that it posits an unrealizable, utopian ideal that bears no relevance for judging actual communicative contexts. The terms of this debate between Habermas and his critics involve highly complex methodological and philosophical issues in the reconstructive sciences, and I am in no position to negotiate them today (or, I suspect, any other day).[14] But let us agree for now that what Habermas calls "the ideal moment of unconditionality" is neither a utopian blueprint nor a hypostatized configuration, and that philosophy can explicate this moment beyond what he calls "the provinciality of the given historical context" (Habermas, 1993a, 146).[15] The question I want to ask is: How meaningful is it to conceive of politics as open to the philosophical achievement of a discourse ethics?

THE MILIEU PROPER TO POLITICS

In responding to this question, I want to return to the intrinsic impurity thesis that has been lying in wait here under the label of a Machiavellian politics of half-truth. For once we move from the subterranean contours of language philosophy to the "provincial" or existential terrain of politics; we are on the Machiavellian's field of actual historical reality. Hence, Machiavellian politics does not focus its challenge to Habermasian discourse ethics at the level of the reconstructive science of language, or the theory of communicative action that this science supports.[16] Indeed, the Machiavellian is quite content to allow the philosophers and underlaborers of discourse ethics—those who journey deep into the construction of language, normativity and the logic of discourse—to go about their business. For the Machiavellian, attending to such philosophical matters is just so much fiddling while Girolamo Savonarola burns.[17]

Where the Machiavellian thesis takes its stand against Habermasian discourse ethics is within "the milieu proper to politics," or what the phenomenologist Maurice Merleau-Ponty imaginatively terms (in deference to Machiavelli) "that knot of collective life in which pure morality can be cruel and pure politics requires something like a morality" (Merleau-Ponty 1964, 211, 214). This shifting of the terms of the debate from the Habermasian to the Machiavellian highlights the distance between a formal *theory* of practical discourse and the concrete complexities of the phenomenal world of politics and political speech.[18] From this vantage point of politics, the Habermasian appears all-too-modern, and *Diskursethik* seems politically naive, if not practically irrelevant. But what is the "range of phenomena," as Sheldon Wolin puts it, that Machiavelli perceived as uniquely peculiar to politics (Wolin 1960, 211), and how is it resistant to the categories of Habermasian discourse ethics?

With this question in mind, we might note (at least) three levels of action in where Machiavelli situates politics in *The Prince*.[19] Each of these levels involves the exercise of what we might call "instituting" and "constituting" acts. On the first and grandest level, Machiavelli's action concept of politics comes to life at the end of the treatise, with the exhortation to "liberate Italy from the barbarians" (Machiavelli 1950, 94). From this vantage point, politics is the activity that aims at the fate of the state, the whole community, or the collectivity, and for a period of time that is, in principle, indeterminate and open to the vicissitudes of fortune (Machiavelli 1950, 92-93; see also Castoriadis 1992, 255).[20] Politics in its grandest sense thereby undertakes the initiation of innovations or even, at its most transformative, a "new system" (94) or "order of things" (21). Under these circumstances, Machiavelli writes, it is sometimes necessary for the prince "to disturb the existing condition and bring about disorders . . . in order to obtain secure mastery," as Alexander VI did in Italy (25). It is one of the paradoxes of politics that sometimes acting contrary to a goal enables one to reach it. Disorders can bring order.

However, disorders can undermine order as well. Hence, on a second level, politics demands the astute exercise of power and an acute sense of what works in practice (*verita effettuale*), always with a view toward avoiding ruin (Machiavelli 1950, 14). Machiavelli offers this "general rule" to the prince: "whoever is the cause of another becoming powerful, is ruined himself; for that power is produced by him either through craft or force; and both of these are suspected by the one who has been raised to power" (14). Implicit in this observation is the fundamental view of politics as an arena of conflict and struggle where the political actor must anticipate and detect (as only the prudent man can) "the evils that are brewing" (11). The prince must be prepared to "remedy disorders" that are not of his own making through violence if necessary, and before they become insoluble (8).[21] Yet no certainty attends the politician's capacity to anticipate and counter disorder. "This is found in the nature of things," Machiavelli writes, "that one never tries to avoid one difficulty without running into another, but prudence consists in being able to know the nature of the difficulties, and taking the least harmful as good" (84–85). As Merleau-Ponty observes, "power is always described in *The Prince* as questionable and threatened" (Merleau-Ponty 1964, 212). The world cannot be made unequivocally safe; nothing predestines it for a final harmony.

The achievement of secure mastery, equivocal though it may be, requires a background consensus that Machiavelli repeatedly characterizes as the support of the people (Machiavelli 1950, 38–39, 67, 68, 70, 71, 81; also Merleau-Ponty 1964, 212). "And let no one oppose my opinion in this," he warns, "by quoting the trite proverb, 'He who builds on the people, builds on mud'" (38). Yet this collective consensus is not "interpretive understanding," much less the *end* or goal of politics in Machiavelli's view. Rather, consensus is a means (perhaps the most significant means) that allows politics (as the activity that aims at the fate of the collectivity) to continue. In Merleau-Ponty's words, consensus is "the crystallization of opinion, which tolerates power, accepting it as acquired" (Merleau-Ponty 1964, 212). On a third level of action, then, politics imposes upon the politician the imperative to maintain the consensus that is the support of the people, or at least to work to avoid its dissolution, which can happen at any time. Thus, Machiavelli reiterates, "Well-ordered states and wise princes have studied diligently not to drive the nobles to desperation, and to satisfy the populace and keep it contented, for this is one of the most important matters that a prince has to deal with" (Machiavelli 1950, 69).

I have located the milieu proper to politics on these three levels of action in order to illuminate a primary Machiavellian point. On all three levels of instituting and constituting acts, from the grandest and most visionary (i.e., the institution of new modes and orders), to the gravest and most elementary (i.e., the anticipation and remedy of evils), to the grittiest and most rudimentary (i.e., the maintaining of consensus between politician and public), *politics is an irreducibly strategic concern and a domain of strategic action*. Our basic political commitments notwithstanding, this is the case in princedoms as well as republics, authoritarian as well as democratic regimes, Communist and post-Communist nations. Although there is much that must be said by way of evaluation and critique about how ideals get articulated, power organized, consensus sought, and tensions managed in these various forms of state, there is no prior or more basic "truth of the matter" than the presence of strategic interests in the power struggle that is politics, whatever the regime (Machiavelli 1950, 56).[22]

Nor does the strategic quality of politics embody a necessary distinction between ruler and ruled, or politicians and citizens. As Isaiah Berlin puts it in reference to Machiavelli, "The subjects or citizens must be Romans too . . . if they lead Christian lives, they will accept too uncomplainingly the rule of mere bullies and scoundrels" (Berlin 1982, 55). When it comes to the pursuit of objectives, the feasibility of different courses of action, the struggle for competitive advantage, the contest for mastery, and the likelihood of success, there is no *a priori* or predetermined division between the "strategic" or active state and the "non-strategic" or inert citizenry. Indeed, the very division between the ruler and the ruled is often the outcome of strategic struggles between participants in politics. Once the line is drawn, the relationship between ruler and ruled may be the continuation of this struggle in a different, but always strategic, form. Thus, when Machiavelli counseled the prince against perceiving (much less treating) the people as "mud," he also conveyed the notion that the strategic domain that is politics extends into the people itself—even if the means of containment and control of the subjects differ from princedom to princedom, and the possibilities for transforming princely subjects into republican citizens differ from state to state.

In identifying the strategic dimension of struggle that is politics, however, I do not mean to suggest that politics is fundamentally a context of domination, coercion, aggression, threat and accusation[23]; although no one recognized better than Machiavelli that these means and even worse ferocities may be called for in certain situations. Witness Caesare Borgia's brutal slaying of his minister Remirro (Machivelli 1950, 27); Ferdinand's "pious cruelty" toward the Moors (82); Severus' expeditious and bloody dispatch of Julianus, then Nigrinus, and then Albinus (72–73). "For it must be noted," Machiavelli remarks, "that men must either be caressed or else annihilated . . . the injury that we do to a man must be such that we need not fear his vengeance" (9). Nevertheless, politics in a Machiavellian sense is not reducible to violence any more than it is reducible to the honest delegation of individual wills, or the intersubjective mutuality of reciprocal understanding. Part of the intransigence of politics, as Machiavelli makes clear, involves its refusal to transform, or restore itself into, the philosophical desire of an ethical ideal. Yet politics also resists being factored into the basest of basic functions. Machiavelli can therefore maintain in equilibrium a relation that the Habermasian attempts to break. Thus, he writes: "the character of peoples varies, and it is easy to persuade them of a thing, but difficult to keep them in persuasion. And so it is necessary to order things so that when they no longer believe, they can be made to believe by force" (Machiavelli 1950, 22).

What Machiavelli asks us to recognize, in other words, is that politics alternately tenses and relaxes somewhere in-between pure persuasion and pure force. This collective knot (to return to Merleau-Ponty's phrase) of "vested interests and expectations, privileges and rights, ambitions and hopes, all demanding preferential access to a limited number of goods" (to borrow Wolin's phrase) loosens and constricts in a milieu that is neither pure manipulation (where humans are treated as "means") nor pure communication (where humans are treated as "ends" in themselves) (Merleau-Ponty 1964, 211; Wolin 1960, 221). Within this in-between, reliance upon pure persuasion can be a disastrous thing; witness Savonarola—unarmed prophets fail (Machiavelli 1950, 22). But also within this world, pure violence can only be episodic and force intermittent, used and not used "according to the necessity of the case," lest power fall to ruin under the weight of human hatred and contempt (Machiavelli 1950, 56, 61).

With this in mind, we might now return to the political naiveté of *Discursethik*, which begins by presupposing precisely what the Machiavellian considers not only naive but self-defeating: that it is meaningful to conceive of politics and political speech as open to the vindicative powers of rational claims to validity, coherence and truth, or practically useful to ask participants "to exclude from [their] conversation all strategic and instrumental attitudes toward interlocutors" (Chambers 1996, 100). The Machiavellian throws the coherence of this "intellectualist" presupposition into question by maintaining, in the name of politics, that those who rely upon the consensuality of communicative rationality must necessarily come to grief among so many who are not communicative or, more accurately, always and inevitably strategically communicative and communicatively strategic.[24] Let me now try to say precisely what all of this might mean by returning at last to the intrinsic impurity and partisanship of political speech.

THE INTRINSIC IMPURITY OF POLITICAL SPEECH

Just as the work of politics tends to generate a good many needs for which deeds of varying extremity are required, so political speech—the activity of articulating and justifying these needs and the deeds that spring from them—may prove impenetrable to discourse ethics, if not agonizing to communicative actors of the Habermasian kind. What "kind" of actor is this? Simone Chambers offers a succinct characterization of the participants in Habermasian practical discourse:

"In discourse a participant must recognize his dialogue partner as responsible and sincere in her desire to reach agreement, even if he disputes the validity of her claim. . . . A sincere interest in reaching authentic agreement presupposes that participants are not interested in deception, manipulation, misdirection, or obfuscation" (Chambers 1996, 99). Similarly, Seyla Benhabib writes of "good partners" in moral conversation and notes, "In conversation, I must know how to listen, I must know how to understand your point of view, I must learn to represent to myself the world and the other as you see them. If I cannot listen . . . the conversation stops, develops into an argument, or maybe never gets started" (Benhabib 1990, 359). As a theory of deliberative democracy, Habermasian discourse ethics projects precisely this kind of moral conversation upon political speech, if only to enable the communicative actor to identify and challenge instrumental and strategic effects in situations of political interaction with a view toward approaching truly rational agreement if not absolutely securing it.

Now it is important to recognize that the Machiavellian does not deny the moral value of the notion of sincere interest in reciprocal conversation, nor even rule out the possibility of its realization in certain domains of social interaction. The Machiavellian simply denies the translatability of moral conversation into the practice of political speech and, moreover, warns against developing the capacity "to assume the moral point of view" (Benhabib 1990, 359) as a mode of being (as opposed to acting) in politics.[25] "If men were all good," as Machiavelli puts a related point, "this precept would not be a good one; but as they are bad, and would not observe their faith with you, so you are not bound to keep faith with them" (Machiavelli 1950, 64).[26] This is not so much a theory of human nature as it is an observation about human conduct in the milieu proper to politics and political speech.

Because the politician's world and hence the politician's speech cannot be readily separated from any of the elements that Habermas links to strategic action (the attempt to reach objectives by influencing others' definitions of a situation, the purposeful pursuit of outcomes and consequences, the use of "weapons, goods, threats or enticements" to achieve the "success" of a policy, plan or operation), political speech cannot be cleansed of the elements that present gratuitous obstacles to Habermasian moral conversation. In the political world, if speech is mostly convention and convention is mostly aimed at securing certain strategic ends, then claims to validity, coherence and truth, not to mention "sincerity" and "truthfulness," have to be understood not only as "redeemables" but also as potential rhetorical tools, or "reliables" that enable political actors to go about their work, if not their life.[27]

To put this otherwise, the Machiavellian thesis holds that it is necessary for those who wish to maintain themselves in politics to learn, among other things, how *not* to be open to the argumentative redemption of validity claims, and to use this knowledge and not use it, according to the necessity of the case.[28] I take the import of Machiavelli's advice as underscoring the importance of both adaptability and strategic calculation in political speech. The effective political rhetorician, whether citizen or politician, speaker or hearer, recognizes that political speech is (quite often and necessarily) the rhetorical art of *strategically* deploying claims to "truth" and *instrumentally* appealing to "sincerity" while *calculatingly* disguising the fact that one is acting strategically, instrumentally, or calculatingly. Success in the domain of half-truth hinges on one's ability to grasp validity-claims as reliable techniques of persuasion and to deploy them effectively in response to problematic contexts.[29] It also requires cognizance of the fact that one is doing so.[30] The political actor must be cognizant, that is, of *working* in half-truth, as opposed to "being," in some constant or consistent characterological sense, "half-truthful" (or, for that matter, a "liar" or a "truth-teller"). Working in half-truth is a skill, an art, and a mode of acting, not a mode of being.

In politics, the effective strategic deployment of claims to validity, coherence and truth and the activity of effectively resisting their "redemption," does not necessarily take place in an ethical vacuum, even though it may be a moral one. Indeed, the skillful appeal to moral notions of "reciprocity" or "mutuality," and the rhetorical manipulation of moral values that one does not necessarily believe may, if successfully delivered, mark the difference between order and disorder, security and chaos, freedom and enslavement—even the polity's life or death. "A certain prince of the present time, whom it is well not to name," Machiavelli writes, "never does anything but preach peace and good faith, but he is really a great enemy to both, and either of them, had he observed them, would have lost him state or reputation on many occasions" (Machiavelli 1950, 66).

This does not mean that truth, or truth-seeking and truth-telling have no currency in politics or that politics is the graveyard of communicative principles. Although the prince should discourage unsolicited advice, Machiavelli argues, "he ought to be a great asker, and a patient hearer of the truth about those things of which he has inquired; indeed, if he finds that any one has scruples in telling him the truth he should be angry" (Machiavelli 1950, 88). Politics and political speech are not inherently immune to the deployment of validity claims, or even to their discursive redemption. Yet Machiavelli also reminds us of the peculiar complexity of these matters in politics by offering this telling observation:

> There is no other way of guarding one's self against flattery than by letting men understand that they will not offend you by speaking the truth; but when every one can tell you the truth, you lose their respect. A prudent prince must therefore take a third course, by choosing for his council wise men, and giving these alone full liberty to speak the truth to him, but only of those things that he asks and of nothing else; but he must ask them about everything and hear their opinion, and afterwards deliberate by himself in his own way, and in these councils and with each of these men comport himself so that every one may see that the more freely he speaks, the more he will be acceptable. (Machiavelli 1950, 87)

The compulsions of politics are formed by certain necessities that make it analytically difficult to establish nice distinctions, and practically impossible to sustain them. The Habermasian's distinction between communicative and strategic speech-action seems, in this respect, especially ill-adapted to the fugitive quality of politics, where the elements of the communicative and the strategic are intricately entangled and intertwined. To return to Machiavelli's example: if one of the imperatives of the political world is to avoid surrounding oneself with flatterers, then is not the politician's enlistment of those who "speak the truth" both a communicative and a strategic goal? It is communicative because "speaking the truth," as Machiavelli describes it, is not a mere game; it is a genuinely discursive activity where the politician asks for and hears the opinions of his or her interlocutors "in full liberty," and with a view toward shared counsel. Yet at the same time this communication is not an end-in-itself. It is strategic—not only in content, but also in form. For "speaking the truth" is a scenario that the politician creates, manages, and participates within, in order to "guard against the plague" of flatterers and mitigate "the risk of becoming contemptible," thereby achieving some measure of success in maintaining power (Machiavelli 1950, 87). There is in this sense an entanglement of, if not a complementarity between, strategic and communicative action in politics.[31]

If another of the imperatives of the political world is to avoid becoming contemptible, then speaking the truth is a good, but not an unalloyed good. The paradoxes of politics tend to wreak havoc with the principles of communication because, as Merleau-Ponty observes, "politics is a relationship to men rather than principles" (Merleau-Ponty 1964, 219).[32] Thus in politics an openness toward the opinions of others is sometimes not a condition *of* mutual respect, but antithetical *to* it. It may be a peculiarity of the political domain that "when everyone can tell you the truth, you lose their respect," but it is a peculiarity that discourse ethicists ignore to their peril (Machiavelli 1950, 87). One might say, then, that speaking the truth is an indispensable element in politics, but not the point of it. To make communicative action, or the enactment of principles of discourse ethics, or moral conversation, the end or goal of politics is to mistake the nature of working in half-truth and thereby misconstrue "the milieu that is proper to politics" itself.[33]

The supervenience of strategic (speech) action on communicative (speech) action in politics that I have been alluding to here is what I also think Timothy Garton Ash meant to convey when, in the aftermath of the PEN Congress, he referred to the "qualitatively different responsibility" that the intellectual has for "the validity, intellectual coherence, and truth of what he says and writes," as opposed to the politician, who invariably works in half-truth. The point is not that the intellectual lives in a communicative world of validity, coherence, and truth while the politician does not. (Although Habermas's ideal communication situation *might* stand a better chance of realization in a scholarly conference or a graduate seminar, as opposed to a press conference, an election campaign, or even a neighborhood caucus.) The politician also inhabits a world of validity, coherence, and truth. Yet validity, coherence, and truth take on different colorations working in the context peculiar to politics—where strategic imperatives and the exercise of power, conflicts of interest and drives of ambition, are ineliminable aspects of collective action. Hence, it is one thing to encourage (or even insist upon) the intellectual's responsibility to keep providing us with various practical (or even imaginary) means for judging the health or sickness of the body politic, and quite another to expect the politician—or the citizen—to "live" them.

POSTSCRIPT

Whatever we make of the philosophical status of *Diskursethik,* we might notice in Habermas's theorizing an attitude or orientation that is fundamental to a strain of Western thought generally, and perhaps particularly in the German tradition from Immanuel Kant to Karl Marx, and quite contrary to the disposition toward politics I have been calling Machiavellian. The philosopher Bernard Williams describes this attitude as indicative of theorists who think that:

Somehow or other, in this life or the next, morally if not materially, as individuals or as an historical collective, we shall be safe; or, if not safe, at least reassured that at some level of the world's constitution there is something to be discovered that makes ultimate sense of our concerns. (Williams 1993, 164)[34]

Yet, whatever its power against the alleged naiveté and intellectualism of the Habermasian, the Machiavellian thesis is also vulnerable to a modern form of critique. Insofar as Machiavelli "did not seek very energetically to define" a power which would not be unjust (Merleau-Ponty 1964, 221), so we might take the Machiavellian thesis as "Machiavellian"—as little more than a premodern nihilistic relativism incapable of furnishing any norms for politics beyond either strategic efficiency or perhaps perspectival art. Without question, Machiavelli's "tough-minded wisdom" (idem.) accepted politics as a field of struggle for which our best preparation is to study "war and its organization and discipline" (Machiavelli 1950, 52). This pre-Clausewitzian thesis, to the effect that the arbiter of politics is a kind of power which is no respecter of truth, puts one in mind of Michel Foucault (Taylor 1988, 223–224; Ingram 1994). And Foucault has drawn on Nietzsche to present the will to truth itself as a manifestation of the will to power. From this purchase in post-modernity, then, we might imagine a series of grapnels, first from Carl von Clausewitz, then Nietzsche, then Michel Foucault, heaved over modernity, and thrown back to the Florentine.

I am not sure whether Machiavelli really did bracket the question of truth and the values of humanism, as at least Nietzsche and Foucault tried to do.[35] But the contestation between premodern and postmodern will have to wait another day. In any case, it is true that Machiavelli gives us no clear guidelines or philosophical principles as to how to choose the lesser of evils among powers in politics, or the relatively best, much less the "good" and the "best." His distinction between cruelties "well-committed" and "ill-committed" does not seem, to moderns, to offer much by way of guidance for political work (Machiavelli 1950, 34). But perhaps neither definitive nor moral guidelines are available from "outside" the action context of politics, and that is the point Machiavelli wants us to grasp. Even so, as Sheldon Wolin puts it:

There was no hint of child-like delight when Machiavelli contemplated the barbarous and savage destructiveness of the new prince, sweeping away the settled arrangements of society and "leaving nothing intact." There was, however, the laconic remark that it was better to be a private citizen than to embark on a career which involved the ruin of men. (Wolin 1960, 223)

Whatever we might count as the "civilizational norms" that modern constitutional democracy has bestowed upon us, I do not believe they offer any excuses for misconceiving or deceiving ourselves about that "knot of collective life" that is politics. Machiavelli, who lived within the historical moment of a dazzling and dynamic Renaissance, a "rebirth" of politics, understood this very well.

NOTES

1. This paper was first prepared for presentation in March 1995 as part of the Symposium on Partisan Politics, organized by Edward Portis at Texas A&M University, and also presented at the American Political Science Association Meetings in San Francisco, August 1996. My thanks to Ed Portis, John Burke, and the other symposium participants at Texas A&M for insightful comments and suggestions, to Stephen White for additional helpful commentary, and to Terence Ball and James Farr for numerous and seemingly endless discussions of the challenges Habermas presents for our thinking about discourse and politics.

2. In fact, Timothy Garton Ash reports, Klaus misquoted his distinction by finding "incredible" the notion that politicians "*live* in half-truth." As Ash proceeds to clarify, "what I said was that politicians *work* in half-truth. The phrase characterizes the professional party politician's job, not his life" (Ash 1995, 35). Klaus's misquotation was revealing, insofar as it reprised Vaclav Havel's pre-1989 formula "living in truth" and thereby jumbled the meaning of *both* Havel's and Ash's perspectives on politics.

3. The phrase "new spirituality" comes from a speech that Havel made in Tokyo in April 1992, where he took issue with "a British friend" (Ash) and resisted the either/or of "independent intellectuals" and "practicing politicians" (Ash 1995, 37). Identifying a "historic challenge," Havel speculated upon the possibility of introducing a "new dimension into politics" that would draw a "new wind, [a] new spirit, a new spirituality . . . into the established stereotypes of present-day politics" (37). It is up to intellectuals, among others, Havel concluded, "to demonstrate whether my British friend has shown foresight, or has simply been too influenced by the banal idea that everyone should stick to his own trade" (37).

4. In a speech delivered on this theme at New York University in October 1991, Havel acknowledged that "in politics, as anywhere else in life, it is impossible and pointless to say everything, all at once, to just anyone." But he immediately qualified this remark by adding, "This does not mean having to lie. All you need is tact, the proper instincts, and good taste. . . . I have discovered that good taste is more useful here than a degree in political science" (Ash 1995, 37). I will refrain from remarking upon the insight involved in at least the last part of Havel's observation.

5. Michel Foucault amplifies this point on principles when he recounts coming across a text devoted to *Fuhrertum* by Max Pohlenz, the philosopher

who "heralded the universal values of Stoicism all his life." "You should read the . . . book's closing remarks on the *Fuhrersideal* and on the true humanism constituted by the Volk under the inspiration of the leader's direction," Foucault remarks to his interviewer, "Heidegger never wrote anything more disturbing." He also adds, "Nothing in this condemns Stoicism . . . needless to say" (Foucault 1984, 373–374). The phenomenologist Maurice Merleau-Ponty expresses a similar insight when he suggests that politics is a relationship "to men rather than principles." . . . "Has not history shown even more clearly after Machiavelli than before him," Merleau-Ponty asks, "that principles commit us to nothing, and that they may be adapted to any end?" (Merleau-Ponty 1964, 219).

6. In his definitive chapter "Machiavelli: Politics and the Economy of Violence," Sheldon Wolin introduces this phrase in order to characterize Machiavelli's theory (Wolin 1960, 211). "To possess a political metaphysic without a philosophy," Wolin argues, "may initially strike us as paradoxical or trivial . . . but in discarding philosophy [Machiavelli] was freed to create something new: a truly 'political' philosophy which concentrated solely on political issues and single-mindedly explored the range of phenomena relevant to it" (211). Wolin amplifies this point by asking, "What would be the implications if man's whole existence were defined by a world of fleeting sense impressions and phenomenal flux, a world having precious little in the way of a firm foundation for knowledge?" (212)

7. I hasten to add that by emphasizing the "intrinsicalness" of politics I mean to specify it along the lines of an action concept, but not in a way that focalizes a spatially bounded "sphere" or "realm" that is (in either an Arendtian or Rawlsian sense) "public" rather than "private" or "social." Since all of these realms (however they are delimited) are both externally and internally open to struggle, conflict and the play of relations of power, they might be understood as (actual or potential) sites of strategic maneuver as well as dissensus, dispute, deception, manipulation, half-truth—that is, as political. Specifying the site of such struggles is impossible in advance for, as Isaiah Berlin observes, "the possibilities of action are not discrete entities like apples which can be exhaustively enumerated" (Berlin 1991, 42). For an example of how the private realm (of familial, marital, intimate, reproductive, sexual, and gender relations) exhibits the overall effect of strategic positions and maneuver as politics, see Machiavelli's domestic comedy *Mandragola* (1957). Also see Ian Shapiro for an intelligent discussion of how politics can be specified and at the same time understood as "ubiquitous to human interaction" and "permeat[ing] every facet of human interaction" (Shapiro 1994, 127–130).

8. That is to say, Habermasian citizens are not truth-seekers with a capital T since, for Habermas, truth is not an objective transcendent aspect of some metaphysical reality. Rather, truth is the outcome of agreement reached through critical discussion or rational consensus. Still, politics is truth-seeking insofar as discourse theory has the success of deliberative politics depend on the institutionalization of certain procedures geared toward the achievement of consensus.

9. Although Habermas certainly recognizes that communicative action is a never-ending aspect of human interaction, there is nevertheless a sense of purification, if not finality, implicit in his understanding of what constitutes any given instance of X questioning what Y is saying. This orientation toward purification is evident in Habermas's vocabulary of "vindicating" and "redeeming," validity claims. An act of *vindication* involves (a) clearing someone or something of accusation, censure, suspicion, and so forth; (b) supporting or maintaining, as a right or claim; and (c) serving to justify. (Although the obsolete usage in which vindicate means "avenge" or "punish" is telling.) In addition to its theological connotation as salvation from sin, *redemption* carries a propertarian reference, for example, regaining possession by paying a price; an ethical reference, for example, fulfilling an oath or a promise; or a reference to setting free, rescuing, or ransoming from hostile forces. Therefore, the negotiation and resolution of breakdowns in speech-communication appear, in Habermas's thinking, to take on the character of a cleansing from "suspicion" or "sin" that aligns rather nicely with the "new spirituality" that Vaclav Havel commends.

10. Jügen Habermas specifies this as follows: "Anyone who seriously engages in argumentation must presuppose that the context of discussion guarantees in principle freedom of access, equal rights to participate, truthfulness on the part of participants, absence of coercion in adopting positions, and so on. If the participants genuinely want to convince one another, they must make the pragmatic assumption that they allow their "yes" and "no" responses to be influenced solely by the force of the better argument" (Habermas 1993a, 31). Again, Habermas deploys these as *anticipatory* suppositions that are constitutive of a practice that, without them, would degenerate "at the very least into a surreptitious form of strategic action" (31). As such, this "ideal speech situation" is quite a bit more than a "mere de facto acceptance of habitual practices" and yet less than an externalized, transcendent Ideal.

11. Habermas clarifies the distinction further by saying that actors are *strategic* if they "are interested solely in the *success*, i.e. the *consequences* or *outcomes* of their actions." As such, strategic actors "will try to reach their objectives by influencing their opponent's definition of the situation, and thus his decisions or motives, through external means by using weapons or goods, threats or enticements" (Habermas 1993b, 133). At issue in strategic situations, Habermas suggests, is the meshing of "egocentric utility calculations" (133) in which the degree of cooperation is determined by the "interest positions" of the participants (134). By contrast, actors are *communicative* if they "are prepared to harmonize their plans of action through internal means, committing themselves to pursuing their goals only on the condition of an agreement . . . about definitions of the situation and prospective outcomes" (134).

12. Because the Machiavellian thesis that I am developing operates on the terrain of political action and not the philosophy of language, I will not pursue this aspect of Habermas's distinction between communicative: strategic action here. But it is important to note that, to date, Habermas has not developed the linguistic "priority" of communicative over strategic speech-

action to any sufficient degree, or adequately addressed the charge that linguistic communication cannot be so easily separated from purposive activity. As Jonathan Culler notes, "To understand 'Could you close the window' is to grasp that it could be used to get someone to close the window as well as to inquire about their abilities" (Culler, 1985, 137). The problem this example raises is that, in the absence of an account that can show how strategic action possesses a "derivative" status (Rasmussen 1990, 40), the positing of communicative consensuality as "primary" is likely to boil down simply to a matter of preference for its norms as better, or more appealing, or more "basic" to language. But that is precisely what has to be proven.

13. The analogy between the chivalric codes and Habermas's theory of communicative action ultimately breaks down on a substantial point—the strict protocols that governed medieval combat themselves presupposed a common, shared normative consciousness and an existing communal *ethos* in which the question of *honor* (among other significant norms and practices) was taken very seriously. Constructed in the context of the technicization of the modern world, Habermas's "code" presupposes no equivalent *ethos*; it relies instead upon theoretical criteria and knowledge of the correct norms that are, for Habermas, part and parcel of the very nature of language itself. For a discussion of the dilemmas that attend Habermas's theoretical grounding of a philosophical ethics without *ethos*, see Gadamer's letter to Richard Bernstein (Bernstein 1983, 261–265), as well as Ronald Beiner (1989).

14. In an earlier (1990) interview with Torben Hviid Nielsen, Habermas regretted what he called his "dubbing" of certain conditions under which idealizing presuppositions would be fulfilled as an "ideal speech situation" because it suggests a "kind of hypostatization" that he resolutely rejects (1993a, 163–164). Habermas goes on to allow that he even hesitates to call the communication community "a regulative idea in the Kantain sense," since these conditions must be satisfied to a sufficient degree "here and now" if we want to engage in argument at all (164). He then tries this "paradoxical" formulation: "the regulative idea of the validity of utterances is constitutive for the social facts produced through communicative action" insofar as it transcends the limits of social space and historical time '*from within the world*'" (165).

15. Habermas makes this argument in response to Albrecht Wellmer's contention that discourses are always social, historical, and *institutionalized*. That is, institutions impose obligations regarding argumentation that are constructed within the institutions themselves. Habermas agrees that institutions (such as "courts, university seminars, and parliamentary hearings) carry "practical obligations"; but he also distinguishes the former from the "transcendental constraints" that characterize the "general pragmatic presuppositions" that *presuppose* institutionalized argumentation (Habermas 1993a, 31). These presuppositions differ from institutional norms insofar as they do not impose obligations to act rationally; rather the presuppositions "*make possible* the practice that participants understand as argumentation" (31). In a Machiavellian mode, I will leave this universalizing idea behind and follow Cornelius Castoriadis in allowing that: "It is actual historical universality with which we

are concerned when we confront the political question, not 'transcendental universality' " (Castoriadis 1992, 253).

16. Habermas maintains that his discourse ethics, based on a theory of rationality that is itself based on language, is open to falsification by scientific evidence; hence, he opens his argument to empirical falsification. This draws Habermas's theory into a number of difficult issues, none of which I will consider here. But see Alford, "Is Jügen Habermas's Reconstructive Science," 1985 and Rasmussen, *Reading Habermas*, 1990.

17. Girolamo Savonarola, Dominican monk, political ruler of Florence, and unarmed prophet, was burned at the stake as a heretic by the Florentine citizenry in 1498. Shortly thereafter, the republic was resurrected and Machiavelli assumed the office of Second Chancellor and Secretary to the Ten.

18. Ronald Beiner (1989) makes a related and equally valuable point in his defense of Gadamer's neo-Aristotelian ethics against Habermas's appeal to universal postulates of linguistic reason. Beiner concludes that, "the dispute between Gadamer and Habermas ultimately comes down to a question of the relative priority of theory and prudence" (Beiner, 239), or science over *phronesis* (240). See also Aryen Botwinick, who contends that Habermas's "philosophy-of-language theorizing" "raises the specter of an unbridgeable gap between theory and practice—since even the most detailed and elaborate of theoretical texts cannot substitute for the context of decision-making and application that confront an agent at the moment of practice, the moment of actual doing or responding" (Botwinick 1993, 76, 77). In political theory, the text that comes closest to achieving a grasp of the complexities involved in the dynamic and indeterminate interplay of events and personalities that is political speech is Thucydides, *The Peloponnesian War* (1982).

19. Machiavelli writes of politics in an age in which the entire chivalric system is nearly collapsed, and to no little extent because of certain techno-logical advances that mark the "premodern" world, in-between medievalism and modernity. The elaborate conventions on ransom-giving and -taking (how one knight accepted the surrender of another, the promise of "safe quarter" to the surrendering knight, etc.) disintegrated as a result of material develop-ments (first in archery, and later in artillery and gunfire) that reduced face-to-face combat and, with it, the possibility of capture and ransom (Meron, 1993). The accompanying break-up of the unified Christian culture of Europe, the Crusades (where chivalric norms were not extended to infidel Arabs) only hastened the process, which may have reached its climax in 1415, on the fields of Agincourt (Weschler 1996). Thus, in contrast to both the medievalism of the Christian chivalric and the modernism of the Habermasian communicative codes, Machiavelli asserts a mode of conduct that can only be known by understanding the codeless code of politics—a realm that, as Benedetto Croce wrote, "has its own laws against which it is futile to rebel, which cannot be exorcized and banished from the world with holy water," nor tempered, we might add, with a reconstructive science of language (Berlin 1982, 53).

20. For many of these formulations, I am indebted to Castoriadis' (im-plicitly Machiavellian) discussion of politics, which he terms "the activity that

aims at the transformation of society's institutions in order to make them conform to the norm of the autonomy of the collectivity" (1992, 254), and uses to counter what he takes to be the excesses of Habermas's theory of communicative action and ideal speech situation. Insofar as he stresses the institutional context of intersubjective communication, Castoriadis echoes Wellmer's critique of Habermas's argument; but he also challenges, as "totally inadequate," Habermas's efforts to found a theory of social action on the ideas of communicative action, interpretive understanding and ideal speech situation (Castoriadis 254, 255). The latter, Castoriadis argues, are "only the atmosphere indispensable to *political* life and creativity—and their very existence depends upon instituting acts. The *end* or *goal* of these acts goes far beyond the establishment of an ideal communication situation, which is only part of that end, and really just a mere means" (256).

21. As both Berlin and Wolin argue, Machiavelli believes in a permanent "economy of violence" (Wolin 1960, 220)—the need for a "consistent reserve of force always in the background" (Berlin 1982, 66). Wolin links Machiavelli's view of violence to the nature of the context in which power was exerted: "the tightly-packed condition of political space which mocked any *merely verbal attempt* at translating power into simple direction or supervision of the affairs of society" (Wolin 1960, 221, italics mine). The metaphor of a "tightly-packed condition" that Wolin associates with politics recalls Merleau-Ponty's "collective knot," and both in turn capture the constricted milieu of conflicting ambitions, demands, fears, hatreds, hopes, and vested interests that is politics.

22. How these strategic interests are theorized is a broader question that is not predetermined by my argument. However, I endorse Ian Shapiro's warning not to thematize strategic interests too reductively, especially solely in terms of game theory or rational choice. Machiavelli's observations about fortune (*fortuna*) as "the ruler of half our actions" remind us that even the most astute strategic actions are intertwined with time and circumstances in ways that confound even the most judicious attempts to formalize underlying norms of human rationality (Machiavelli 1950, 91).

23. One of the problems with Habermas's distinction between communicative-strategic action is that it tends to construe too narrowly the strategic type of action, and wrongly characterize it, as David Ingram notes, as "manipulative, egoistic and atomistic, as opposed to the openness, impartiality, and consensuality of communicative rationality" (Ingram 1993, 308; also 1993).

24. Here, of course, I am paraphrasing Machiavelli's famous line in chapter fifteen of *The Prince*, "A man who wishes to make a profession of goodness in everything must necessarily come to grief among so many who are not good" (Machiavelli 1950, 56). The message concludes with this consummately strategic advice: "Therefore it is necessary for a prince, who wishes to maintain himself, to learn how not to be good, and to use this knowledge and not use it, according to the necessity of the case" (56).

25. In any case, knowing exactly what it means to say that discourse ethics is the "practical activity" of redeeming validity claims is greatly impaired by the fact that Habermas and his commentators rarely offer very

complex examples of the activity of discourse, and certainly none that are equal to the multilayered and multivocal dynamics of political speech. Indeed, most efforts to clarify what constitutes the redemption of validity claims or moral conversation rely either on abstract examples of communicative interaction between two individuals (Bernstein 1983, 186) or interacting parties (McCarthy 1981, 288–289), or on prosaic examples of communicative interaction between two individuals, such as Anthony Giddens's example of the traveler and the ticket clerk at a railway station (1985, 128–129), or Seyla Benhabib's example of the admonition of a parent to a child (Benhabib 1990, 358–359). Simone Chambers's example of the giving and taking of commands, although political, hardly begins to capture the complex dynamics of "break down" in irreducibly particular speech situations where authority is challenged (Chambers 1996, 95–96). Of course to expect that it *could* do so is to demand far too much of a political theory—and perhaps too little of the politician.

26. Or, as Stephen Macedo bluntly puts this point in his review of Moon's discourse-generated liberal theory: "Neither Moon, Rawls, nor any other political theorist will have much to say to those who regard their particular truth as more important than arriving at a reasonable consensus with other people" (Macedo 1995, 391).

27. In returning to Timothy Garton Ash's observation that politicians work (rather than live) in half-truth, I am mindful of Charles Taylor's observation that "the affirmation of ordinary life" is one of the "great revolutionary forces of modern culture" (Taylor 1988, 227). Under "ordinary life" Taylor includes "the belief that the central point of human existence and human fulfillment is to be found in the life of production and reproduction, or work and the family, or labour and sexual love" (idem). Taylor does not include politics in his homage to ordinary life, nor (for different reasons) does Ash; nor does Machiavelli. Habermas presents a different, although inconclusive, case. Given both his frequent references to communicative action as "day-to-day" or "everyday" discourse, and the linkage he draws between communicative action and discursive democracy, it may be that Habermas absorbs politics into everyday life, thereby obliterating the difference that the Machiavellian maintains between two conflicting systems of value (Berlin 1982, 58).

28. Failing to recognize this may lead those who partake in politics to grief. A contemporary example is found in Walter Mondale's sincerity and truth-telling about the necessity of raising taxes, made in the course of what would be his disastrous presidential bid against Ronald Reagan in 1984. As Mondale allowed in speculating upon the reality of raising taxes and Reagan's response to this fact, "Ronald Reagan will raise your taxes, and so will I. He won't tell you, I just did." The way of a truly moral or honest politics, as Havel avers and Mondale discovered, is neither simple nor easy. From a partisan perspective it may also be self-defeating, if not disastrous, for the politician, if not the body politic.

29. Perhaps the most compelling (premodern) and literary example of this peculiar and complex dimension of political speech is provided in Thucydides' presentation of the debate in Athens between Cleon and Diodotus

concerning the fate of the Mitylenians (1982, Bk.III). With a view toward per-suading the *demos* to uphold its earlier decision to put the Mitylenians to death (and thereby sustaining his own imperialist ambitions), Cleon launches a series of rhetorical speech-maneuvers. Not the least of these maneuvers is his rhetorical attack on rhetoric and rhetoricians themselves (III [38]). In Cleon's speech, Thucydides offers a brilliant example of how the principles of com-municative action can be rhetorically deployed in the service of strategic ends. Thus, Cleon ("the most violent man at Athens") charges the Athenian *demos* with what we might call certain failures in communicative competence and "discursive democracy": "[you] go to see an oration as you would to see a sight, take your facts on hearsay, judge of the practicability of a project by the wit of its advocates, and trust for the truth as to past events not to the fact which you saw more than to the clever strictures which you heard; you are the easy victims of new-fangled arguments, unwilling to follow received conclu-sions" (III [38]). Cleon also accuses the *demos* of betraying "strategic" rather than "communicative" sensibilities: "the first wish of every man among you is that he could speak himself, the next to rival those who can speak by seeming to be quite up with their ideas by applauding every hit almost before it is made, and by being as quick in catching an argument as you are slow in foreseeing its consequences . . . you are very slaves to the pleasures of the ear" (III [38]). Cleon's appeal to the *demos* to be more like "the council of a city" than "the audience of a rhetorician" is not, however, a case for genuinely discursive democracy in the Habermasian sense. Rather, his appeal is instru-mentally calculated to blunt the force of what he fears (rightly, as it turns out) will be Diodotus' more skillful rhetoric geared toward persuading the Athe-nians to spare the Mitylenes.

The brilliance of this piece of political literature has to do with Thucydides' recognition of the way strategic action supervenes upon communicative action in political speech. In the domain of political speech-struggle that Thucydides brings to life in the agonal contestation between Cleon and Diodotus, the "end" is mediated not only by an immediate and urgent question of life or death, but also by the clashing ambitions and vested interests of the participants in the dialogue, who include not only Cleon and Diodotus, but also these leaders and the Athenian *demos*. Under these circumstances (which might be understood not as incidental to but, to varying degrees, *inherent in* politics) we must (at the very least) recognize the tension between communicative and strategic action that is embedded in political speech. At most, we might recognize that the "resolu-tion" of this tension never admits of the achievement of "pure" communicative action or the banishment of strategic action, but rather takes place along a continuum of "more or less." Indeed, Thucydides' history might be read as representing various nodal points along this continuum in its narrative of the complex unfolding of speeches and events that mark the politics of the Peloponnesian War and Athenian Democracy.

30. Thus, working in half-truth involves, in rhetorical form, the art of creating illusions or a "false world" that others will accept as real. As Wolin notes, however: "Where the actors were all intent on creating false worlds,

success depended not only on the ability to distinguish the true world from the false, but also in avoiding the trap of one's own deceptions"(1960, 213; italics mine).

31. Chambers recognizes this when she allows that, "It is not entirely correct to say that discourse does not contain any instrumental calculation. Discourse is goal-oriented in the sense that participants are looking for the best means of attaining the goal of mutual understanding. *Thus, it is not means/ ends rationality that is excluded from discourse but only viewing one's dialogue partner as the means to attaining one's own ends*" (Chambers 1996, 100, Italics mine). Similarly, Benhabib attempts to soften what she calls "the stark opposition between political utopianism and political realism" that is introduced by the distinction communicative:strategic by formulating the relationship in this way: "Communicative ethics anticipates *nonviolent strategies of conflict resolution* as well as encouraging cooperative and associative methods of problem solving" (Benhabib 1990, 354, italics mine).

Whether or not these qualifications align with Habermas's views, they certainly weaken the practical (if not the analytical) strength and coherence of the communicative-strategic distinction upon which Habermas's defense of the "priority" of communicative (i.e., non-instrumental, non-means/ends, non-strategic) action depends. In any case, once Chambers and Benhabib allow "instrumental calculation" and "nonviolent strategies" of action into communicative ethics, as they do in these respective passages, the game is up. In effect, what they both finally if indirectly articulate (despite their Habermasian leanings) is precisely what I have been calling the "Machiavellian view" of the "intrinsic impurity of politics." See also Foucault, "The Subject and Power," 1982.

32. Ingram develops this thought significantly, as follows: "No set of political principles can assure against tyrannical outcomes. Democracy governed by the principles of discourse ethics is no exception, for the demand that all needs be validated through public discourse favors the political activist (and orator) over the domestic caretaker" (Ingram 1993, 320 n.45).

33. This is not to say that Machiavelli posits some (much less one) other "end" of politics. In fact, *The Prince* countenances a heterogeneity of ends in politics, not the least of which is "the majesty of his dignity," in bearing and demeanor, of the prince himself (Machiavelli 1950, 85).

34. Isaiah Berlin makes a similar and even broader claim when he identifies the "one major assumption" of Western thought: "That somewhere in the past or the future, in this world or the next, in the church or the laboratory, in the speculations of the metaphysician or the findings of the social scientist, or in the uncorrupted heart of the simple good man, there is to be found the final solution of the question of how men should live" (Berlin 1982, 76). Berlin maintains that Machiavelli "lit the fatal fuse" that finally "split open" this rock upon "Western beliefs and lives had been founded" (68).

35. Merleau-Ponty is quite sure that Machiavelli is a humanist, but of a very particular kind. "If by humanism we mean a philosophy of the inner man," he writes, " . . . Machiavelli is not a humanist. But if by humanism we

mean a philosophy which *confronts* the relationship of *man to man* and the *constitution of a common situation* and a *common history* between men as a problem, then we have to say that Machiavelli formulated some of the conditions of any serious humanism" (1964, 223, Italics mine).

REFERENCES

Alford, Fred. 1985. "Is Jürgen Habermas's Reconstructive Science Really a Science? *Theory and Society* 14: 321–340.

Ash, Timothy Garton. 1990. *The Magic Lantern*. New York, NY: Random House.

———. 1995. "Prague: Intellectuals and Politicians." *The New York Review of Books*, 12 January.

Beiner, Ronald. 1989. "Do We Need a Philosophical Ethics? Theory, Prudence, and the Primacy of *Ethos*." *The Philosophical Forum* 20(3):230–243.

Benhabib, Seyla. 1990. "Communicative Ethics and Current Controversies in Practical Philosophy." In *The Communicative Ethics Controversy*. Edited by Seyla Benhabib and Fred Dallmayr. Cambridge, MA: MIT Press.

Berlin, Isaiah. 1982. "The Originality of Machiavelli." In *Against the Current: Essays in the History of Ideas*. New York, New York: Viking Press.

———. 1991. "Two Concepts of Liberty." In *Liberty*. Edited by David Miller. Oxford, Eng.: Oxford University Press.

Bernstein, Richard. 1983. *Beyond Objectivism and Relativism: Science, Hermeneutics, and Praxis*. Philadelphia, PA: University of Pennsylvania Press.

Botwinick, Aryeh. 1993. *Postmodernism and Democratic Theory*. Philadelphia, PA: Temple University Press.

Castoriadis, Cornelius. 1992. "Individual, Society, Rationality, History." In *Between Totalitarianism and Postmodernity*. Edited by Peter Beilharz, Gillian Robinson, and John Rundell. Cambridge, MA: MIT Press.

Chambers, Simone. 1996. *Reasonable Democracy: Jürgen Habermas and the Politics of Discourse*. Ithaca, NY: Cornell University Press.

Culler, Jonathan. 1985. "Communicative Competence and Normative Force." *New German Critique* 35.

Foucault, Michel. 1982. "The Subject and Power." In *Michel Foucault: Beyond Structuralism and Hermeneutics*. Edited by Hubert Dreyfus and Paul Rabinow. Chicago, IL: University of Chicago Press.

———. 1984. "Politics and Ethics: An Interview." In *Foucault Reader*. Edited by Paul Rabinow. New York, NY: Pantheon Press.

Giddens, Anthony. 1985. "Jürgen Habermas." In *The Return of Grand Theory in the Human Sciences*. Edited by Quentin Skinner. Cambridge: Cambridge University Press.

Habermas, Jürgen. N.d. "Three Normative Models of Democracy." Paper prepared for the Conference for the Study of Political Thought.

———. 1990. *The Philosophical Discourse of Modernity: Twelve Lectures*. Cambridge, MA: MIT Press.

———. 1993a. *Justification and Application: Remarks on Discourse Ethics*. Cambridge, MA: MIT Press.

———. 1993b. *Moral Consciousness and Communicative Action*. Cambridge, MA: MIT Press.

Ingram, David. 1993a. "The Limits and Possibilities of Communicative Ethics for Democratic Theory." *Political Theory* 21(2): 294–321.

———. 1994. "Foucault and Habermas on the Subject of Reason," In *The Foucault Companion*. Edited by Gary Gutting. New York, NY: Cambridge University Press.

Lyotard, Jean-François. 1984. *The Postmodern Condition: A Report on Knowledge*. Minneapolis, MN: University of Minnesota Press.

Macedo, Stephen. 1995. "Review of Moon." *Political Theory* 23(2).

Machiavelli, Niccolo. 1950. *The Prince and the Discourses*. New York, NY: Modern Library.

———. 1957. *Mandragola*. Translated Anne Paolucci and Henry Paolucci. New York, NY: Bobbs-Merrill.

Merleau-Ponty, Maurice. 1964. "A Note on Machiavelli." In *Signs*. Evanston, IL: Northwestern University Press.

McCarthy, Thomas. 1981. *The Critical Theory of Jürgen Habermas*. Cambridge, MA: MIT Press.

———. 1991. *Ideals and Illusions: On Reconstruction and Deconstruction in Contemporary Critical Theory*. Cambridge, MA: MIT Press.

———. 1994. "Kantian Constructivism and Reconstructivism: Rawls and Habermas in Dialogue." *Ethics* 105: 44–63.

Meron, Theodor. 1993. *Henry's Wars and Shakespeare's Laws: Perspectives on the Law of War in the Later Middle Ages*. Oxford, Eng.: Oxford University Press.

Rasmussen, David. 1990. *Reading Habermas*. Cambridge, MA: Basil Blackwell.

Rawls, John. 1985. "Justice as Fairness: Political Not Metaphysical." *Philosophy and Public Affairs* 14(3): 223–251.

Shapiro, Ian. 1994. "Three Ways to be a Democrat." *Political Theory* 22(1): 124–152.

Taylor, Charles. 1988. "The Hermeneutics of Conflict." In *Meaning and Context: Quentin Skinner and his Critics*. Edited by James Tully. Princeton, NJ: Princeton University Press.

Thucydides. 1982. *The Peloponnesian War*. Translated by Richard Crawley. New York, NY: Modern Library.

Weschler, Lawrence. 1996. "Take No Prisoners." *The New Yorker*, 17 June.

White, Stephen K. 1988. *The Recent Work of Jürgen Habermas: Reason, Justice and Modernity*. Cambridge: Cambridge University Press.

Williams, Bernard. 1993. *Shame and Necessity*. Berkeley, CA: University of California Press.

Wolin, Sheldon. 1960. "Machiavelli: Politics and the Economy of Violence." In *Politics and Vision: Continuity and Innovation in Western Political Thought*. New York, NY: Little Brown.

PART III

Political Theory as Politics

CHAPTER 7

Secularism, Partisanship and the Ambiguity of Justice

William E. Connolly

TWILIGHT OF THE IDOLS

The self-destruction of Communist states, the internationalization of capitalist relations, the migration of former colonials to the centers of declining empires, the expansion of tourism, the globalization of communication media, the porosity of population flows across territorial boundaries, the re-intensification of contending nationalisms, the amplification of religious controversies, the acceleration of speed in military actions, cultural transactions and political movements—these contemporary compressions of time and complications of territorial space squeeze several idols of the Western state. The territorial nation-state, universal reason, the primacy of the individual, the separation of church and state, the jagged line of division between private and public, the practice of secular justice, and the experience of nature as a medium susceptible to human mastery are all up for grabs. Indeed, the curtain is falling down on the historic compromise between advocates of religious purity and defenders of worldly activity. The compromise formation known as secularism—a political culture in which an assortment of faiths, identifications, and relations circulate in the private realm and generic persons, reason, principles, rights, interests, and justice convene in the public realm—is coming apart at the seams.

Contemporary Anglo-American political theory registers these effects, in its way. The individualist/communitarian debate, for instance, has recently devolved into a series of exchanges over the appropriate shape of pluralism. Contractual theories founded on reason have collapsed into "reasonable" conceptions of justice grounded on the overlapping consensus of a pluralist culture. The ideal speech situation from which a rational consensus might emerge has faded toward the herme-neutic circle within which responsible dialogue revolves. The inde-pendent individual of rights is rapidly becoming the ambiguous subject of agency and cultural delineation. And a "third wave" in IR theory now challenges presumptions inside both the "realism" of the sover-eign, national security state, and the "idealism" of a world regime. Replies and responses are issued quarterly to these foreign imports and domestic upstarts. But these intellectual challenges combine with unexpected events to put pressure on the old idols. It becomes neces-sary either to reconfigure the idols or to return them to their privi-leged places by compulsion.

To put it briefly, today a new *pluralization* of subjects, creeds, cul-tures, values, and sites of political action is often countered by the *fundamentalization* of old radical, liberal, and conservative idols. These debates between pluralization and fundamentalization form some of the most crucial conflicts of our time: they occur within us as well as between us; and these struggles rewrite old debates between radicals, liberals, and conservatives. Liberalism, under these conditions changes its shape even as it strives to remain the same. For liberalism is now caught in a cultural bind. It can either try to secure its old cultural standing by illiberal means or rescue its liberality by reconstituting itself. It cannot remain the same.

Chantal Mouffe's (1993) book, *The Return of the Political,* helps to expose this shift in the cultural circumstances of liberalism. Mouffe is a democratic pluralist. She finds the liberal pluralism of John Rawls and his friends to be too universalist, too apolitical, and too stingy. Indeed, she identifies violences and exclusions hidden inside the lib-eral grammar of reasonableness and rationality. Her critique of Rawls invokes neither the priority of the individual nor the quest for na-tionhood. Rather, she deploys Carl Schmitt's understanding of "the political" to expose arbitrary exclusions in liberal delimitations of reasonableness and diversity, and she deploys an appreciation of the "constitutive outside" that operates within every practice, associa-tion, and judgment, to attenuate the decisionism of Carl Schmitt. One mark of Mouffe's capacity to redistribute the spaces of political possibility is that the reservations she awakens in me pull me back neither to Rawls nor to Schmitt. They inspire me to try to draw selective sustenance from Rawls while rewriting him radically to ward off Schmitt.

Society, says Mouffe, pursuing the line developed in her book with Ernesto Laclau, *Hegemony and Socialist Strategy* (1985), is neither a unified whole, an association of rational cooperation, nor an incomplete unity realizing itself dialectically. Indeed, "society" never is. There is, rather, "a fundamental antagonism" in every associational form, a division internal to the construction of every social identity that enables it to function while simultaneously defeating its ability to realize itself as a rational, cooperative, unified or non-antagonistic whole. Every identity and culture is founded on the exclusion of differences it constructs and alienates to be. "The political," then, consists in those mechanisms and decisions through which such exclusions are effected and, often, effaced by the state. This means:

> There is no identity that is self-present to itself and not constructed as difference, and that any social objectivity is constituted through acts of power. It means that any social objectivity is ultimately political and has to show traces of the exclusion which governs its constitution, what we call its "constitutive outside." As a consequence, all systems of social relations imply to a certain extent relations of power, since the construction of a social identity is an act of power. (Mouffe 1993, 141)

This (Schmittian) conception of the social serves Mouffe pretty well in her engagements with Rawls. For Mouffe repeatedly reveals the political element inside Rawlsian justice and reasonableness. The engagement with Rawls also explains why Mouffe, a pluralist and a democrat, leans so heavily on Schmitt, a sovereign decisionist and defender of cultural homogeneity through state decisionism. For Schmitt purports to expose those arbitrary "decisions" through which every unity, apparently grounded in reason or justice, is actually maintained. Mouffe's deployment of this "antagonistic" conception of the social disrupts the Rawlsian claim to offer a theory of justice without drawing upon any particular "comprehensive doctrine." Mouffe at once contests the fundamental Rawlsian conception of society as a "system of social cooperation" and confounds his division between political theories that reflect a comprehensive view and those, like his own is said to be, compatible with several, overlapping, reasonable metaphysical perspectives. The fundamental doctrine of Mouffe denies the possibility of a comprehensive view of society by asserting society to be fundamentally split. And yet she still projects a fundamental perspective that might be called "metaphysical," not in the sense of the two world metaphysic offered by Saint Augustine in one way and Immanuel Kant in another. But in the sense of a set of fundamental convictions within which everything else she says about modern ethics, identity and politics is set. Is the Mouffeian doctrine "political, not metaphysical," then? Or does its metaphysic rule out a comprehensive doctrine of politics? Mouffe presses Rawls to enter a conversation for which he is not well prepared.

But while Mouffe deploys Schmitt to challenge the Rawlsian pretense to a theory of justice rising entirely above the partisanships it adjudicates, the very terms of that critique may disable her from filling a vacancy in her own analysis. For Mouffe needs *a positive ethos of politics* to inform and enable the open-ended pluralism she endorses. She needs an *ethos* of engagement between partisans that plays the role in her conception of democracy that an overlapping consensus plays in Rawls'. But her repudiation of Rawls combines with her endorsement of Schmitt to make it very difficult to achieve this result.

Schmitt celebrates exclusionary political decisions that consolidate social identity amidst the play of centrifugal forces. As I read Schmitt, his text is governed by a covert aesthetic of homogeneity—an identification of the beautiful with unity and strength and the ugly with diversity and weakness—that exacerbates the logic of political exclusion. Schmitt *argues* that the unity of a state is held together by sovereign decisions which cannot be derived from any kind of higher principle, and he *wants* those decisions to produce an artificial unity by defining various diversities to be outside the pale. But Mouffe seeks a democratic pluralism in which multiple identities coexist and interact. She concedes the impossibility of eliminating decisionism from politics while resisting the Schmittian drive to artificial homogeneity. The difficulty is that Schmittian conceptions of the social and the political do not support the pluralism Mouffe endorses. They are hostile to it. And the countervailing forces Mouffe invokes to support pluralism may not be powerful enough to challenge the Schmittian agenda. Mouffe herself may sense this. Note, for instance, the equivocation in the formulation quoted earlier. Social identity (with Schmitt) "is an act of power," but (now more quietly against Schmitt) all "systems of social relations imply to a certain extent power." The first formulation forecloses Rawlsian normativity; the second creates a little space for a Mouffeian normativity *that still remains to be articulated*. There are other places, too, where Mouffe first states the logic of social antagonism in implacable terms and then softens it to make room for a positive alternative whose moral compass is never quite set.[1]

Mouffe's agenda may be to convert fixed relations of social antagonism into multiple lines of difference and connection in which, you might say, relations of agonistic respect, partial collaboration, and studied indifference soften, multiply, and ambiguate antagonistic divisions of friend and enemy.[2] But to get there Mouffe needs to delineate possibilities of social conflict less implacable than those she draws from Schmitt. In particular, Mouffe needs a positive conception of public ethics that goes beyond the Rawlsian secular rendering of persons, reasonableness, and justice without falling into the Schmittian conception of the political.

AN ETHOS OF ENGAGEMENT

I concur with Chantal Mouffe, Judith Butler, Carl Schmitt, Jacques Derrida, Michel Foucault, and Friedrich Nietzsche in contending that every identity and every culture is punctuated, surrounded, and traversed by a constitutive outside that is neither teleological in character nor fully contained by the habits through which it is organized and regulated. But this thesis is neither located beyond metaphysics nor one that anyone has demonstrated to be true. To insist otherwise in either respect is to offer an essentialist critique of essentialism; it is to recapitulate at one point the essentialist mode of argumentation Mouffe opposes at others. The alternative to essentialism is not to find a place beyond metaphysics, in any generous use of that latter word. It is to articulate a metaphysic of politics that breaks with the dominant and teleological alternatives. This alternative would not seek to provide *the* authoritative cultural source of ethics. Rather, it would enter into competition and collaboration with others now existing and others yet to come within the same civilization. Invocations, for instance, of a constitutive outside present the world as if it were both without an inherent purpose *and* replete with energies that exceed every social organization of humans and things. That is, it asserts something fundamental about the character of being. And this fundamental assertion enables some sources of ethics while calling others into question.

The Mouffeian perspective remains, like its competitors, a highly *contestable* rendering of the fundaments of being. Strategies of genealogy or deconstruction might draw us closer to the fugitive experience of excess or fundamental difference which Mouffe emphasizes. But we cannot demonstrate that experience to be undeniable or necessary. At least, no one has done so to date. The fundament stands, then, as an article of faith that informs concrete interventions into public life, one that can be defended in competition with other fundamental perspectives (e.g., Augustinian Christianity, Kantian Christianity, secular contractualism, teleological conceptions), but not one that can be located somewhere above the fray.[3] For where you and I uncover protean energies and nontheistic excess, they may project a loving god, or an inscrutable suprasensible realm of the Kantian sort, or a harmonious design of being in the last instance, or the ultimate plasticity of nature, or the susceptibility of things to law-like explanation. It may be possible to chasten and soften partisanship—as I think it is—but its terms go all the way down to the metaphysical level.

Nietzsche communicates these two meta-convictions—the unavoidable invocation of fundaments in interpretation and the persistent contestability of the deepest invocations—when he presents his fundamental projections in phrases such as, "*Suppose* the world as will to power, what then?" Or, "Suppose truth is a woman." Nietzsche vigorously interprets through these suppositions; he acts *as if* they were true. But he refuses to claim they are either the unavoidable result of transcendental arguments of the Kantian sort or intuitively undeniable like the Kantian conception of morality as law. Indeed, Nietzsche, at his best moments, *seeks* communication with others who base alternative interpretations on different suppositions about the fundamentals of being and who then affirm the contestable character of those projections. These would be *noble* adversaries, capable of practicing "forbearance" and "thoughtfulness" in their relations with others. They would say, if they were Christian, "Suppose Jesus as the Savior, What then?" Or, if Rawlsian, "Suppose society as a scheme of rational cooperation, What then?" This voice in Nietzsche (there are others) would not *exclude* Christianity if it had the power to do so. Nor would it command Christians (of various sorts) to keep their faiths out of the public realm or to translate them into either the Rawlsian vocabulary of persons and justice or his vocabulary of will to power. Nietzsche would contend with and against Christians and Rawlsian in relations of agonistic respect, to the extent they would allow it. This Nietzsche (the Nietzsche of *The Gay Science* and *Thus Spoke Zarathustra* more than *The Antichrist*) seeks noble Christians with whom to enter into relations of agonistic respect. Only when such an invitation is adamantly refused does he try to "pass by the poisonous flies" of dogmatism.

Nietzsche concurs in advance with Mouffe, Rawls, and Schmitt that the collapse of the medieval world of signs—a world which encountered its own dissenters and competitors even in its heyday—means that moderns are unlikely to converge upon a single conception of the good. But while Schmitt experiences the collapse of a metaphysics of harmony as *a lack* to be closed by sovereign decisions that artifice a more homogeneous unity, and while Rawls repairs this rent with the reasonableness of justice as fairness to "persons," one powerful strain in Nietzsche experiences it not only as an abyss, but also as *an abundance* that can enable the cultivation of greater diversity and generosity in life. This difference in mood or temper is fundamental, since it has the most effects on the tone of the ethical sensibility of the parties involved. Once you negotiate the tricky move (with plenty of help from Foucault) of moving *this* affirmative Nietzsche onto the register of the democratic Left, significant differences open up between a post-Nietzschean ethos of generous pluralism, Schmittian homogenization through decisionism, Rawlsian secular reasonableness, and Mouffeian pluralist decisionism.

Mouffe might draw considerable ethical sustenance from Nietzsche and Foucault to pursue the generous pluralism she endorses if only she would let Schmitt—who resents the world for not offering the unity he once projected into it—swing in the breeze once her critique of liberal universalism has been executed. As things stand now, however, Mouffe tells us what we need in the way of political ethics, but she does not do enough to fill the need. Here is a formulation in which she both recognizes the need and exposes a vacancy in her response to it. The words are hers:

> We do *need* to re-establish the lost connection between ethics and politics, but this *cannot* be done by sacrificing the gains of the democratic revolution. . . . But *we must also be able* to formulate the ethical character of modern citizenship in a way that is compatible with moral pluralism and respects the priority of the right over the good. What we *share* and what *makes us fellow citizens* in a *liberal democratic* regime is not a substantive conception of the good but *a set of political principles* specific to such a tradition: the principles of freedom and equality for all. *To be a citizen* is to recognize the authority of such principles and the rules in which they are embodied, *to have them informing* our political judgment and our actions, *to be associated* in terms of the recognition of the liberal democratic principles: this is the *meaning of citizenship* I want to put forward. It implies seeing citizenship not as a legal status, but as a form of identification. (Mouffe 65-66, italics mine)

Mouffe marks the moral perspectives she resists. And she insists that the democratic commitment to "equality and freedom" is compatible with contestation over the concrete meanings of these indeterminate terms. I concur. But Mouffe first grounds this ethos of democratic citizenship in the implicit logic of our already *constituted practices* and then slides rapidly toward the admission that these are pretty much identifications she *hopes we will endorse*. But the initial insinuation of a logic of necessary implication within the democratic tradition of citizenship is at odds with the Mouffeian recourse to a constitutive outside that disrupts and exceeds every attempt to move from the implicit to the explicit dialectically. Mouffe solicits an ethic by cultural implication that the Mouffeian philosophy of a constitutive outside that inhabits our practices but is never adequately captured by our concepts cannot accommodate. The resulting oscillation between the constative and the performative consolidates itself finally in a phrase: "this is *the meaning* of citizenship *I want* to put forward."

Here is the bind that drives Mouffe to preserve and obscure that oscillation: If she pushes the constitutive "our" hard the democracy she endorses will require a lot of (Schmittian) exclusions; for there are many who now participate in democratic politics who are either deeply at odds with Mouffe's commitments or whose implicit implication in them is profoundly qualified by other commitments. Alternatively, if Mouffe presses the "I want to put forward" too hard, her conception of citizenship loses its inspirational power; it becomes one "we" may or may not "want to put forward" with her. The "I want" now both gains prominence *and loses its power to inspire.* This power loss occurs because Mouffe fails to elaborate any more profound perspective, a perspective that might inspire more of us to democratic pluralism even in circumstances where *that tradition* has become mixed, ambiguous or weak, that is, even in circumstances where the logic of citizenship does not already incline overwhelmingly in that direction. And Mouffe hesitates at this point, I think, because she does not want to implicate herself. Mouffe is rather close to Rawls in this respect, as his ethical theory becomes increasingly dependent on an overlapping consensus that might crack or break with a sharp shift in the governing conventions of American life. Of course, any generous ethic will be in trouble if such a development occurs. But some perspectives may have positive ethical resources to draw upon in resisting it, resources that augment the "implicit presumptions" of a political culture if and when that "logic" becomes blurred.

I doubt that any practice of ethics ever entirely frees itself from the equivocations apparent in Mouffe's position. But Mouffe, by refusing to promote her political metaphysic as a positive, contestable interpretation, also loses access to the distinctive ethical sustenance it might offer. She may forget to peel off resentment against disenchantment of the world sticking to the Schmittian problematic *in time* to mine the positive ethical possibilities residing within a post-secular affirmation of the protean diversity of life.

Nietzsche and Foucault draw their respective ethics of reciprocal generosity between diverse constituencies from existential care for the fundamental abundance of being, an abundance that is never entirely exhausted by any particular organization of cultural life. Neither tries to secure the epistemological necessity of the care he cultivates. There is no god or transcendental imperative available to either from which a final command to be moral could be issued. Both are glad of that. Each is moved by an existential source of ethical *inspiration and moti-*

vation rather than by a transcendental source of moral *love, authority,* or *command.* So each pursues an *ethic of cultivation* in which care for the abundance of being precedes the assumption of obligation and responsibility rather than the other way around. Both, in their different ways, strive to cultivate more deeply and broadly a care for the diversity of life which—according to these faiths—already inhabits almost everyone part of the time to some degree or other. They then try to move that care in specific directions. Michel Foucault, for instance, first cultivates care "for what exists and might exist" and then struggles to identify new ways in which diverse constituencies might coexist and interact with less violence in the same social matrix. He knows that eventually he will bump into the political necessity of delimitation and exclusion. But he seeks to draw sustenance and inspiration from the rich diversity of being *before* closing on a systemic set of limitations. He combats, you might say, the Schmittian aesthetic of unity by affirming the wonder of the sublime.

SECULARISM, PERSONS AND JUSTICE

A vibrant democratic culture is marked by the productive tension it maintains between *pluralism* as the set of identities, moral codes, and practices of justice already on the cultural register of legitimacy and *pluralization* as the disruptive politics by which new identities and codes, enacted out of differences, injuries, and energies, subsisting below the existing threshold of justice, are placed on the register of legitimacy, morality, and justice. An *ethos* responsive to the politics of pluralization is thus never entirely reducible to any established moral code. *For it is the* protean spirituality *you draw upon to adjust vague principles and old codes to* new and surprising movements *under changed circumstances of life.* Critical responsiveness to the enactment of new identities out of old differences, then, exposes the constitutive ambiguity of justice. It respects the role justice as fairness plays in adjudicating conflicts between established constituencies, but it remains alert to calls to modify an established practice of justice in response to the enactment of new possibilities of being. In a democratic culture marked by periodic tension between already existing pluralism and the politics of pluralization, existing codes of justice and morality are periodically subject to revision by an *ethos* of critical responsiveness neither entirely reducible to them nor sufficiently derivable from any generic conception of the person.

We might trace the constitutive ambiguity of justice by addressing elements in John Rawls' theory that disable him from recognizing it.

For Rawls is a marvelous advocate of a "reasonable pluralism" whose interconnected categories of persons, private, public, justice, and the secular also render him tone deaf to the politics of becoming. The loss of traditional grounds for "the good" means, Rawls says, that the public practice of justice must be insulated as far as possible from irresolveable debates over the good. So Rawls seeks a fixed conception of persons appropriate to justice as an internal practice, dependent only on the (supposedly modest) externality of cultural "reasonableness." But such a quest effaces the fundamental ambiguity of justice and, thereby, obscures how the politics of pluralization periodically reconfigures its practice. I know Rawls says a thin conception of the person allows concrete persons to develop rich, individual selves. But the very formality of this permission obscures how dense *cultural differentiations* and *rankings of types of self* (identities) precede and configure the *operative practice of justice.* It therefore deflects ethical attention from thick cultural demarcations of what is inside, marginal to, and excluded from personhood *before* justice as fairness arrives on the scene. A veil of ignorance shrouds the constitutive ambiguity of justice.

Rawls now acknowledges how a fortunate modus vivendi set the historical conditions of possibility first for secular liberalism and eventually for the doctrine of justice as fairness. Religious toleration was not part of public morality in the sixteenth century: "At that time, there was not an overlapping consensus on the principle of toleration. Both faiths (Catholics and Protestants) held that it was the duty of the ruler to uphold the true religion and to repress the spread of heresy and false doctrine" (Rawls 1993, 148). Toleration, where it developed, emerged first as a modus vivendi between contending religious forces. Out of this delicate, contingent set of balances, a principle of tolerance could then develop. That development was inspired by a new, generalized appreciation of rationally irresolveable differences of faith between alternative religions within Christianity; it was motivated in part by weariness with the disastrous effects of civil war between contending claimants to represent the will of God in public life. This general recognition across religious lines of difference, in turn, opened the possibility for general principles of justice not entirely dependent upon any "particular" religious view within the Christian tent. Eventually a public, secular practice of justice could emerge, free from exclusive dependence upon any "comprehensive" religious or philosophical view. To some extent, justice as fairness reflects a general, public conception of the person shared by all reasonable members of society, without reference to the particular faiths they adhere to in private life; and yet to a certain degree (the proportions here are, reasonably enough, not clearly marked): "We hope to make it possible for all to accept the political conception as true or reasonable from the standpoint of their own comprehensive view, whatever it may be" (Rawls 1993, 150). A variety of comprehensive views, including Judaism, Christianity, Kantianism, and Millianism are, when not too dogmatically or exclusively advanced, supportive of this public conception of persons and justice. Once this effect is achieved you no longer normally need to draw any of these religious/metaphysical faiths directly into public discourse. They form its implicit background, or, better, the theological premises of each are compatible with a public practice of justice that does not invoke those premises. However, as Rawls reluctantly acknowledges, there are times and issues when the protection of public civility itself may require drawing some parts of those comprehensive doctrines most supportive of secularism into public discourse.

This is the key to a secular culture of public justice. Religious and metaphysical doctrines now slide into private life, providing the tropical undergrowth from which the clean air of justice emanates. But these doctrines themselves need not become central objects of public discourse. It is because an "overlapping consensus" now becomes possible that profound social divisions over such questions as the highest good, damnation, and salvation become avoidable. For "by avoiding comprehensive doctrines, we try to bypass religion and philosophy's profoundest controversies so as to have some hope of uncovering a basis of a stable overlapping consensus" (Rawls 1993, 152).

When you underline "to have some hope" within Rawlsian thought it becomes clear just how insecurely grounded and uncertain is the cultural background from which Rawlsian ethics draws sustenance. The account seems to acknowledge the messy blending in public ethics itself of moral motives and historically contingent balances between overlapping and contending forces. Rawls, however, does not attend to the uncertainty and changeability of this background once it has played the role needed in his theory. Active attention to such historical contingencies beyond and within ethics might open up the need to rethink whether the historic modus vivendi, from which secular liberalism was formed, remains sufficiently in place today. But Rawls evinces no interest in this question. The compromise formation of *secularism* is the last historical moment in the politics of becoming Rawlsian categories allow him to acknowledge. Rawls now wants to *freeze* in place those interconnected conceptions of the secular, the person, private, public, tolerance, and justice enabled by this historic formation. Thus, he first acknowledges some nonmoral conditions of possibility for the public morality he admires and then struggles to place under arrest the complex of basic conceptions he draws from it. But the world keeps changing and issuing new surprises, even as the central Rawlsian conceptions remain set in cement. The fragile stability of Rawlsian theory rests upon an uncanny combination of remembering and forgetting, remembering the historicity of the occidental settlement he prizes and forgetting how history keeps moving even after that settlement has been established.

How does Rawlsian forgetting proceed? Rawls now treats the secular, public, liberal conception of "the person" as a universal above the fray. Persons *just are*, for Rawls, at least after the modus vivendi of liberalism and in those respects that count for the practice of justice. "No constructivist view, including Scanlon's, says that the facts that are relevant in practical reasoning and judgment are constructed, any more than they say that the conceptions of person and society are constructed."[4] But, revealingly, Rawls supports this judgment by referring to a historic struggle in which this very conception of persons was still subject to contest; the outcome of that struggle itself helped to consolidate the modern, American, secular view of persons. The case is slavery:

> In claiming that slavery is unjust the relevant fact about it is not when it arose historically, or even whether it is economically efficient, but that it allows some persons to own others as their property. *That is a fact about slavery, already there, so to speak, and* independent of the principles of justice. The idea of constructing facts seems incoherent. (Rawls 1993, 122)

"So to speak." Rawls may sense the cruel closures that accompany his quest for moral closure in the domain of slavery. He levels persons to flatten social facts. And he pursues these two agendas to freeze a secular conception of justice endorsed by all reasonable persons in public life regardless of the density and variety of their private worlds. But the problem is that slaveholders and defenders could endorse a highly abstract view of "persons" while contesting its full application to some human constituencies. The most relevant moral fact about slavery, to its defenders, was that slaves were not deemed Christian enough or intelligent enough or sufficiently capable of self-mastery to count as full-fledged moral beings. And while the locus of such claims keeps shifting historically, the introduction of "persons" into the lexicon of Western moral thought has proved quite compatible with finding some human beings and, especially, some traits, dispositions, or dimensions of selective constituencies to fall below the historically operational threshold of the person.

Defenders of slavery fleshed out what is essential to civilized humanity itself differently than Rawls does; and they placed the differential capacities of human beings within a hierarchical order of being at odds with the secular doctrine in which Rawlsian persons are placed. The Rawlsian conception of personhood is both an effect of this political struggle and one of the considerations antislave forces brought to that struggle. The irony is, as we shall see shortly, that the Rawlsian purification of these categories disables him from engaging ethically new and unexpected forms of suffering shuffled below the operational threshold of abstract lovers of the person.

Rawls, of course, would contest this reading. He would say that slaveholders and defenders brought a "controversial doctrine" of world hierarchy into public discourse. The Rawlsian judgment fits the facts about persons as such while slaveholders represent them through the lens of a controversial doctrine. I thoroughly support the Rawlsian opposition to slavery without, however, being content with the icy conception of persons in which that opposition is couched. That is, I both resist the hierarchical view of the world Rawls opposes and find the Rawlsian conception of persons to provide an insufficient alternative to it. The comparative ethical advantage of the hierarchical view was that it sought to reach deep into the complexity of cultural life by engaging ethically each particular cultural formation; its disadvantage was that it found it impossible to identify any particular identity without placing it somewhere in a fixed hierarchy of being. The comparative ethical advantage of Rawlsian theory is that it engenders respect for persons as such; its disadvantage is that it does so by placing beyond the effective reach of ethics and justice those multifarious relations of identity\difference that both constitute the actual density of cultural life and often generate modes of unnecessary suffering. A commitment to the univocality of justice drives Rawlsian doctrine to forget the relevance of cultural density to the judgment of justice. And the reduction of concern for the density of culture to a hierarchical doctrine disables him from engaging other perspectives that do appreciate this density.

The Rawlsian model of persons needs to be revamped because it functions *today* to render Rawlsians hard of hearing with respect to injuries and movements placed below the established practice of justice. That is, it places Rawlsianism in a poor position to probe critically and responsively the dense tropical undergrowth of cultural discriminations between traits that now fall *inside* the recognized orbit of personhood and numerous afflictions, inferiorities, liabilities, perversities, disorders, and defects shuffled, to one degree or another, *outside* that orbit. These latter modes of subsistence below the protection of justice often contain cruelties and suffering missed or devalued by the practice of justice. They also sometimes mobilize intense energies to place emerging formations of identity onto the register of justice. When a new cultural movement succeeds in reconfiguring the register of legitimate identities, then, it also modifies the cultural configuration of what falls inside and outside the circle of the regular, reasonable person. It thereby alters the practice of justice.

The flat conception of persons is not a pure philosophical category, but the complex historical effect of the secular formation itself. That uncertain formation raised persons, rights, interests, tolerance, and justice onto the public realm by tamping down into the private realm a thick undergrowth of cultural injunctions, discriminations and intolerances. The secular formation promoted several positive effects, including the chastening of Christian enthusiasm in public life and the advent of greater tolerance and plurality. But it also concealed the profound ambiguity of justice as fairness from secularists. Rawlsianism remains incapable of probing this ambiguity as long as it refuses to disturb the historic formation of secularism in which the ambiguity is set.

It may seem risky to unsettle the secular formation during an age in which so many enthusiasts already press intense religious convictions into the public sphere. But that is one of the reasons the risk must be run. For the secular barrier against "comprehensive doctrines" in public life has broken; only a small number of *academic* liberals and post-metaphysical radicals today pretend to abide by this dubious principle of self-restraint. Everyone else has already breached it.

The second reason the risk must be run is more compelling ethically. For the secular, Rawlsian practice of justice is insufficient unto itself. Each time a new political movement inspires changes in established ethical sensibilities, it also modifies the existing formula of eligibility for inclusion on the register of justice. In reconfiguring the existing practice of justice and "reasonable pluralism" it suggests *retrospectively* that the previous practice inadvertently placed severe and unnecessary modes of suffering beyond its pale. Modes of conduct and affiliation previously obscure, monstrous, morally uncertain, or intolerable now become enacted into new traits, practices, identities, and affiliations falling within the range of tolerance. They now become, say, new objects of cultural indifference, or rights against which it is unjust to discriminate, or identities it is perfectly legitimate to include in an electoral coalition. To rework the historic modus vivendi of secularism would be to open the door to explore more profoundly and responsively the constitutive ambiguity of secular justice.

Numerous examples are available of new movements that have changed the register of identities eligible for inclusion in the American practice of justice. Thus, slaves were said to be inhabited by natural inferiorities pushing them below the threshold of personhood in the hierarchy of being; Indians were said (e.g., by Tocqueville and the America he registered) to lack the requisites of Christian civilization to enable them to participate in American democracy; atheists were (and often still are) said by Tocquevillian America to be governed by a narcissism, materialism, restlessness, and selfishness effectively disqualifying them from consideration for public office, though they were persons enough to participate in employment, commerce, and military liability; women were (and sometimes are) said to be qualified for household responsibility but not the responsibilities of full citizenship; "homosexuals" were (and still are) said to deserve justice as persons *and* to be marked by an objective disorder and/or sin locating their *sensualities* below the reach of justice; "post-modernists" (today occupying the subject position heretofore reserved for atheists) are said to lack the needed epistemic base for moral judgment or to refuse to articulate positive ideals, rendering questionable their competence as responsible social scientists and public intellectuals; those demanding the right to medically assisted death when life is no longer tolerable were (and sometimes are) defined as sinful or sick; and Rawls himself treats the mentally retarded as something less than full persons because they cannot participate fully in the practice of "fair cooperation" upon which his scheme of justice rests.

In each of these domains a successful movement of pluralization reconfigures the dense cultural experience of personhood, placing a new practice, identity or right on the register of justice by folding it within the revised compass of legitimate personhood. Moreover, each success in modifying the cultural field of moral eligibility also affects the self-identities of heretofore regular, unmarked persons. The shape of their ethnicities, faiths, sensualities, household organization, orientations to death, and models of masculinity/femininity may or may not change, but the very presentation of reasonable alternatives in these domains dims the aura of natural necessity, civilizational indispensability or moral universality that previously shone upon these practices. This loss of aura creates the basis for those outbursts of moral outrage that so often overcome regular persons when such changes are underway. To the extent such constituencies overcome resentment against loss of the halo effect, they (we) now become more open to selective political alliances with constituencies previously outside their range. And such a pluralization changes the terms of public discourse in another way. For the fervent claim to moral purity by those who insist that what they already say in the domains of morality, ethnicity, faith, gender, sensuality, and so on expresses the model of personhood itself is now open to the challenge that it represents a strategy to manage the symbols of moral regularity to its own advantage. One deleterious effect of the Rawlsian focus on persons as if it were a sufficient category, then, is its depreciation of a public *ethos* of critical responsiveness in which a variety of constituencies become more thoughtful and receptive to new movements that challenge the sufficiency of an existing practice of justice. The very terms of the Rawlsian division between public and private life relieves ethical pressure on dominant constituencies to denaturalize what they are to some degree in order to become more attuned to alternative possibilities of being negated by the politics of naturalization. It deflates the ethical importance of *tactical work upon ourselves* to disperse the implicit equation we often make between our own identities and the universal dictates of personhood as such. Such tactics of self and constituency are profoundly underestimated by a perspective confined to the person, universal/particular relations, and retrospective examples; they are valorized more actively by one built around appreciation of deep diversity, the social construction of identity\difference relations, the constitutive ambiguity of justice, and cultivation of critical responsiveness to new drives to identity that periodically come into being.

We can now see more clearly why Rawls is superb at acknowledging the justice of claims after the politics of pluralization has reconfigured the cultural matrix in which justice is set and why he remains so forgetful about the *politics of* cultural reconfiguration each time it has already been accomplished. Commitment to stability of the person and the univocality of justice require such forgetfulness. Within a period of thirty years or so Rawlsians have acknowledged generously the claims of Indians, women and gays *after* a series of social struggles made considerable strides in reshaping their cultural identifications. But Rawls pretends (and his categories suggest) that justice as fairness is in the same position today with respect to new injuries and new movements that it is with respect to constituencies whose previously degraded identifications have already been redefined through the politics of becoming. This, then, is the unconscious element of conservatism in Rawlsian justice. It renders Rawlsians unalert both to the constitutive ambiguity of justice and to the dependence of this ambiguous practice upon an *ethos* of critical responsiveness that exceeds it.

The point is not to criticize "oversights" of Rawlsians, *as if we* have a clear moral view above the fray they lack. Such a model of moral criticism, still abundantly familiar, would reiterate Rawlsian insensitivity to the politics of becoming. The point, rather, is to press Rawlsians to cultivate *a bivalent ethical sensibility* responsive to the radical insufficiency of *justice to itself.* For it is extremely probable that all of us today are unattuned to modes of suffering and exclusion that will have become ethically important tomorrow after they have been moved by politics across the threshold of cultural attentiveness. This is so, again, because a morally effective movement of pluralization breaks a constituent in its official identity that previously placed it below the reach of justice by representing it to be immoral, unnatural, abnormal, irresponsible, perverse, narcissistic, or sick.

Often enough, of course, such a movement fails; and sometimes many concur that it should not succeed even after they have explored closures and dogmatisms in their own identities. Thus, a movement by the citizen's militia, attacking the state violently in order to renationalize the American people, may both express grievances of those who initiate it and point toward the future closure of cultural pluralism. I would resist such a movement while exploring other ways to speak to the grievances from which it proceeds. But this constitutive uncertainty at the center of the politics of pluralization does not defeat the central point.[5] It underlines it. For once you come to terms with the constitutive ambiguity of justice you are in a better position to cultivate critical responsiveness. You are no longer assured that every new issue can be appropriately settled by reference to a set of preestablished conceptions and principles. You now come to terms both with the fragility of ethics and the insufficiency of abstract principles and codes to ethical judgment.

It is not exactly that ethical judgment is "particular," "situational," or "contextual" *rather than* flat, contextless, and universal. The universal/particular duality itself is unsettled by these considerations. For cultivation of responsiveness to unpredictable movements of difference may disrupt existing contexts or established conceptions of the universal or both. Decontextualization is sometimes crucial to an *ethos* of agonistic respect and critical responsiveness. For, recall that the hierarchical conception of being was extremely attentive to particular contexts and classes; but it responded to them within a fundamental conception of being that many of us would contest. In general contextualism is too unalert to the politics of becoming. For often enough, obscure pains, objective disorders, low levels of energy, perverse sexualities, basic inferiorities, uncivilized habits, hysterical symptoms, inherent abnormalities, nihilistic drives, irrational disbeliefs, objective inferiorities, and unreliable moral dispositions, defined so closely within the particular contexts in which they are set, become reconfigured through a politics of becoming and critical responsiveness that first exceeds both those contexts and the official reach of justice and then places new possibilities of cultural life on its register. These effects suggest contexts to be constitutively ambiguous practices, insufficient to guide ethical judgment.

The Rawlsian theory of justice recognizes this condition. But it does not yet appreciate how the practice of justice is indispensable to adjudication of conflicts between parties already on its register and insufficient to the ethics of responsiveness when the question is what kinds of conduct are to be *eligible* for placement on that register. No general concept of the person or reference to settled cultural context dissolves this ambiguity. Every attempt to do so will either (like the Rawlsian model) be too formal to reach deeply into dense cultural networks of identity\difference or (like the communitarian model) too context-bound to respond to diverse possibilities of being that may turn out to be tolerable or admirable after a new turn in the politics of becoming.

Rawls is pulled by a wish that things be still at bottom. He wants—after the historical modus vivendi of secular liberalism—persons and generic facts about them to remain placid so that liberal justice can be (nearly) sufficient onto itself. One should offer a moment of tribute to those who cling to such a winter doctrine during difficult times. They honor one important dimension of ethical life in the face of contemporary forces that press relentlessly toward a redogmatization of culture. But it is even more important to emphasize how things keep moving, often in surprising, disruptive ways. Any doctrine of secular liberalism built around the pretense that existing codes of personhood and justice are sufficient puts the politics of becoming on ice. This will to stillness is the crucial, secular, Rawlsian sensibility to contest by nontheistic, postsecularists (and others) who think the politics of becoming is never finished in a world that is itself perpetually unfinished. Because Rawls hides his comprehensive doctrine inside a closet in the private realm, this contestation must proceed through symptomatic readings of effects the underlying doctrine has on politics.

Nietzsche and Foucault, you might say, follow the teleological tradition of ethics in contesting Augustinian/Kantian/Rawlsian moralities of command and contract. They then pursue an ethic of cultivation comparable to the hierarchical, teleological tradition of "virtue" in some respects but grounded in a fundamental conception of being at odds with that tradition. They join teleologists in calling into question the sufficiency of the dominant categories of secular ethics; but they break with them in cultivating (nontheistic) care for the abundance of being over historically specific practices of identity, justice, and rationality. In doing so, they need not deny the pertinence of persons, reasonableness, or justice to ethics. Far from it. But they refuse to convert any of these media, in its current cultural configuration, into the final court of appeal.

In such an ethic *goodness as generosity* proceeds from appreciation of the abundance of being and *obligation to difference* proceeds from that source as well as acknowledgment of the indebtedness of your cultural identities to a range of differences that render them possible. *Receptive* generosity grows out of the sense that movements of difference are often capable of teaching something new and surprising to those who will listen.[6] These post-Nietzschean sources of goodness, obligation, and receptivity are fragile and fugitive. They do not have epistemological anchors. That is a *strength* of post-Nietzschean interventions into ethics. We appreciate the persistence of ethics, the fragility of goodness, justice, obligation and critical responsiveness, and the contestability of the ethical sources we and others draw upon. And we point to more generous possibilities of diversity and diversification than often sanctioned by a variety of theistic, contractual, teleological, and rationalist traditions.

A related point must be made. The post-Nietzschean ethic endorsed here is anchored in a partisan reading of the fundamentals of being. The claim is that it is unlikely that partisanship and contestation can be eliminated from alternative readings of the sources of ethics. So now the *key* question of political ethics becomes not, "What is the universal anchor?" but "How can we construct an *ethos* of engagement between independent constituencies who honor different (partisan) sources of ethics?" The first and most noble move involves the reciprocal acknowledgment by the parties involved of the contestability of the sources each honors the most. It is this acknowledgment of the problematic status of its own perspective and its invitation to other partisans to so the same that allows post-Nietzscheans to open up numerous lines of communication with the ethical perspectives of contemporary monotheists, secularists, atheists, neo-Kantians, Rawlsians, Habermasians, and Taylorists. For, as deconstructionists, critical theorists, and genealogists have shown repeatedly over the last three decades, these latter ethics are also grounded in unstable, fugitive, and contestable sources. In specific contexts they may advance claims with which we can collaborate and teach us some things we need to learn. But like the post-Nietzschean alternative, none of these traditions is entirely reducible either to the preferences of its advocates or to the implicit dictates of the fractured traditions of democracy in which we reside.

PLURALISM AND FUNDAMENTALISM

When such a line is pursued,[7] a positive ethical case can be built for a bi-valent, robust *ethos* of politics. This would be one in which an enlarged number of constituencies acknowledge more vigorously comparative elements of partisanship and contestability in their own identities and fold *this* shift in self-recognition into pursuit of greater forbearance and generosity in social relations. It would also be a pluralism in which new drives to *pluralization,* say, in the domains of gender, sexuality, household organization, ethnicity, metaphysical faith, and orientations to death, were met with greater responsiveness than some traditions of secular pluralism now authorize. For, if the possibilities of life are as protean and diverse as some of us project them to be while historically contingent dictates of social organization regularly narrow their range, we can expect existing formations to be challenged periodically by new movements that seek to transfigure injuries, grievances, energies, and uncertain hopes, circulating through them into new possibilities of being.

Appreciation of such a pluralist/pluralizing *ethos* need not draw upon Nietzschean sources alone, though they do provide an excellent source for it, and they do deserve agonistic respect from those not moved by them. It can draw selective support from a variety of currents flowing through theistic doctrines, particularly those which emphasize the mystery of God or the place of love in a faith receptive to the surprise of alterity. It can also draw sustenance from a modest rewriting of the Rawlsian problematic. In this refigured Rawlsianism, we pursue restrained terms of contestation and collaboration between multiple, overlapping traditions, each of which recognizes a certain reciprocity between the element of contestability in its own faith and in the alternative faiths with which it contends and collaborates. Such a rewriting touches the Rawlsian idea that the modern age is incompatible with a fixed conception of the good. But it no longer calls upon each constituency to leave its metaphysical/religious doctrine in the private sphere before it enters public, secular life. Rather, it calls upon it to acknowledge the contestability of its own presumptions and to allow that acknowledgment to infuse restraint, agonistic respect, and responsiveness into its relations with other constituencies. That is, it calls upon each to revise its self-understanding in the light of these considerations. Such an *ethos* of pluralism neither rises above partisanship nor reduces politics to unfettered partisanship. It fosters restrained partisanship within and between multiple constituencies, each of which may be able to identify lines of connection and collaboration with a series of others.

This is, then, a political ethic, an ethic in which politics plays a constitutive role and a politics in which ethics plays a constitutive role. It does not, of course, provide an accurate description of the contemporary condition in America, with its steep inequalities and large classes of people closed out of effective participation in political life. It is a critical ideal. As such, it is perhaps more appropriate to the times in which we live than the Rawlsian model it rewrites. It is presented not as *the* standard to which every ethic must appeal but as *an* ethical sensibility able to enter into critical dialogue and selective collaboration with a variety of other perspectives. The very indispensability and contestability of contending onto-theo and onto-non-theistic stances in the late-modern world supports the case for cultivating relations of agonistic respect and selective collaboration between multiple, overlapping constituencies, *each of which draws pertinent aspects of its* fundamental doctrine *into public life when, as so very often happens,* the occasion demands it. And several of which also invoke the essential contestability of the ethical sources they honor the most. Out of these diverse lines of connection across multiple lines of difference, a politics of creative coalitions might even be forged to enable action in concert through the state to support the economic and cultural preconditions of justice and pluralism.[8]

We urgently need a new modus vivendi today. For the secular idol now gives off a hollow sound whenever it is tapped. At a minimum, timid forms of secular liberalism can no longer succeed in calling upon others to leave their "comprehensive doctrines" at home when they enter the public sphere. Nor will secular liberals so readily be believed when they purport to do so themselves. Still, those who think a new imagination of a more multi-valent pluralism is imperative today must also seek to draw the most vibrant ideals of justice, tolerance, creativity, and plurality into the new matrix. What is called for is a rewriting of liberal ideals, not their elimination. If contemporary political culture does not become more ambiguous and expansive in something like the way suggested here, it seems likely either to decline into a cramped, stingy, exclusionary regime or degenerate into a series of cultural wars between dogmatic contenders.

Let us set aside for today the predictable question: "How could action in concert be possible in such a regime?"[9] It is possible to respond to that question, once the elements of this perspective are delineated more fully. But here is a related, Mouffeian, question: "Doesn't such a vibrant and fluid pluralism generate its own imperatives of delimitation and exclusion?" Yes. Among other things, fundamentalism in the domains of religion, aesthetics, reason, race, sexuality, and nationality can be permitted, but none of these movements must be allowed to gain political hegemony. We (Rawlsian, Habermasian, Mouffeian, Foucauldian) pluralists and pluralizers must collaborate to resist the hegemonization of such Schmittian movements. In doing so, we can appeal to the contestability of the grounds from which they proceed; we can affirm corollary points of contestability in our own faiths as part of an invitation to forbearance and receptive generosity in political relations; we can appreciate multiple sources from which reflective moral sensibilities might develop; we can show how possibilities for coexistence and selective collaboration among numerous constituencies expand when agonistic appreciation becomes reciprocal across multiple lines of interdependence and difference. But if and when the issue is on the line, we must stand against the violent hegemony of fundamentalism. A variety of secularists, monotheists, closet polytheists, Rawlsian, Mouffeians, Foucauldians, and Habermasians may soon find themselves drawn together into a general political assemblage to resist the fundamentalist onslaught.

NOTES

1. For example: "Once we have abandoned the rationalist idea that a formula can be found through which men's different ends can be harmonized, we have to come to terms with the fact that a society from which antagonism has been eliminated is radically impossible. This is why we have to accept with Carl Schmitt that 'the phenomenon of the political can be understood only in the context of the ever-present possibility of the friend-and-enemy grouping (Mouffe 1993, 128).' "

2. I pursue these objectives in Connolly, *Identity/Difference*, 1991. The objective there is to convert relations of antagonism into relations of agonistic respect and, sometimes, the latter into relations of partial collaboration.

3. The difference between Chantal Mouffe and me here may flow from the fact that the form of "essentialism" she has engaged in is a Marxism that may postulate the full intelligibility of a social form. That claim can be dismantled, if anyone actually advances it. But there is another form of "essentialism," one often invoked by Christian monotheists, in which that excess

which is God is not fully knowable, but still provides humanity with some guidance through cultivation of the arts of attunement, prayer, confession, and so forth. This tradition recognizes the constitutive outside in a big way while investing it with a diffuse purpose with which the Augustinian communes. One point in engaging this tradition is that it compels us (Mouffe and me, among others) to identify contrasting points of faith in our nontheistic, non-teleological invocations of excess. Another is that it reminds rationalists and secularists that they are messing around with theists, too, when they dismiss "postmodernism." We ask rationalists merely to give us the same respect they publicly bestow upon theists. And, while they stumble through adult life without the generosity our faith sustains, to raise their kids to have it.

4. See Rawls, *Political Liberalism*, 1993: 118. Wow, that Scanlon must be a wild guy.

5. It actually reinforces the central point. For if you could devise a sufficient *code* in advance to adjudicate between acceptable and unacceptable movements of difference, critical responsiveness would not be required as an ethical counter and supplement to justice. An additional point. The language I have emphasized in this essay focuses on the relation of "critical responsiveness" to the politics of becoming. I do so because this dimension has been underplayed by both theorists of sufficient justice and defenders of the politics of becoming. But of course agents of *initiation* are extremely crucial to the politics of becoming. You might be on one side of that line in some instances, for example, a woman involved in feminist initiatives, and on the other side on others, for example a white, Christian, heterosexual woman responding to the politics of becoming by blacks, gays/lesbians, and atheists. Often, you will be on both sides to different degrees on the same issue. The politics of becoming probably has a better chance in a culture where most "subject positions" are multiple, and where most people find themselves on the initiating side in some domains and the responsive side in others. But these are elaborations.

6. Romand Coles, *Rethinking Generosity* (1997), shows how Kantian philosophy sets unreasonable limits to the ethics of receptive generosity while the work of Nietzsche, Adorno, and Habermas, in various ways and to various degrees, prepares the way for such an ethical orientation. This is a superb book, very relevant to several issues noted briefly here.

7. I do pursue it in Connolly, "Beyond Good and Evil," 1993. That essay compares this perspective to the teleological tradition it has affinities with in some respects and dissents from in others. What is missing in it, however, is a critical engagement with the Levinasian tradition. For the latter founds obligation on the relation of indebtedness to "alterity" in ways that must be engaged by the post-Nietzschean tradition if it is to sustain itself. In an early essay, "Violence and Metaphysics," Derrida, *Writing and Difference* (1979), explores this relation of contact and tension between Nietzsche and Levinas.

8. I pursue this question in Connolly, *The Ethos of Pluralization*, 1995: chap. 3. The claim there is that "social fragmentation" is least likely to emerge out of the restrained differences between contending and interconnected identities reciprocally marked by appreciation of the contestability of the deepest sources

each draws upon, most likely to emerge from contention between dogmatic, exclusionary identities, each of which insists it *must* provide the universal matrix of action in this culture. This latter demand for coddling and special treatment is one no culture can afford to honor anymore. Moreover, the suggestion is that in the late-modern age, these are the basic alternatives "we" face. The economic/political conditions for a unitary, harmonious culture grounded in the same single are no longer available, if they ever were. Today the nostalgia to reinstate them can only intensify cultural wars.

9. In Connolly, Ibid., 1995, I argue that a culture of civic pluralism in which many participating identities acknowledge elements of contingency in their own identities and, particularly, affirm without resentment the contestability of the presumptions in which they invest the most faith, holds the most promise for the formation of political coalitions to support the educational and economic conditions of cultural pluralism. It is not that the perspective advanced here simply favors diversity while others seek the unity needed to govern, we disagree over the extent to which the drive to unity fosters cultural fragmentation and the degree to which inclusive majority assemblages are compatible with extensive cultural plurality of the right sort. See particularly chap. 3.

REFERENCES

Coles, Romand. 1997. *Rethinking Generosity: Critical Theory and the Politics of Caritas*. Ithaca, NY: Cornell University Press.

Connolly, William. 1991. *Identity/Difference: Democratic Negotiations of Political Paradox*. Ithaca, NY: Cornell University Press.

———. 1993. "Beyond Good and Evil: The Ethical Sensibility of Michel Foucault." *Political Theory* 21:365–389.

———. 1995. *The Ethos of Pluralization*. Minneapolis, MN: University of Minnesota Press.

Derrida, Jacques. 1979. *Writing and Difference*. Chicago, IL: University of Chicago Press.

Laclau, Ernesto, and Chantal Mouffe. 1985. *Hegemony and Socialist Strategy*. New York, NY: Verso Press.

Mouffe, Chantal. 1993. *The Return of the Political*. New York, NY: Verso Press.

Rawls, John. 1993. *Political Liberalism*. New York, NY: Columbia University Press.

CHAPTER 8

Political Theory and the Postmodern Politics of Ambiguity

Ruth Lessl Shively

Do not go about as a demagogue, encouraging triangles to break out of the prison of their three sides. If a triangle breaks out of its three sides, its life comes to a lamentable end. . . . The artist loves his limitations: they constitute the *thing* he is doing.

—Chesterton, *Orthodoxy*

"Is political theory a form of politics?" This essay looks critically at one form of thought that answers "yes." My criticism of this answer takes its inspiration from Chesterton's insight above. I will argue that those who would "free" theory and politics from the prison of rational order, would bring both to a lamentable end. For this order is to politics and theories of politics as the three sides are to the triangle. It is one of the "limitations" that constitutes the thing we are doing.

POLITICS OF AMBIGUITY

The theorists I address in this essay—those who answer "yes" to the question above—go by different names. They include in their ranks "militant" or "politicized" liberals like William Connolly and Richard Flathman, "*virtu* theorists" like Bonnie Honig, poststructuralist feminists like Judith Butler, "extravagance" theorists like William Corlett, and others who generally fall into the postmodernist camp. What they share, of importance to this essay, is the conviction that political theorists' attempts to order the world—and, in particular, their efforts to make it conform to the ideals of reason and community—are inherently ambiguous. In one sense, these attempts are taken to be

173

ambiguous because the ideals of reason and community are not what theorists generally take them to be: they are not objective insights into truth and order, but are formed out of, and sustained by, issues of power and control. In another, more normative sense, these attempts are taken to be ambiguous because the humane goals toward which they are directed lead to inhumane results. That is, because most people are unwilling to admit to the ambiguity of their ideals, they are driven to silence and exclude those who call attention to this fact: those, for example, whose irrationality or disruptiveness underlines the fragility of all reasons and harmonies. Political theory is political, then, in two key ways: first, in that its seemingly apolitical ideals about reason and community take their form only out of the political realities of power and conflict; and second, in that its efforts to impose rational and social order on the world inevitably involve it in the coverup of ambiguity and, as such, in the political activities of exclusion and control.

This is the gist of the argument made by the enthusiasts of ambiguity—or the "ambiguists" as I will hereafter call them (not with an intent to be disparaging, but to accentuate the set of assumptions that most distinguish and drive this group).[1]

To flesh out this argument a bit, let us add some detail to each of its key ideas. First, what is it that makes reason ambiguous for the ambiguists? Or why might they say that the ideal of reason is not what it seems to be? The key answer given here is that reason is formed and sustained by its oppositions: by irrationality, madness, chaos, flux. In William Corlett's words, rational forms can emerge only "by sequestering the mysteries, accidents, and madness of flux"; or by creating a temporary "border between reasonable order and epistemological insanity (Corlett 1989, 88–89, and 149)." Thus, to exist and to accomplish its ends, reason must silence or "sequester" nonreason. It must create a dividing line—however arbitrary and unstable—between the rational and irrational.

But then this is where the ambiguity of reason enters in, for, from this perspective, reason can never completely do away with nonreason. Its oppositions—insanity, mystery, flux, disorder—remain in the background, in the margins, because they are necessary to it. Madness, Corlett (1989, 180) argues, does not simply connote the absence of reason, but "plays a constitutive role in the possibility of reason and order." It is that against which we define ourselves as sane and our ideas as ordered. It is both "the death of reason and also its most profound resource" (Corlett 1989, 160). Which is to say, in other words, that reason is ambiguous because it must do what it cannot do: it must exclude the chaos and madness from which it springs and is sustained.

Second, what is it that makes the formation of community ambiguous for this group? The answer is that community also emerges from the silencing or sequestering of its oppositions—in this case, from the conflicts, differences or deviancies that threaten its identity and ends. To exist and to accomplish its ends, communities must impose "order on the chaos and multiplicity which would otherwise prevail" (Connolly 1983, 241). They must set boundaries that distinguish people and behaviors—as good or evil, licit or illicit, normal or abnormal, and so on—according to their contributions or costs to the communal order. And, more ominously, they must establish means of controlling and punishing those who stray from these norms. Yet, as with reason, the ambiguist finds that community needs the contraries it seeks to exclude: it takes its form by defining itself against that which is different; it achieves its unities and communal sensibilities by punishing that which is dissolute and dissenting. It is sustained by its conflicts. Hence, its ambiguity. Communities need, and yet cannot abide, their oppositions.

Thus, the ambiguists find that our attempts at rationally and socially ordering the world are built on permanent contradictions and are, as such, foundationally ambiguous. They also find that there is a certain *moral* ambiguity in these attempts. That is, they observe that most human beings dislike ambiguity, for most of us do not want to believe that our intellectual and social decisions are arbitrary, or that our categorizations are created by us out of our own fears and needs rather than out of a solid, objective reality. We do not want to acknowledge that we need the irrational and the deviant to have our sense of reason and community—or that our identities are not possible without these excluded others. Thus, the argument goes, the more insecure we become about the ambiguity of our foundations, the more insistent we become about the absoluteness of our truths. As William Connolly (1990, 60) puts it, we are driven by our insecurities to

> fix the truth of identity by grounding it in the commands of a god or the dictates of nature or the requirements of reason . . . to constitute a range of differences as *intrinsically* evil, irrational, abnormal, mad, sick, primitive. . . . As other.

And to make matters worse, the more insistent we become about our truths, the more we feel the need to control and punish those who call attention to the pretense behind them. That which is different is thus converted "into a form of deviation which must be improved, excluded, punished, or conquered" (Connolly 1983, 158). And the drive to truth and order inevitably turns into a drive to cruelty and the subjugation of others.

Like all attempts to impose order on the world, then, political theorists' attempts to order the world of politics—to manage or tame its disorders by making it rational and harmonious—are foundationally and morally ambiguous. To the extent that theorists attempt to provide for harmonious community by silencing and managing conflict and deviance, they overlook the community's foundations in conflict and deviance and participate in the cruelties discussed above. And to the extent that they claim to provide secure, rational foundations for political life, they overlook the irrational elements that constitute and sustain reason, clinging to the false reassurance that their truths are grounded in a solid, intelligible reality. J-F. Lyotard sums up this ambiguist sentiment when he writes that this philosophical "quest for a constituent order that gives sense to the world, to society, to discourse . . . is the mental illness of the West." For it is this kind of quest that holds out the false "hope that in time the fullness of meaning will emerge; that the problems facing Western civilization will be solved by reasonable and orderly minds put to the task of assembling the remaining pieces of the human puzzle; that madness, chaos, and bewilderment, like a frontier will eventually be settled" (Corlett 1989, 155–156).

Political theory is a political, not a philosophical, endeavor then because it is one more arena in which rational and social orders are presented as invariable and absolute goods while, in reality, being matters of variable and arbitrary power. And it is one more arena in which we are reassured of the mind's ability to triumph over disorder when, in fact, disorder remains a permanent and vital feature of our situation.

What then should we do? If we accept the fundamental ambiguity of reason and community, what becomes of the role of the political theorist? The ambiguists vary somewhat in their answers to this question, but they agree that the theorist's role is *not* about building the perfect, harmonious society or the ideal, rational order, and that a theory's success is not measured by its ability to manage or resolve conflict and difference. Rather, the theorist's role is about unmasking and delegitimizing the forms of power and subjugation that lie behind the aims of reason and harmony and a theory's success is measured by its embrace of difference and support for the goods of political conflict.

In fact, from this perspective, political confrontation is something to be positively celebrated. In the first place, it is a permanent and constitutive feature of our communities. It is inescapable. And those who attempt to escape it only end up deceiving themselves and subjugating others. And in the second place, it is a source of vitality for human society. To be truly alive is to be conflicted and conflictual, for, as Stuart Hampshire warns: "Harmony and inner consensus come with death, when human faces no longer express conflicts but are immobile, composed, at rest" (Hampshire 1989, 189). While to live vitally is to be willing "to accept and embrace the perpetuity of contest . . . to give up on the notion that one day a constitutive truth . . . will emerge and settle the ambiguities and struggles that mark the lives of most men and women" (Honig 1993, 210–211).

Thus, the ambiguists favor an expansion of the sites of political conflict in society. They would foster a general "enmity toward order,"[2] teaching us to reject the idea of a highest good or final harmony to be achieved in society, to purge "rational foundational truths from the public realm,"[3] and to embrace "the unruly conflicts and contests of democratic politics" (Honig 1993, 14). In this light, then, the public realm is not the place to resolve differences or ambiguities, but the place to welcome, and work with, them: "the medium through which . . . ambiguities can be engaged and confronted, shifted and stretched" (Connolly 1990, 82).

> What is aimed at is what Lyotard has christened "la sveltesse": the exhilaration of a discordant diversity or "difference" metamorphic enough to prevent the rootedness that engenders serious conflict but simultaneously strong and purposeful enough to "contaminate" and subvert the hegemony of rationalist, technologically regimented existence. (Pangle 1992, 48)

By embracing diversity and disorder as such, the ambiguists hope to unsettle the human drive toward conformity and control, and to undermine rationalist claims to truth and order. They would teach us to resist closure and the "all-too-human yearning for a freedom from politics or contest," to challenge and "problematize" society's categorizations while supporting and expanding the goods of disruption and subversion.[4]

I hope this brief summary fairly captures the postmodern approach to the inevitably political nature of all political theory. I personally believe that there is much to admire in this project. It has helped to uncover real elements of cruelty and arbitrariness in assumptions about reason and community and to create a new and deeper appreciation for the goods of diversity and contest.

But while I am sympathetic to these ends, I am doubtful about the means the ambiguists use to achieve them. In particular, I am doubtful that the maintenance of a deep skepticism or antifoundationalism is the best way to enhance political contest (using "contest," here, as shorthand for the various ambiguist projects of resistance, subversion, dissonance, disruption, and the celebration of difference).

My argument is twofold. First, I will suggest that a closer look at the nature and needs of political contest reveals an activity requiring certain clear, *uncontested* foundations. And second, a closer look at the ambiguists' own assumptions reveals that some such foundation is implicit and implicitly protected from contest or subversion. In other words, even those who would build a politics of radical resistance and subversion must acknowledge and justify their own *un*resisted and *un*subverted foundations.

"JUST SAYING NO"

The first point here is that the ambiguists cannot embrace all disruptive actions or resist all attempts to categorize activities in terms of "good" and "bad," "legitimate" and "illegitimate," "civil" and "uncivil." For if their aim is to give voice to those who have been silenced or marginalized, they must, at the very least, distinguish between activities that silence and marginalize versus those that do not. They must tell us, for example, what makes an act an act of resistance rather than of cruelty or tyranny, or what defines behavior as contestation as opposed to mere bullying or ostracization.

They do not tell us these things, of course, since their own assumptions require them to resist such attempts at closure and categorization. Yet, an answer is implied. It is implicit in their democratic vision of society and, indeed, in any democratic vision of society. "Good" political acts—acts of legitimate resistance and contest—are, for them, as for most other people, civil acts: meaning, essentially, acts that are respectful of the goods of democracy and liberty; acts that are nonviolent and designed to increase others' freedom and knowledge. For example, no ambiguists (in my readings) seek or sanction acts of "contest" that involve behaviors like burning crosses on people's lawns, lying to the public, shouting others into silence, hitting or killing or threatening political opponents, or the like. Rather, their political examples uniformly suggest that the expansion of contest would involve only civil kinds of resistance and subversion: things like teaching, protesting, demonstrating, arguing, raising awareness, questioning and the like. After all, the point of being in the ambiguist camp in the first place is to protest acts of tyranny and compulsion. So, despite strong rhetoric about disrupting *all* orders and undermining *all* rules, they cannot, and do not, contest or undermine basic rules of civility (rules which I will define further in a moment). In keeping with their democratic ambitions, they do not seek to annihilate or silence opposition, but to diversify and increase its voices and opportunities.

My point here is not just to say that the ambiguists are nice people who happen to reject violent and tyrannical tactics. It is to say that their goals imply and require this. For certain subversive or disruptive political activities—like threatening others with violence or shouting opponents into silence—are such that they undermine any further subversions and disruptions. In this sense, some disruptions turn out to solidify the status quo and some subversions turn out to be countersubversive. Which is why the ambiguists must stop short of celebrating all differences or disorders, for what would be the point of rejecting the old system for its supposed tyrannies—its bullying and silencing tactics—only to take up more of the same?

To put this point another way, it turns out that to be open to all things is, in effect, to be open to nothing. While the ambiguists have commendable reasons for wanting to avoid closure—to avoid specifying what is *not* allowed or celebrated in their political vision—they need to say "no" to some things in order to be open to things in general. They need to say "no" to certain forms of contest, if only to protect contest in general. For if one is to be open to the principles of democracy, for example, one must be dogmatically closed to the principles of fascism. If one would embrace tolerance, one must rigidly reject intolerance. If one would support openness in political speech and action, one must ban the acts of political intimidation, violence or recrimination that squelch that openness. If one would expand deliberation and disruption, one must set up strict legal protections around such activities. And if one would ensure that citizens have reason to engage in political contest—that it has practical meaning and import for them—one must establish and maintain the rules and regulations and laws that protect democracy.

In short, openness requires certain clear limits, rules, closure. And to make matters more complex, these structures of openness cannot simply be put into place and forgotten. They need to be taught to new generations of citizens, to be retaught and reenforced among the old, and as the political world changes, to be shored up, rethought, adapted, and applied to new problems and new situations. It will not do, then, to simply assume that these structures are permanently viable and secure without significant work or justification on our part; nor will it do to talk about resisting or subverting them. Indeed, they are such valuable and yet vulnerable goods that they require the most unflagging and firm support that we can give them.

Thus far, I have argued that if the ambiguists mean to be subversive about anything, they need to be conservative about some things. They need to be steadfast supporters of the structures of openness and democracy: willing to say "no" to certain forms of contest; willing to set up certain clear limitations about acceptable behavior. To this, finally, I would add that if the ambiguists mean to stretch the boundaries of behavior—if they want to be revolutionary and disruptive in their skepticism and iconoclasm—they need first to be firm believers in something. Which is to say, again, they need to set clear limits about what they will and will not support, what they do and do not believe to be best.

As G. K. Chesterton observed, the true revolutionary has always willed something "definite and limited." For example, "The Jacobin could tell you not only the system he would rebel against, but (what was more important) the system he would *not* rebel against . . ." He "desired the freedoms of democracy." He "wished to have votes and *not* to have titles . . ." But "because the new rebel is a skeptic"—because he cannot bring himself to will something definite and limited— "he cannot be a revolutionary." For "the fact that he wants to doubt everything really gets in his way when he wants to denounce anything" (Chesterton 1959, 41). Thus, the most radical skepticism ends in the most radical conservatism.

In other words, a refusal to judge among ideas and activities is, in the end, an endorsement of the status quo. To embrace everything is to be unable to embrace a particular plan of action, for to embrace a particular plan of action is to reject all others, at least for that moment. Moreover, as observed in our discussion of openness, to embrace everything is to embrace self-contradiction: to hold to both one's purposes and to that which defeats one's purposes—to tolerance and intolerance, open-mindedness and close-mindedness, democracy and tyranny.

In the same manner, then, the ambiguists' refusals to will something "definite and limited" undermines their revolutionary impulses. In their refusal to say what they will *not* celebrate and what they will *not* rebel against, they deny themselves (and everyone else in their political world) a particular plan or ground to work from. By refusing to deny incivility, they deny themselves a civil public space from which to speak. They cannot say "no" to the terrorist who would silence dissent. They cannot turn their backs on the bullying of the white supremacist. And, as such, in refusing to bar the tactics of the anti-democrat, they refuse to support the tactics of the democrat.

In short, then, to be a true ambiguist, there must be some limit to what is ambiguous. To fully support political contest, one must fully support some uncontested rules and reasons. To generally reject the silencing or exclusion of others, one must sometimes silence or exclude those who reject civility and democracy.

SAYING "YES" TO PERSUASION

The requirements given thus far are primarily negative. The ambiguists must say "no" to—they must reject and limit—some ideas and actions. In what follows, we will also find that they must say "yes" to some things. In particular, they must say "yes" to the idea of rational persuasion.

This means, first, that they must recognize the role of agreement in political contest, or the basic accord that is necessary to discord. The mistake that the ambiguists make here is a common one. The mistake is in thinking that agreement marks the end of contest—that consensus kills debate. But this is true only if the agreement is perfect—if there is nothing at all left to question or contest.

In most cases, however, our agreements are highly imperfect. We agree on some matters but not on others, on generalities but not on specifics, on principles but not on their applications, and so on. And this kind of limited agreement is the *starting* condition of contest and debate. As John Courtney Murray writes:

> We hold certain truths; therefore we can argue about them. It seems to have been one of the corruptions of intelligence by positivism to assume that argument ends when agreement is reached. In a basic sense, the reverse is true. There can be no argument except on the premise, and within a context, of agreement. (Murray 1960, 10)

In other words, we cannot argue about something if we are not communicating: if we cannot agree on the topic and terms of argument or if we have utterly different ideas about what counts as evidence or good argument.

At the very least, we must agree about what it is that is being debated before we can debate it. For instance, one cannot have an argument about euthanasia with someone who thinks euthanasia is a musical group. One cannot successfully stage a sit-in if one's target audience simply thinks everyone is resting or if those doing the sitting have no complaints. Nor can one demonstrate resistance to a policy if no one knows that it is a policy. In other words, contest is meaningless if there is a lack of agreement or communication about what is being contested. Resisters, demonstrators, and debaters must have some shared ideas about the subject and/or the terms of their disagreements. The participants and the target of a sit-in must share an understanding of the complaint at hand. And a demonstrator's audience must know what is being resisted. In short, the contesting of an idea presumes some agreement about what that idea is and how one might go about intelligibly contesting it. In other words, contestation rests on some basic agreement or harmony.

The point may seem trite, as surely the ambiguists would agree that basic terms must be shared before they can be resisted and problematized. In fact, they are often very candid about this seeming paradox in their approach: the paradoxical or "parasitic" need of the subversive for an order to subvert.

But admitting the paradox is not helpful if, as usually happens here, its implications are ignored; or if the only implication drawn is that order or harmony is an unhappy fixture of human life. For what the paradox should tell us is that *some* kinds of harmonies or orders are, in fact, good for resistance; and *some* ought to be fully supported. As such, it should counsel against the kind of careless rhetoric that lumps *all* orders or harmonies together as arbitrary and inhumane. Clearly some basic accord about the terms of contest is a necessary ground for all further contest. It may be that if the ambiguists wish to remain full-fledged ambiguists, they cannot admit to these implications, for to open the door to some agreements or reasons as good and some orders as helpful or necessary, is to open the door to some sort of rationalism. Perhaps they might just continue to insist that this initial condition is ironic, but that the irony should not stand in the way of the real business of subversion.

Yet difficulties remain. For agreement is not simply the initial condition, but the continuing ground, for contest. If we are to successfully communicate our disagreements, we cannot simply agree on basic terms and then proceed to debate without attention to further agreements. For debate and contest are forms of dialogue: that is, they are activities premised on the building of progressive agreements.

Imagine, for instance, that two people are having an argument about the issue of gun control. As noted earlier, in any argument, certain initial agreements will be needed just to begin the discussion. At the very least, the two discussants must agree on basic terms: for example, they must have some shared sense of what gun control is about; what is at issue in arguing about it; what facts are being contested, and so on. They must also agree—and they do so simply by entering into debate—that they will not use violence or threats in making their cases and that they are willing to listen to, and to be persuaded by, good arguments. Such agreements are simply implicit in the act of argumentation.[5]

Imagine, then, that our two discussants have the following kind of exchange:

> Mary: Guns don't kill people; people kill people.
>
> Tom: Yes, but guns make it a lot easier for people to kill one another.
>
> Mary: That's not necessarily true. There are lots of other murder weapons—knives or rat poison, for instance—that may be just as handy and lethal.

At this point, the argument reaches an impasse. Tom has presented a claim that Mary does not accept. Thus, if the argument is to continue, Tom must either find a way to convince Mary of this claim or he must go on to a different line of argument. Let us say that, in this case, Tom backs up his initial claim with further evidence. Perhaps he has some evidence to show that people are less apt to survive a gunshot wound than they are to survive being stabbed or poisoned. Mary then relents on this point:

> Mary: All right, I'll grant you that gun shot wounds are more apt to kill people. But that's exactly the reason I want to own a gun—so I can effectively protect myself and my family.
>
> Tom: Well I sympathize with that motive, but I don't think owning a gun is the best way to protect yourself. In fact, I've heard that people who own guns are more apt to get injured or killed themselves than to protect themselves against an intruder.
>
> Mary: What?! I find that very difficult to believe.

Here, again, our discussants reach an impasse. If the argument is to go further, they must either find a way to agree on the disputed claim, or move on to another claim (if there is one). Thus, if Tom has some further evidence that Mary will find convincing, they can continue this line of reasoning; if he does not, then they must move on to something else or give up the argument completely.

This is the ordinary ebb and flow of debate. Argument continues as long as there is some hope of progress in coming to agreement or as long as there are other lines of argument to be explored. But if there comes a point at which the two sides run out of new claims or cannot agree about the facts supporting claims already made, the argument is effectively over. The participants may continue to shout at one another, as they often do, but there is no longer anything positive or informative that can come from their interaction. There is nothing more to be learned and nothing that either side will find convincing.

The point here is that in arguing—and the point holds equally for other forms of contest—we assume that it is possible to educate or persuade one another. We assume that it is possible to come to more mutual understandings of an issue and that the participants in an argument are open to this possibility. Otherwise, there is no point to the exercise; we are simply talking at or past one another.

At this point, the ambiguists might respond that, even if there are such rules of argument, they do not apply to the more subversive or radical activities they have in mind. Subversion is, after all, about questioning and undermining such seemingly "necessary" or universal rules of behavior.

But, again, the response to the ambiguist must be that the practice of questioning and undermining rules, like all other social practices, needs a certain order. The subversive needs rules to protect subversion. And when we look more closely at the rules protective of subversion, we find that they are roughly the rules of argument discussed above. In fact, the rules of argument are roughly the rules of democracy or civility: the delineation of boundaries necessary to protect speech and action from violence, manipulation and other forms of tyranny.

Earlier we asked how the ambiguists distinguish legitimate political behaviors, like contest or resistance, from illegitimate behaviors, like cruelty and subjugation. We find a more complete answer here. The former are legitimate because they have civil or rational persuasion as their end. That is, legitimate forms of contest and resistance seek to inform or convince others by appeal to reasons rather than by force or manipulation. The idea is implicit in democracy because democracy implies a basic respect for self-determination: a respect for people's rights to direct their own lives as much as possible by their own choices, to work and carry on relationships as they see fit, to participate in community and politics according to decisions freely made by them rather than decisions forced on them, and so on. Thus, to say that rational persuasion is the end of political action is simply to acknowledge that, in democratic politics, this is the way we show respect for others' capacities for self-direction. In public debate, our goal is to persuade others with ideas that they recognize as true rather than by trying to manipulate them or move them without their conscious, rational assent.

Of course, to say that this is the implicit end of political action is not to say that we always recognize or act in accord with it. Like most ideals, it is, strictly speaking, unattainable. Yet, like most ideals, it nonetheless defines our judgments on the subject. It is the gauge against which we judge progress or decline.

Nor is this recognition of rational persuasion a rejection of the role of interest or power in politics. Clearly, the reasons we may give in persuading others may be based on issues of interest or power. We may try to convince others, for example, that a certain policy position is in their self-interest or that a certain action will increase their bargaining power. Though I should quickly add that, in a democracy, there must be other reasons recognized beside power and interest. For if power trumps everything, then those with the most power will always win and those with less will always lose (unless, by happy chance, their interests coincide), and there is no point in talking about democratic concepts like rights or equality or freedom. Democracy necessarily assumes that certain ideas trump power: for example, that ideas like the right to assemble, the right to free speech and representation, the rights of the accused, and so on, are to be rendered to people regardless of their positions in society.

I should also say that by calling these activities "rational" I do not mean to conjure up universal, rational principles or Rawlsian original positions, but only to say that democratic political activities have as their end persuasion by appeal to shared reasons. The "rational" tag simply serves to distinguish voluntary from less-than-voluntary kinds of persuasions. Thus, for example, I may "persuade" a man to do something by hypnotizing him or by holding a gun to his head, but I would not be using rational persuasion; I would not be giving him reasons upon which he might make his own judgment. Instead, I would be deciding for him. Again, the point is that in order to respect the self-determination of others, we must give them reasons they can recognize, or grounds that allow them to weigh their own thoughts and choose.

Nor, finally, should the "rational" or "civil" tag suggest that democratic actions are always inoffensive or acceptable to the majority. There are many actions that can be considered persuasive and political in the broad sense used here, while yet being offensive to majorities: we might list among these gay rights groups' disruptions of church services, animal rights groups' splashing of blood on fur owners, or anti-abortion groups' attempts to block clinic entrances.

Leaving aside legal or moral questions about these tactics, we can say that they are political in a way that burning crosses is not. That is, they are political to the extent that they are aimed at rational

persuasion of some kind: at communicating or heightening awareness of an idea, at enhancing others' understandings of an issue, and
thus at enhancing others' freedom and ability to make political decisions—rather, that is, than being aimed at merely intimidating them.
We can further grasp the intuition here by noting the different response we would have upon learning that an animal rights activist
was splashing blood on people with the intent merely of bullying
them or frightening them out of the habit of wearing furs. In such a
case, most of us sense that the action is no longer legitimately political because (or to the extent that) it is aimed at intimidation rather
than rational persuasion.

To sum up the argument thus far, the ambiguists cannot support
political contest unless they are willing to say "no" to—or to bring
closure to—some activities, and unless they are willing to say "yes" to
the rational rules of persuasion. Like all other democratic theorists,
they must make some foundational assumptions about the goodness
of self-determination, the preferability of reasons over force, and the
evils of tyranny, among other things. All democratic visions presuppose that politics is about rational persuasion. Thus, talk of resisting
or subverting *all* orders or *all* rational foundations is incoherent. At the
very least, the foundations of rational persuasion must be rigidly
upheld.

It will not do, then, to say we simply need more contest or more
"politics" and less rationality or foundationalism. It will not do to
invoke contest as a kind of talisman against the need to make difficult
judgments about good and bad, healthy and unhealthy, political actions. For inasmuch as the conditions necessary to political contest
require constant support and protection and inasmuch as we require
constant education and improvement in upholding and effectively
applying them, the conditions necessary to political contest require
these judgments.

CATEGORIES OF ANTI-CATEGORIZATION

In response to these arguments, the ambiguists might counter that
they do not mean to contest the basic structures of democracy—that
they mean simply to resist the cruel and subjugating tendencies that
prevail *within these structures*. Thus, assuming that we live in an open,
democratic society, they may simply set out to challenge our categorizations of people and behaviors as good or evil, licit or illicit, normal
or abnormal, and so on. And within our given system, they may simply seek to remind us that these categories are our creations—that we

need the irrational and the deviant to have our own sense of rational and communal identity. Thus, perhaps it is possible to pursue a general policy of contest and subversion—a policy designed to resist social pressure to categorize and judge others—without contesting or subverting the basic structures of openness and democracy.

I would like to finish this discussion by briefly suggesting why such a policy of general subversion is not the best answer to the important issues the ambiguists raise, or why a policy of rational judgment is a preferable approach to these issues. The first problem with the ambiguists' position here is one that they typically acknowledge. The problem is that it is impossible to subvert all categorizations, for in subverting one categorization, one necessarily embraces another. Thus, in subverting traditional categories—like good versus bad, normal versus abnormal, right versus wrong— the ambiguists necessarily embrace the alternative categories of the ambiguist: categories like those of open-mindedness versus close-mindedness, flexibility versus rigidity, creativity versus conformity, skepticism versus trust, tolerance versus intolerance, and the like. Which is to say that in denouncing anything, theorists cannot help but suggest what it is that they are *not* denouncing—or what they are accepting as preferable.

While, as I said, the ambiguists acknowledge the impossibility of subverting all categorizations, they do not think that this undermines their general policy of subversion. Rather, they maintain that the acknowledgment of this fact should make us approach our own (and others') ideas with skepticism and flexibility, prompting us to see our ideas not as justified truths but as useful positions from which to unmask truth claims and not as enduring grounds for political theory but as temporary resting points from which to unsettle others— points that can themselves be expected to be challenged and changed down the road.

The problem with this position is that even temporary and unstable positions need justification. That is, even if we acknowledge that our categorizations are apt to be undermined and overthrown, they must be given reasons at the moment we are using them. If we are denouncing others' choices, we are necessarily commending our own and, as such, we need to say why we think our own commendable. Likewise then, in denouncing traditional categories, the ambiguists cannot avoid suggesting that their own categories are superior; and, as such, they cannot avoid making positive moral claims or presenting a general, alternative theory about humanity and society. Thus, they are obligated to present their reasons for this alternative vision.

This is why the ambiguists need to do more than call for a whole-sale resistance to categories. Because resistance to some categorizations always involves acceptance of others, they need to own up to, and justify, their own choices.[6] If they propose that we choose their version of reality and their favored categorizations, they must give us reasons. If they think we ought to be skeptical ambiguists rather than truth- or harmony-seekers, they must make a case for this prescription. Simply being against established categories is disingenuous when the argument is designed to establish new categories in replace of the old.

We are brought back, then, to the issues of rational judgment and persuasion. Earlier I argued that political contest rests on certain un-contested foundations or rational conditions. Here I have added that the policy of anti-categorization rests on certain stable categories of its own. Thus, the subversives are not free from the responsibility of choosing and justifying the subversive categories that define and guide them. For once we recognize the inescapability of choosing categories, we see that subversion or any other political project is a matter of choosing the right categories, not of escaping them. Thus, to be truly subversive requires taking a stand: judging what is good and bad, legitimate and illegitimate, allowed and disallowed, in the best sub-versive society.

The desire to avoid this sort of judgment is understandable, for it tends to be associated with intolerant and oppressive attitudes and behaviors. And the situations within which we must judge are often dauntingly complex and uncertain. Rarely can we be certain that our judgments are right.

Nonetheless, judgments must be made—not only in the develop-ment of political theory, but also in confronting the decisions of every-day political life. Thus, even in the face of great uncertainty and ambiguity, we are compelled to act and, in so doing, to judge what is good and bad, reasonable and unreasonable, and so on. The ambiguity of our situation does nothing, as such, to alter the need for judgment.

As John Courtney Murray writes, to say that uncertainty and complexity must keep us from judging or acting is as senseless as

> a surgeon in the midst of a gastroenterostomy [saying] that the highly complex situation in front of him is so full of paradox ("The patient is at once receiving blood and losing it"), and irony ("Half a stomach will be better than a whole one") and dilemma ("Not too much, nor too little, anesthesia") that all surgical solutions are necessarily am-biguous. (Murray 1960, 283)

The point, of course, is that there is no avoiding judgment and action here, and that in political theory and politics, as in surgery, we are often compelled to deal with the complexities we meet as best we can.

Thus, if we must judge, there is no point in trying to avoid the task through a policy of indiscriminate subversion. Our choice is not whether to judge, but whether to judge through open, reasoned argument or not. And the point of this essay has been to say that the former option is best.

NOTES

1. I borrow the term "ambiguist" from John Courtney Murray in his book, *We Hold These Truths* (1960, 284-286), who used it to describe a form of thought that was popular in the late 1950s and that is, in many ways, startlingly similar to the form I examine in this essay. In describing this approach, Murray writes that, for the ambiguist, "the factual situation always appears as a 'predicament,' full of 'ironies,' sown with 'dilemmas,' to be stated only in 'paradox,' and to be dealt with only at one's 'hazard,' because in the situation 'creative and destructive possibilities' are inextricably mixed, and therefore policy and action of whatever kind can only be 'morally ambiguous.' "

2. Or, expanding on a Nietzschean phrase, a resistance to "the efforts of political and moral orders to stabilize themselves as the systematic expressions of virtue, justice, or the telos of community." See Honig, *Political Theory and the Displacement of Politics*, 1993: 3.

3. "For fear," Honig, ibid., (1993, 9) adds, "that their irresistible compulsion will shut down the agon [the sites of political contest]."

4. In such a setting, Robert Hollinger, "Postmodernism and Politics," (1993, 170), writes, "difference is preserved and commonality is in some sense always a temporary stopping place that grows out of the interactions among the irreducibly other voices in the conversation. There is no utopianism, no consolation, no telos to history, society, human life."

5. For an excellent discussion of this point, see McCloskey, *Rhetoric of Economics*, 1985: 24–25. McCloskey sums up the rules that are implied in argument and conversation as follows: "Don't lie; pay attention; don't sneer; cooperate; don't shout; let other people talk; be open-minded; explain yourself when asked; don't resort to violence or conspiracy in aid of your ideas." And he adds, we "cannot imagine good conversation or good intellectual life deficient in these."

6. As J. C. Murray in *We Hold These Truths* (1960, 283), put it, "the dilemmas and ironies and paradoxes [of the ambiguists] are, like the beauty of the beloved, in the eye of the beholder. They represent a doctrinaire construction of the facts in terms of an antecedent moral theory."

REFERENCES

Chesterton, G. K. 1959. *Orthodoxy*. New York, NY: Doubleday.

Connolly, William. 1983. *The Terms of Political Discourse*. Princeton, NJ: Princeton University Press.

Connolly, William. 1990. "Identity and Difference in Liberalism." In *Liberalism and the Good*. Edited by R. Bruce Douglass, Gerald M. Mara, and Henry S. Richardson. New York, NY: Routledge, Chapman, and Hall.

Corlett, William. 1989. *Community Without Unity*. Durham, NC: Duke University Press.

Hampshire, Stuart. 1989. *Innocence and Experience* Cambridge, MA: Harvard University Press.

Hollinger, Robert. 1993. "Postmodernism and Politics." In *Paradigms in Political Theory*. Edited by Steven Jay Gould. Ames, IA: Iowa State University Press.

Honig, Bonnie. 1993. *Political Theory and the Displacement of Politics*. Ithaca, NY: Cornell University Press.

McCloskey, Donald. 1985. *Rhetoric of Economics*. Madison, WI: University of Wisconsin Press.

Murray, John Courtney. 1960. *We Hold These Truths*. New York, NY: Sheed and Ward.

Pangle, Thomas. 1992. *The Ennobling of Democracy: The Challenge of the Postmodern Age*. Baltimore, MD: Johns Hopkins University Press.

CHAPTER 9

Political Theory as Metapractice

John G. Gunnell

Fine fellows—cannibals—in their place.

—Joseph Conrad, *Heart of Darkness*

UNDERSTANDING ANTHROPOPHAGI

In his *Notes Toward a Definition of Culture*, T. S. Eliot evoked the dilemma of an anthropologist studying cannibals.[1] I will embellish this image as a way, analogously and metaphorically, of entering an analytical and historical discussion of the relationship between political theory and partisan politics, and more generally, between (what I will call) "metapractices" and their object. My purpose is to explore the complexities of this relationship and to examine critically some of the images that characterize contemporary discussions.

The most immediate problem, of course, is the danger of being consumed by one's subject matter. To avoid becoming a delicacy requires a delicate unobtrusive approach, if not the abandonment of fieldwork altogether in favor of library research. But the peril of being swallowed up or absorbed by one's work is hardly a one-dimensional issue. While one concern of an investigator of such an exotic culture is that of becoming a menu item, there is also the potential of being devoured either in the sense of idealizing the subject and adopting its values, maybe because of its primitive innocence, or even developing a taste for the cuisine and going native. The very idea of understanding implies a distinction between the interpreter and the interpreted, but there is always the nagging belief, and fear, that truly to understand requires identity, that to apprehend fully the subject requires becoming what we study.

As Eliot noted, however, the person "who, in order to understand the inner world of a cannibal tribe, has partaken of the practice of cannibalism has probably gone too far." Like Kurtz's atavistic regression in Joseph Conrad's *Heart of Darkness*, "he can never quite be one of his own folk again" (Eliot 1949). Those who investigate cannibals are always looked upon with some suspicion, and they adopt circumspect behavior with regard to their colleagues as well as their subjects. There is at least the problem of gaining tolerance, and even sympathy, for what would likely be understood by one's peers as less than seemly practices. In the end, it is difficult to be at once a good anthropologist and a good cannibal, or, as Max Weber might have put it, the vocations of studying one's kind and eating one's kind are ultimately incompatible and involve different kinds of commitments.

There is also, however, the issue of ingesting one's subject matter. As a cultural practice, cannibalism is not the social aberration associated with events such as the Donner (one may hesitate to say) party. There is a certain reverence for such curiosities and sometimes a belief that they should not be disturbed—that what is conventionally natural deserves, like other ecological objects, to be sustained no matter how reprehensible it may appear by more civilized standards. Is it not part of the human condition and an expression of individual realization? And functionalism offers a more scientific basis for this sentiment. After all, cannibal "theory," such as believing that one absorbs the strength of digested enemies, may have been rooted in false beliefs, but, at least as an intergroup practice, it had the prudential value of deterrence, and, symbolically, it offered a certain sense of closure.

While studying cannibals may have become largely a purely academic pursuit, the impetus was originally missionary zeal and a dedication to human emancipation. The endemic conflict between the disparate cultures of inquiry and its object, between two different visions of reality and rationality and between two sets of social norms, is not easily dissipated. Even if the existence of practices such as cannibalism is the professional raison d'être of anthropology, the scholarly ethic of relativism can only be extended so far, and even when intrinsic value is assigned to what is different, few would ultimately defend incommensurability. Even the posture of objectivity does not adequately either inhibit evaluation or insulate the object of inquiry. How long can one hold it steady and pristine in order to gain a cognitive grasp? And simply the fact of prolonged contact is bound to create conditions where the concepts and values of the observer intrude into the world of the observed. What is involved here are paradoxes of distance and proximity, purity and contamination, attraction and repulsion. The strangeness of cannibal life requires immediacy and propinquity in research, and maybe even something like participant observation in pursuit of "thick" description, but there are the dangers of the loss of impartiality on the part of the investigator and of the pollution of the object. Advocacy is viewed both as unprofessional and as hazardous to the integrity of the subjects, and science seems to provide only authority for understanding and explaining rather than evaluating and prescribing.

With respect to these issues, the anthropologist finds solace not only by maintaining some physical remoteness, camping outside the village and engaging in only seasonal visits, but also by creating quite elaborate forms of theoretical, conceptual, and methodological distance. The imposition of social scientific categories also creates practical distance, but, maybe less felicitously, it opens up a cognitive gap. Some may believe, like Peter Winch, that "it is unjust to give any action a different name from that which it used to bear in its own times and amongst its own people" (Winch 1958), but it is ultimately the language as well as the values of anthropology that separate it from the practices it studies. And eventually maybe cannibalism becomes less an empirical phenomenon than a theoretical product, like kinship, which evolves in the conceptual practice of professional anthropology, remote from the jungle of its origins and performance. While the original purpose of anthropology may have been to transform the minds and actions of the subjects, they often end up unrecognizable to themselves and conceptually transfigured in the form of discursive disciplinary objects. "Cannibal," after all, derives from Columbus's Spanish rendering of an Arawakan tribal name and his application to the practices observed.

I have probably reached, if not exceeded, the limits of this metaphor, although I cannot resist noting that the problem manifest in the puerile story about the cannibal who passed the anthropologist in the woods is more than syntactical. But, without pointing out the parallels at every juncture, I do want to suggest that the metaphor illuminates the relationship, both in principle and historically, between social science, or political theory, and politics. Discussions of this relationship have, however, often been obfuscated by decontextualization and a resistance to recognizing the discreteness of practices such as political theory and politics and the, often conflicting, constraints that govern each. Political theorists have tended to adopt a dual, and sometimes contradictory, strategy: on the one hand, claiming that political theory and politics can be assimilated and, on the other, asserting that political theory is both distinct and epistemically privileged.

POLITICAL THEORY AND POLITICS: IDENTITY

There is a propensity among political theorists to blur the line between theory and practice or between academic and public discourse—to find theory in politics and to find politics in theory. It is not that this boundary is in fact all that clear or impervious, but neither is it merely analytical. This search for identity between the two realms is, I will suggest, nearly an endemic feature of those practices of knowledge that study other forms of human activity, and it is rooted in both cognitive and practical motives. Jacques Derrida (1982, 213), for example, tells us that "every philosophical colloquium necessarily has a political significance" and that the "essence of the philosophical" and the "essence of the political" are "always entwined" and joined by an "a priori link." Although claims about political theory as a form of political discourse or phrases such as the "politics of interpretation" may be illuminating in some instances and in some dimension, they also often reflect conceptual strategies for displacing or repressing the issue of their relationship to their object of inquiry (See, for example, Mitchell 1982).

It is sometimes suggested that political theory is simply a more abstract and reflective form of political discourse, that, as some literary critics claim about their own activity, it is "politics by other means" (Mitchell 1982, 1); that politics is ultimately a linguistic practice and therefore not really unlike political theory in a universe of intertextuality; that human affairs are, at least in the modern world, a seamless web, and that, as George Orwell noted, "in our age there is no such thing as 'keeping out of politics.'" Since there is no clear boundary between the academy and politics, theory in various ways has practical consequences, for example, that a cultural and historical object like politics only gains identity in relation to other cultural objects, and thus neither disciplines nor their subject matters can be viewed in isolation; or that academic analysis and prescription with respect to public issues is a kind of political practice. All of these propositions may have some general merit, and each may be true in some set of historical circumstances. But they often are pleas for an excuse not to confront the real issue of theory and practice. The assumption seems to be that to admit difference is to prejudice negatively the case for relation, but it is impossible to speak of relationships without assigning criteria of difference and identity to the things in question.

There might seem to be some intuitive basis for suggesting that political theory can be construed as a means or form of political action. Politics is a relatively familiar activity and one that is often encompassed by the culture of both observer and observed. Under these circumstances, problems of practical and cognitive distance seem mitigated. We might, however, be less inclined to think, for example, of the anthropologist as engaging, except vicariously, in cannibalism. But we would also probably not think of a sociologist studying the family, in a professional capacity, as engaging in family life. Suggestions of an identity between politics and political theory seem, in the end, to have little more than a lexical basis.

One of the difficulties in approaching this issue derives from the fact that there is a prismatic ambiguity attaching to the term "politics" and its cognates. The concept refers not only to a historically and culturally circumscribed activity and its attributes but also to abstract and functional extensions that are reflected in phrases such as "academic politics." It is also easy to be seduced, or seduce others, into believing that by talking *about* politics, one is in some manner engaged *in* politics, that such commentary is at least a virtual politics if not a microcosm of political life. A recent article in the *New Yorker* magazine comparing President Clinton with the political philosopher Michael Oakeshott noted that "these days, political philosophy exists in two varieties—as a specialized subject taught in universities and as a thing that every politician just has."[2] But the image of assimilation is often joined to the image of separation and superiority.

POLITICAL THEORY AND POLITICS: DIFFERENCE

One notion of theory and practice is to conceive of both as contained within, as elements of, a field or activity. One might speak, for example, of the theory and practice of literary interpretation. Here theory is understood as a set of principles of inquiry and as something that can both guide the practice of interpretation and serve as a basis for judging it. This notion of theory and practice is often extended, sometimes consciously and sometimes unreflectively, to the relationship between two different practices or to what is usually referred to as the spheres of theory and practice. The idea of theory as a guide to practice may be dubious (as anti-theorists in literary criticism, such as Stanley Fish, have argued and as anti-epistemologists in political theory have claimed), but the extension of this image to the relationship between discrete practices and the claim of epistemic and, consequently, practical authority on the part of a theoretical practice such as social science or political theory is even more contentious.[3]

A sub-text common to political theory and most other metapractices, such as philosophy, is the theme of relativism. While some, such as postmodernists, may, like earlier liberals, embrace relativism as a liberating stance, it is more often presented as a danger to the integrity of activities such as politics and science. What is really at issue, however, is the relationship between, for example, social science and its subject matter. Social science's claim to practical authority with respect to its object of inquiry is usually cognitive, that is, a claim to know it better than it knows itself and to be in a position to judge it by virtue of the possession of a special kind of knowledge. The specter of relativism threatens this transcendental status. The problem of relativism is the displaced, philosophical, residue of the theory/practice problem.[4] The question that is posed is whether there is some way to escape the hermeneutic circle and privilege an idea of theory or reason that can underwrite a critique of the *sensus communis* or various specific social practices. Anti-foundationalism and various forms of contextualism, hermeneutics, post-structuralism, and postmodernism are viewed as threatening theoretical practice and as implicitly, if not explicitly, endorsing a conservative, or at least status quo, attitude. How, it is asked, can philosophy, literary theory, and other such enterprises retain, what Christopher Norris (1985, 10) has called, a "radical edge" and the ability to demystify texts or, more generally, everyday beliefs in an intellectual climate that engenders skepticism about the possibility of distinguishing between appearance and reality.

It is instructive that while most images of critical theory are predicated on some version of rationalism or foundationalism, Norris finds a basis for critical inquiry in desconstructionism and the work of Derrida. Such a move indicates, in part, that the issue is less foundationalism per se than a philosophical justification of the cognitive authority of theory. While Jürgen Habermas (1987) and others maintain that postmodernism is an instance of a wider crisis of reason, precipitated by H-G. Gadamer, Richard Rorty, J-F. Lyotard, and others, which denies the possibility of philosophical privilege and undermines the idea of critical theory, postmodernism is sometimes invoked as a kind of reverse transcendentalism. Rather than empowering, for example, political theory with privileged access to knowledge, the claims to truth in the practices it studies are devalued or transfigured so that both seem to occupy the same playing field. Yet theory seems to retain an attenuated but still superior reflective position such as that implied in Rorty's (1978) image of an "edifying" philosophy that would join in the "conversation of mankind."

The assumption that academic political theory is in some way relevant to, or may have an effect on, politics is based less on evidence than hope. When the same claims are made for literary criticism, and this enterprise is advanced as a critical social practice, credulity seems more strained. But one activity has as great, or small, a claim as the other. Asking whether political theory has a closer tie to politics than literary criticism is something like asking which liberal arts major is the best preparation for law school. They are both academic enterprises that are subject to the contextual restraints and possibilities of such pursuits, and they both make texts their object of analysis and seek to construe textual interpretation as social inquiry. Since arguments about political theory as a means to or form of political action are so familiar, it may be interesting to look at an extended argument from this other sphere of the academy where it has become common to claim that literary interpretation is not only a way of exposing ideology but "itself a way of changing the world" (Mitchell 1982, 5).

Frank Lentricchia, like Christopher Norris, Terry Eagleton (1983; 1985; 1978), and others, has argued strongly for the idea of literary criticism, and university education, as not only *means* of social change but *modes* of social action. He asks if it is possible to "do radical work *as* a literary intellectual," that is, a person "who works mainly on texts and produces texts," that is, to be a significant actor in a wider social realm by simply doing what comes naturally, that is, what scholars do. He concludes, but without a particle of evidence, that they, "in their work in and on culture, involve themselves inescapably in the political work of social change and social conservation." Lentricchia claims that the role of the "university humanist . . . as a social and political actor has been cynically underrated and ignored." He refers not to an academician who engages in supplementary extrinsic political activity but rather the person whose work "is carried on at the specific institutional site where he finds himself and on the terms of his own expertise, on the terms inherent to his own functioning as an intellectual" (Lentricchia 1983).

Lentricchia in his book, *Criticism and Social Changes*, argues that "our potentially most powerful political work as university humanists must be carried out in what we do, what we are trained for."

> I would go so far as to say that those of us in the university who conceive of our political work . . . not as activity intrinsic, specific to our intellectuality (our work as medieval historians, for example) are being crushed by feelings of guilt and occupational alienation. We have let our beliefs and our discourse be invaded by the eviscerating notion that politics is something that somehow goes on somewhere else, in the "outside" world, as the saying goes, and that the work of culture that goes on "inside" the university is somehow apolitical— and that this is a good thing. (1983, 1–7)

Borrowing from Karl Marx's aphorism, he claims that "the point is not only to interpret texts, but in so interpreting them, change society" and the structure of power through the transformation of culture. By doing what they quintessentially do, academicians can play, and play upon, politics. It is scholarship without guilt. Theory in literary criticism becomes a form of rhetoric and persuasion and a vehicle for a radical and "oppositional critic, seeking to amplify and strategically position the marginalized voices of the ruled, exploited, oppressed, and excluded" and to create a new "community." In the end, it is claimed, "all literary power is social power" (Lentricchia 1983, 10–12, 15, 19).

This vision is often less audaciously articulated but nevertheless pervasively implicit in much of the literature of political theory. My claim is not that theory has no consequences, and I do not deny that there may be, or have been, places where this image fits the facts—such as Eastern Europe or nineteenth-century Germany. But most of those who embrace generically the notion that textual analysis can be a form of social criticism offer little in the way of evidence. They rarely confront the analytical dimensions of the relationship between theory and practice, let alone examine the actual institutional and historical setting and the operative relationship between the orders of discourse.

This kind of argument has begun to surface in a number of areas such as cultural studies. The claim of this program is that it is necessary to break down disciplinary boundaries, because the identity of a cultural object is a matter of its affiliations with other cultural objects. Carried one step further, this becomes an argument for the nonidentity and mutuality of theory and practice whereby various kinds of oppositional literary theories are presented as forms of social criticism and "cultural politics" (see, for example, Brantlinger 1990; Agger 1992; Grossberg, Nelson, and Treichler 1992). What this kind of image encourages is a neglect of the actual boundaries of discursive practices and of the relationships between them. The assumption is that to recognize boundaries and relationships, and, consequently, the intrinsic identity of activities, is to defend insulation within and between both theory and practice. But what is actually taking place is the legitimation of theory.

Immanuel Kant's defense of the preeminence of theory, more than two hundred years ago, may be the paradigm and classic case, and there can be little doubt about his immediate concern. He was apprehensive both about the status of philosophy among the university faculties and about the depreciation of academic discourse. Statesmen, and other practitioners, he claimed, were "of one mind in going after the *academician*, who concerns himself with theory on their behalf and for their good; but since they imagine themselves to understand this better than he, they desire to banish him to his academy . . . as a pedant, who, unfit for practice, only stands in the way of experienced wisdom" (Kant 1983, 62–63). Kant, like many after him, set out to demonstrate that although theory and practice represented different activities, the spheres of truth and power, there was a kind of functional unity which established the priority of the former and its relevance to the latter. Since theories, or rules and principles, were indigenous to practice, theory and practice were, in effect, one, but the activity of theory retained a privileged position because of its self-consciousness. It is no accident that Kant was the founder of modern philosophical foundationalism.

THE THEORETICAL DISTORTION OF POLITICS

I would insist that there is no kind of politics other than partisan. This is not a claim about the inability of actors to reach a position beyond interest but rather an insistence on what I will call the "historical particularity and conventionality" of politics and a warning about the confusions, and strategic conflations, involved in various functional and figurative extensions of the concept of politics. In this respect, I may be taking issue with the premise reflected in the title of this anthology, since I can no more take literally the idea of "political theory as a form of partisan politics," or as a "means" of such politics, than I can countenance a serious discussion of anthropology as cannibalism—or as a means of engaging in it. We might also find it provoking and illuminating to think about politics as political theory in action— or even about cannibalism as, at least physical, anthropology with its particular version of carnal knowledge. After all, anthropology and anthropophagy, like political theory and politics, have at least an alliterative connection. The problem with such images is that they tend to repress and obscure real distinctions and relationships.

What has happened in much of the literature of academic political theory is that politics has been rendered in terms of analytical frameworks and philosophical images that have little more to do with its existential and historical practice than, for example, the extent to which the account of science that was conjured up by logical positivism was an adequate representation of the practice of natural science. Similarly, the image of social science, as, for example, a critical mode of inquiry, has often been presented with little attention to the actual situation and character of its contemporary practice (see, for example, Fay 1987).

Both political theory and politics have become reifications, and the problem of the relationship between them has been transformed into a metatheoretical issue with metatheoretical solutions.

"Politics" belongs to the language of both inquiry and its object, and this sometimes leads us to suppose some aspect of identity between the two that is less persuasive in cases such as the relationship between, for example, anthropology and the rituals of alien society. "Political theory" has been characteristically used to refer both to the study of politics and to something internal to politics. But it is in part the ambiguity of the concept of politics that mystifies and seduces us when we think about the issue of political theory and politics and which, at the same time, facilitates more self-conscious discursive strategies of assimilation and conquest.

Politics can be infinitely idealized and demonized with varying degrees of attention to its phenomenological particularity. But politics is a conventionally constituted and historically circumscribed activity. It has no essential universality. To say that it is just another game is, of course, an irritating oversimplification. Its social significance and scope is greater, its defining membranes are considerably more permeable, its internal constitution less well-defined, and its instances less identical. But politics has no truly theoretical status—there cannot be a theory of politics in the sense that there can be a theory of human action. "Politics" refers to a historically limited configuration of human action, and the criteria of identity and similarity are conventional—whether imposed from without or generated from within.

Politics, in addition to the big stories on television and in the newspaper, is what people do in local elections, what takes place at school board meetings, what happens in city councils, and so forth. This profane world, however, is rarely directly represented in the discursive universe of political theory except in a derivative manner. There is, of course, nothing *ultra vires* about using the word "politics" in any way one wishes, but metaphorical and functional extensions of meaning can become troublesome in a manner that extends beyond, for example, speaking of diplomacy as playing chess. What characteristically takes place is that a familiar image of politics, or some attribute often associated with it, such as power or interest, or some promise of its ideal form, such as democratic deliberation and human realization, is abstracted and universalized. Politics then becomes, by definition, present or possible, across time and space and a necessary dimension of human life, but this often has little to do with how, or whether, politics is existentially either externally or internally perceived and discriminated.

While this kind of descriptive and explanatory disjunction between what may tentatively be called conceptual and lived politics has been a significant problem in mainstream comparative political science, political theory, more broadly conceived, and often with more normative and conscious motives, has embraced metaphorical and functional definitions of what is political and even assigned to such constructed realms the more essentialist name of *"the* political." Such fixed transhistorical images inhibit confronting the actual or historical relationship between political theory and politics. What, then, can be said about social science or political theory and politics that is, so to speak, theoretical or universal and not dependent on their particular character and circumstances?

METAPRACTICES

I have, so far and to some degree, retained the familiar terminology of "theory and practice," but it is necessary to recognize that this usage is very problematical. Like dichotomies such as thought and action, it both implies that the former is superior and that the latter is lacking, that knowledge *about* is the key to knowledge of *how*. When we are talking about theory and practice, we are actually usually talking about two realms of practice (and theory) whose identity, and the relationship between them, are matters that cannot be settled a priori. A better approach would be to discriminate more carefully between what I will call the "orders of discourse."[5]

Political theory belongs to a genre that I will speak of as metapractices which includes a large variety of activities ranging from the philosophy of science to sportscasting. Metapractices are, for the most part, practices of knowledge which have another conventional or discursive practice as their object of inquiry. They also are not functionally necessary, or given, in the very concept of human society. Parasitic may be too strong a word, but they are commensal and distinctly supervenient and contingent. We might want to say that without nature, we could not have natural science, but that would not be to say very much. And, in fact, it would probably be more significant, epistemologically if not metaphysically, to say that without natural science, there would be no nature, since nature is largely a discursive product of natural science. On the other hand, it is difficult to imagine drama critics without theater. Maybe in a Jorge Borges novel we might find something as fanciful as paleontology without artifacts. One might argue that there have been historical instances in which there was political theory after the demise of its object—possibly the case of

Aristotle. But, for the most part, we must seek the character of political theory in terms of its relationship to its subject matter.

Although some metapractices are what might be called "third (or even fourth)—order" types, in that they have another metapractice as their object (the philosophy of social science would be a case in point), political theory, or political science, belongs to the second-order variety. No matter how they theoretically construe their object or in what language they describe it, that object, unlike, for example, the phenomena posited by natural science, is not merely a conceptual by-product of the practice of knowledge. There are, at least in principle, inherent constraints on how it is conceived. While it may be tempting to suggest, for example, that there is no "text" against which to check interpretations (Fish 1980) and to extend this idea to social science and its objects, we must be careful on both counts. Abstract claims about original meaning and authorial authority are as indefensible as those about the indeterminacy of meaning and the banishment of the author—which is in effect the banishment of the text.

Within a second-order, or interpretive, discipline, there is not, anymore than within a natural science, a transtheoretical access to the subject matter, but that subject matter is not simply a creation of theoretical practice. While we might, metaphorically, wish to say that there is no text without an interpreter, we cannot allow this image to be extended to the point that we forget that the text has been already conceptually constituted. By the same token, we may deny that there is any definitive interpretation of an instance of politics, but we cannot deny that it has already been interpreted by the actors and by others in the social milieu. While in natural science, the battle over the "interpretation" of nature is fought out between scientists, there is in metapractices not only a lateral competition between accounts of the object but also, at least potentially, a battle between them and their subject matter—a battle between two interpretations and two theoretical universes that is not only cognitive but potentially practical.

Since it is impossible to speak about metatheoretical practices, either specifically or generically, except relationally, any general account must address the nature of first-order practices. The latter, as historical types and tokens, are infinitely variable, but there are certain distinguishing features. First, they are given in that they are preconstituted and preinterpreted by the participants and possess their own image of themselves. Second, they also embody a vision not only of their own identity but of an external world. Between, and within, these forms of life there may be different and changing paradigmatic accounts of the "world," but it makes no sense to ask what the world is except as a theoretical construction of first-order practices such as science, religion, politics, common sense, and the like. There is no automatically privileged description.

It is difficult to speak generically about the character of the *relationships* between second- and first-order practices, since this is a quintessentially practical, cultural, and historical issue. There is neither a metatheoretical nor a theoretical solution to the problem of theory and practice, as much as philosophers have believed it possible either through grasping the meaning of history or discovering the authority of transcendental imperatives. Certain generalizations are, however, worth venturing.

Although, as I will indicate later, there are circumstances in which one might say that first-order practices make second-order activities objects of scrutiny, as in the case of the apocryphal missionary boiled up in the proverbial pot, it can be assumed that for the most part the reverse is almost definitively the case. It is also probably safe to suggest that in many instances the discourses that become institutionalized as autonomous second-order practices, such as the philosophy of science and social science, have their origins in first-order practices from which they, at some point, break out or float free. But second-order practices are seldom content with simply their cognitive relationship to their subject matter. As Nietzsche noted, philosophy is always characterized, as least latently, by a will to power over the universe of discourse that it makes its object. And this is even more true of social science.

It is not, however, simply political science and ethics that have an end in action, even though their claims to knowledge might seem to carry greater urgency for application. There is always a conflict between second and first-order claims—between knowledge *about* and knowledge *in*. In second-order discourses, there is also, as I have already stressed, characteristically an urge toward assimilation, or reassimilation, to its object, since its identity and authority are tied to that object. But, at the same time, the authority of second-order claims must be won by seeking grounds that trump or transcend those inherent in first-order practices, and this means, paradoxically, seeking identity through difference.

I will defer any further generic discussion of first and second-order practices, and the relationship between them, and attempt to make the issues more historically concrete. And part of such an endeavor is to acknowledge that what is involved is not a relationship between a world-historical vocation of political theory and some fundamental dimension of the human condition but, for the most part, a more mundane one between the university and an academic practice, on the one hand, and everyday political life, on the other hand. The case that I will address is that of the relationship between political theory (and political science) and politics in the United States.[6] The story would be very different in other places and times and with respect to other second- and first-order discourses. I will, however, introduce the discussion of the United States by addressing a somewhat parallel, but yet quite different, situation.

THE HISTORY OF A PRACTICE OF KNOWLEDGE

Max Weber's distinction, in 1919, between the vocations of science and politics has often been condemned and praised, frequently for the same reason, but seldom viewed contextually. Much of Weber's life, as a public person and a scholar, had, despite his ambivalence about his own calling, been devoted to finding a bridge between the university and politics. At the time that he wrote the famous essays on the vocations of science and politics, he had seldom been more simultaneously involved in both realms. It is a mistake to assume, as many critics and defenders of his position have, that his distinction was a rejection of the goal of linking the two. Quite simply, although paradoxically, he believed that it was necessary to separate them, conceptually and existentially, in order to get them together—both cognitively and practically.

The world of the German mandarins had passed. *Wissenschaft* and politics had parted ways, and it was a matter of coming to grips with this change. Both society and the university were ideologically pluralistic, and the authority of knowledge could no longer be based on cultural homogeneity and coincidence with political authority. Weber chided those on both the left and right who embraced philosophical ideologies, in part because he disagreed with their positions but more generally because it was no longer meaningful or effective to speak from the podium in partisan terms. Only the ethic of the specialized sciences, embracing method and objectivity, could, he believed, provide the practice of knowledge with a legitimate voice and, at the same time, achieve the authority to transcend the claims of politics grounded in power and irrationality.[7] Weber's death, however, bequeathed to the remainder of the Weimar conversation the practical problem of exactly how what had been alienated could be reconciled.

Many of those who remained in Germany, such as Martin Heidegger and Karl Jaspers, as well as those who emigrated to the United States, such as Hannah Arendt and Max Horkheimer, continued to seek grounds for the authority of philosophy. And they approached the problem of theory and practice as a philosophical issue. Karl Mannheim, however, took his cue from Weber and accepted the premise of the nonidentity of the vocations of science and politics. He suggested that a vehicle of articulation could be found in relatively detached, but still partisan, intellectuals trained in the university in the sociology of knowledge. They would recognize and synthesize the diverse values in society and provide a practical science of politics. Part of the appeal of Weber's and Mannheim's work in the United States was that it seemed to validate what, from the beginning, had been the definition of the problem as well as the solution that was embraced, that is, that cognitive authority was the key to practical authority.

The emergence of the social sciences as disciplines in the United States during the late nineteenth century was principally the confluence of two distinct but interconnected tributaries. One was the traditional, and religiously informed, university curriculum in moral philosophy and practical ethics, devoted to training citizens and leaders. The other, also often religiously and even evangelically inspired, consisted of organizations such as the American Social Science Association which pursued broad and diverse programs of social reform. The former sought, especially during the Germanization of social studies, to recast its identity in terms of science, and the latter, seeking metapolitical authority, gravitated toward the university which it saw as representing the authority of the modern scientific enterprise.

The study of partisan politics in this context had one fundamental purpose—to change it, and even abolish it. Understanding was a means to an end. The paradox, however, was that cognitive authority was perceived as the basis of practical authority, and this, in turn, seemed to require objectivity which entailed achieving both intellectual and physical distance. But distance was also a more pragmatic issue. The circumspection accorded politics was in part because it seemed a realm of irrationality and danger. Francis Lieber, the German émigré who founded systematic political studies in the United States, believed that politics was at least in part responsible for the tendency in American life toward what he called the "alienation of the mind." George Beard, maybe our first psychoanalyst, attributed in part what he euphemistically called "American nervousness" to thinking about and engaging in partisan politics. In short, politics, long before Harold Lasswell, was equated with mental pathology.

Theoretical and methodological distance was created through such devices as casting the subject matter in terms of the State—something both more sublime and scientifically accessible than mere politics. This esoteric language estranged political science from the very thing that it wished to address, but it also promised security as well as authority. Politics was not a benign object. The natives were not friendly. As Gene Poschman has pointed out, studying politics was not exactly like studying other activities. "Politics," like "society," may have had a generic abstract connotation, but it also had a specific, concrete, and fearsome reference. History, for example, was not a threat to historians. One representative incident was the University of Kansas's refusal to allow the creation of a department called either "politics" or "political science," since, the trustees noted, there was enough politics in the state already. And many universities had no qualms about dismissing people with untoward social opinions. The institutionalization of social science was in part a search for scientific authority, but it was also a search for professional safety.

There has not been adequate recognition of the structural impact that the fear of reprisal exercised during the formative years of the social sciences. Periodically, from after the turn of the century through the McCarthy era (see Schrecker 1988), the perils would again become concretely manifest, but even when not directly threatened, like Robinson Crusoe, social scientists saw the footprints of the cannibals everywhere. These disciplines became institutionalized in both senses of the term, but for both cognitive and practical reasons, there was a need to gain access to that from which they had become estranged. The path to proximity, however, was circuitous. And the demands of discipline and profession, in terms of impartiality, scholarly production, and other criteria of scientific performance, took their toll on time, energy, and commitment.

By the time that political studies had evolved into a profession, political science was already a relatively conservative field or discipline, both ideologically and with respect to its strategies for reengaging politics. The days of more easy intercourse between academic and public life that had, for example, distinguished the career of Francis Lieber, were gone. The object lessons involving those, such as the radical economist Richard Ely, who had pursued advocacy from the podium, were all too vivid. Ely had returned from his education in Germany full of enthusiasm for what he understood as the participation of the academy in progressive public policy, but he was finally forced to recant publicly his socialist agenda in order to retain his academic status. Those, such as John Burgess at Columbia and Herbert Adams at The Johns Hopkins, who were the most influential in establishing the content and form of graduate studies in political science and political theory, came back from Germany with a different image of the relationship between academic and public discourse. They believed that the modern university would produce the leaders and citizens who would animate public life, but what it produced was basically more scholars.

Europe was a poor model for the United States. After the Civil War and the rise of the modern research university, there never was an integration, or reintegration, of the university into the structure of political power. Both the distance from politics and the fear and trembling, and loathing, that it engendered was reflected in the dominant vision of social science—what was called "social control." Many of the students of both Burgess and Adams were ideologically more to the Left than their mentors, but their basic concerns and purposes were similar. Partisan politics could, ideally, they believed, be replaced by administration, but how reform was to be accomplished, that is, how truth would speak to power, remained a dilemma. When the American Political Science Association was established in 1903, its founding documents reflected what was by then a profound tension. The charter stated that the fundamental purpose of the profession was to advance the scientific study of politics and that it would not take a position on any partisan issue, yet the first president, Frank Goodnow, stated that the fundamental goal was to achieve "authority over practical politics." Much of the history of the discipline could be construed as the story of the continuing attempt to devise strategies that would resolve these less than compatible aspects of professional identity.

Woodrow Wilson's image of the "literary politician" and his attempt to seek a reconciliation between science and politics by designating the department at Princeton "Politics" were symbols of the search for an intellectual resolution. A practical resolution was much more elusive, and he, in the end, was forced to choose between distinct vocations. The Progressive dream, represented, for example, in the work of Charles Beard and Arthur Bentley, was that of social scientific realism as a vehicle of political enlightenment and a catalyst for awakening a dormant democratic public, but the dream was fleeting. The politics of interest was all too real and ineluctable. Some, like Beard, because he made money from textbooks, could afford to maintain his principles and walk away from Columbia when academic integrity was threatened, but for most individuals, the issue remained one of accommodating to the demands, both ideological and professional, of academia, while seeking political effect.

Charles Merriam remained true to Progressive values, but he was disillusioned with the practical strategy. No more than his predecessors was he content with partisan, or what he called "jungle," politics, and his vision of social science was one in which scientific authority would gain the ear of political elites who, in turn, would use the mechanisms of the state for molding public opinion and institutions. The values of democracy were the goal, but democratic processes were not necessarily the means. This vision was radicalized in the early work of Merriam's student, Lasswell. Never had the abolition of politics been more boldly endorsed. His optimism receded, however, and his agonized ambivalent confrontation with the fundamental paradox of academic and public discourse persisted through most of his career.

By the mid-1930s, a nascent democratic theory had begun to be extracted from the realities of partisan politics. Interest group struggle had not only become acceptable, but also was valorized as the new meaning of democratic representation in the work of David Truman and others. Robert Dahl finally provided the theoretical foundation for this image of pluralist democracy, and, in a certain sense, behavioralism achieved a detente between political science and politics by its transformation of the description of politics into a normative thesis. It might be said that political science solved its problem of engaging politics by reconciling itself to the belief that politics was doing fine. Political theory, however, began to take a different course which was largely a consequence of the transplantation of the Weimar conversation. While some such as Carl Schmitt, Martin Heidegger, and a host of far less fortunate individuals became, in various ways, objects of political consumption, others fled the cannibals.

Political theory, like political science as a whole, was an American invention, and it had until now reflected and reinforced the values of the parent discipline. What Leo Strauss, Hannah Arendt, Eric Voegelin, the Frankfurt School, and others brought to the United States was a dissident perspective. They attacked scientism, liberalism, pluralism, pragmatism, relativism, historical optimism, and most of the other defining tenets of the American social-scientific credo. And they reawakened the old antipathy toward partisan politics. They had already been tempted by philosophical distance in Germany, and an endemic disdain for normal politics was accentuated by their image of Weimar as the threshold of totalitarianism—an image which they transposed to American liberalism. In place of partisan politics, they championed a new kind of ontological politics quite foreign to the indigenous culture.

The attack that political theory separatists mounted against political science during the 1960s, on the grounds of the latter's political quiescence and acquiescence, was in many ways an invocation of ancestral values, but, in the end, it did not entail any closer cognitive and practical relationship to political life. And while the émigrés had exited an intellectual world in which the relationship between academic and public discourse was a pivotal issue, their definition of the problem lost much of its meaning in the American context. Both the politics that was criticized and the idea of the political that was idealized were alienated images, and the hope for political theory as a form of political praxis, whether as conceived by the Frankfurt School or as represented in Strauss's vision of the education of gentlemen, had an attenuated practical meaning. All of this had little to do with any existential relationship between academic and political life. The problem of theory and practice was transformed into a trope in the internal conversation of political theory.

Although, at least intellectually, if not professionally, political science and political theory began to go their separate ways by the early 1970s, both the mainstream discipline, represented by David Easton's announcement of a "new revolution in political science," and theoretical dissidents, embracing what Sheldon Wolin had designated as the "vocation of political theory," continued to grapple with the issue of the relationship between political theory and politics. Both Easton and Wolin made pleas for relevance, but neither the reconstruction of political science as public policy analysis nor the idea of political theory as a form of political education managed to transcend the tensions of the past. Easton's hope for a national federation of social science advisers was never realized, and Wolin's attempt, through the short-lived vehicle of *democracy*, to translate the academic idiom into the language of politics is an instructive example of the difficulties involved. But both of these visions raise issues long latent in the history of the social sciences. These include not only the general problem of the relationship between academic and political discourse, but also the compatibility of democracy and the claims of political theory.

TWO CULTURES

What most past and present discussions of theory and practice or knowledge and power presuppose is that there is some manner in which the former are self-validating, that, at least in principle, they have a claim to authority grounded both in their reflective position and in their grasp of something transcendental or universal. I believe that we must engender a basic skepticism about this assumption, but even if the superiority of theory should be accepted, either, in principle or in a particular instance, its precedence, like that of scientific rationality, may be in fundamental conflict with other values such as democratic deliberation. The tension between the social-scientific pursuit of a rational society and the processes of democratic politics has been distinctively a part of the history of American political science, and it is no less manifest in various forms of contemporary academic political theory. Democracy, like cannibalism, has its own logic, and as much as varieties of critical theory, for example, may proclaim the values of democracy, the implied relationship to their subject matter is distinctly elitist.

Michael Walzer has advanced the idea of the theorist as a "connected critic" who while seeking necessary "critical distance" enters the "mainstream" and pursues criticism as "interpretation" and "opposition" and seeks to mediate between "specialists and commoners" or "elite and mass" (Walzer 1987, 39, 60; Walzer 1988, 4, 11). Walzer acknowledges the conflict between the claim of philosophy to "objective truths" and the authority of the political community, but he fails to situate this image. None of Walzer's many historical examples, however, from the Hebrew prophets to Michel Foucault, touch directly upon the circumstances of contemporary institutionalized academic political theory.

The issue of theory and practice has, today, become a very abstract one. While the idea of political science making contact with partisan politics had always been something of fantasy, the respective practices involved were, for at least a century, concrete and recognizable in the literature. Political science pondered, and sometimes struggled with, its relationship to the politics of its time. Increasingly, however, what "political theory" and "politics" came to refer to in the language of political theory were reifications that had little to do with the actual professional academic activity and with the real world of politics. And the fate of academic political theory, since its intellectual escape from political science, has, ironically, been in bondage to varieties of philosophy and other discourses toward which it has migrated in search of grounds of cognitive and normative judgment. The problem of theory and practice has largely been transformed into a conceptual issue and conceived in terms of the problem of epistemological authority.

Claims about the alienation of political theory from politics, and from itself (see Gunnell 1986), are answered in a number of ways which often do not squarely confront the issue. One line of argument is based on the "trickle-down" hypothesis that the university, and maybe particularly political science and political theory, play, through education and other processes of cultural diffusion, a major role in shaping the public consciousness. This is at once the hope and nightmare of those on the ideological right who believe that there is, at present, a hegemonic, pernicious, ultra-liberal academy that must be supplanted by a new form of political education (Bloom 1987; Anderson 1992). But this image of the political efficacy of the university is also shared by many on the left who believe that participating in the esoteric indigenous philosophically generated discussions of postmodernism, multiculturalism, political correctness and the like, represents a form of political action and even a realm of political discourse. Although it would be interesting to know if, to what extent, and in what manner academic discourse reverberates in the world of social practices, such claims remain largely matters of faith and rhetoric. For every claim of this kind, there is a counter argument that suggests that academicians do not really function as public intellectuals and that the key to social change is not to be found in academic contributions to culture (Jacoby 1987).

Another answer, what I will call the "hat-trick" argument, is to suggest that when we carefully survey the work of individual theorists, we find many who are working assiduously on actual political phenomena and speaking to and about pressing political problems, both by confronting the philosophical dimension of these issues and by speaking to and for various concrete and marginalized constituencies. And there is the further claim that many such individuals do not simply give at the office but take their work home and, through their individual efforts, carry it into the relevant communities. My first response to such a claim is to suggest that it is an interesting thesis, but that it remains largely at the level of professional folklore. To the extent that it can be demonstrated empirically, it may indicate something about a few individuals but does not tell us very much about the general structural relationship between political theory and politics. There is, however, a more significant point.

The vision of political theory, in instances as diverse as those of nineteenth-century social science, American images of policy analysis, and Critical Theory, was precisely to transcend the vagaries and unpredictability of individual action and to establish the profession, the vocation, or the science as an institutional social force that would carry authority and inform practice on a systematic basis. To suggest that the functions, for example, attached to the idea of a critical social science are somehow being performed within society by particular individuals or by surrogate means (Leonard 1990), is interesting but hardly an answer to the problem that political theory had set for itself.

A somewhat similar answer is to point to what is sometimes called the "cross-over" phenomenon, but this also fails to take account of what the social science movement has been all about. And it has other difficulties attached to it. While "cross-over" may seem intuitively significant—cases like those of Woodrow Wilson, Henry Kissinger, Hubert Humphrey, in one direction, and those of Jimmy Carter and similar instances, in the other direction—these are exceptions that do not, literally speaking, prove the rule, that is, do not falsify it. What these cases tell us about the general relationship between political theory and politics is that for the most part these realms are actually quite disparate and that we note these incidents because they are so unusual. Even more importantly, however, they represent choices between vocations. Much has been made of the manner in which Straussians found their way into the Reagan administration, and one could point, for example, to the fact that a political theorist of communitarian liberalism, such as William Galston, has joined the Clinton White House. What must be noted, however, is that although academic credentials may have facilitated entry, this was a matter not of their influence in the role of an academic scholar but of their leaving theory, at least temporarily, for practice.

There is, in principle, no reason why political theory should not join political practice or why political practitioners should not enter the world of political theory. There is also no general reason to insulate either culture from the influence of the other. But, as in the case of anthropologists and cannibals, the dangers and complications of contact and interpenetration should not be minimized. What most demands scrutiny, however, are those claims, or assumptions, that suggest that the problem of theory and practice is other than, itself, a practical historically situated issue, that it has an epistemological or metatheoretical solution, that theory can be construed as a form of practice, or that practice can be understood as a mode of theory. If the vocation of political theory is to have integrity and relevance, it must make phenomenal or partisan politics its actual subject matter. Unless it talks *about* existential politics, it makes little sense to dream about speaking *to* it and engaging *in* it.

NOTES

1. I owe this reference, and image, to Gene Poschman's paper (1982) "Emerging Social Science and Political Relevance: Some Extractions from a Less Than Classic Literature," and much of my thinking about the relationship between political theory and politics has emerged from conversations with Gene Poschman.

2. Adam Gopnik, *New Yorker*, October 1996, 194.

3. See Gunnell, *Between Philosophy and Politics,* 1986 for an argument against both these claims about the relationship between theory and practice.

4. For a fuller discussion of this issue, see Gunnell, "Relativism," 1993a.

5. See Gunnell, The Orders of Discourse, 1998 for a more extended analysis of metapractice.

6. The following discussion is drawn from Gunnell, *The Descent of Political Theory,* 1993b.

7. See the discussion of Weber's dispute with Brentano in Portis, *Max Weber and Political Commitment,* 1986.

REFERENCES

Agger, Ben. 1992. *Cultural Studies as Critical Theory.* Washington, DC: Palmer Press.

Anderson, Martin. 1992. *Imposters in the Temple: The Decline of the American University.* New York, NY: Simon and Schuster.

Bloom, Allan. 1987. *The Closing of the American Mind.* New York, NY: Simon and Schuster.

Brantlinger, Patrick. 1990. *Crusoe's Footprints: Cultural Studies in Britain and America.* London: Routledge and Kegan Paul.

Derrida, Jacques. 1982. *Margins of Philosophy.* Chicago, IL: University of Chicago Press.

Eagleton, Terry. 1978. *Criticism and Ideology: A Study in Marxist Literary Theory.* London: Verso Press.

———. 1983. *Literary Theory: An Introduction.* Minneapolis, MN: University of Minnesota Press.

Eliot, T S. 1949. *Notes Toward the Definition of Culture.* New York, NY: Harcourt, Brace.

Fay, Brian. 1987. *Critical Social Science: Liberation and its Limits.* Ithaca, NY: Cornell University Press.

Fish, Stanley. 1980. *Is There a Text in This Class? The Authority of Interpretative Communities.* Cambridge, MA: Harvard University Press.

Grossberg, Lawrence, Cary Nelson, and Paula A.Treichler. 1992. *Cultural Studies.* New York, NY: Routledge and Kegan Paul.

Gunnell, John G. 1986. *Between Philosophy and Politics: The Alienation of Political Theory.* Amherst, MA.: University of Massachusetts Press.

———. 1993a. "Relativism: The Return of the Repressed," *Political Theory* 21: 563- 84.

———. 1993b. *The Descent of Political Theory: The Genealogy of an American Vocation.* Chicago, IL: University of Chicago Press.

———. 1998. *The Orders of Discourse: Philosophy, Social Science, and Politics.* Lanham, MD: Rowman and Littlefield.

Habermas, Jürgen. 1987. *The Philosophical Discourse of Modernity.* Cambridge, MA: MIT Press.

Jacoby, Russell. 1987. *The Last Intellectuals: American Culture in the Age of Academe.* New York, NY: Basic Books.

Kant, Immanuel. 1983. *Perpetual Peace and Other Essays on Politics, History, and Morals.* Translated by Ted Humphrey. Indianapolis, IN: Hackett Publishing Co.

Lentricchia, Frank. 1983. *Criticism and Social Change.* Chicago, IL: University of Chicago Press.

Leonard, Stephen. 1990. *Critical Theory in Political Practice.* Princeton, NJ: Princeton University Press.

Mitchell, W. J. T., ed. 1982. *The Politics of Interpretation.* Chicago, IL: University of Chicago Press.

Norris, Christopher. 1985. *The Contest of Faculties: Philosophy and Theory After Deconstruction.* London: Macmillan.

Portis, Edward. 1986. *Max Weber and Political Commitment: Science, Politics, and Personality.* Philadelphia, PA: Temple University Press.

Poshman, Gene. 1982. "Emerging Social Science and Political Relevance: Some Extractions from a Less than Classic Literature." Presented at the annual meeting of the American Political Science Association

Rorty, Richard. 1978. *Philosophy and the Mirror of Nature.* Princeton, NJ: Princeton University Press.

Schrecker, Ellen. 1988. *No Ivory Tower: McCarthyism and the Universities.* New York, NY: Oxford University Press.

Walzer, Michael. 1987. *Interpretation and Social Criticism.* Cambridge: Cambridge University Press.

———. 1988. *The Company of Critics.* New York, NY: Basic Books.

Winch, Peter. 1958. *The Idea of a Social Science and its Relation to Philosophy.* London: Routledge and Kegan Paul.

EPILOGUE

In one of the rare instances of memorable rhetoric in our discipline a well-known political theorist, after likening the supposed scientific study of political affairs to Nero's fiddling, added that its practitioners might be excused because they realized neither that they fiddled nor that Rome burned (Strauss 1962, 327). This was thirty years ago. Today such rhetoric would be pointless because the great majority of political scientists no longer read or listen to political theorists. This disregard is reciprocated. Many, perhaps most political theorists, irrespective of whether they think Rome burning, no longer concern themselves with whether the discipline of which they are a part is fiddling. They tend to write for one another, for philosophers, and for the politically committed intellectual.[1]

In the initial years of the estrangement between political theorists and the increasingly influential champions of a strictly empirical science of politics, the former often accused the latter of being apolitical if not anti-political (e.g., Morgenthau 1946; McCoy and Playford 1967). They argued that to advocate a "value-free" science of politics inevitably is to trivialize its subject matter because it excludes from serious consideration that which makes politics important to its practitioners. And by concentrating upon behavioral arrangements or mechanisms rather than ends, political science is unlikely to serve whatever higher purposes might be affirmed by serious reflection on rational priorities (see Brecht 1959).

Whether rational reflection really can conclusively affirm such priorities, or whether it is possible to even think about social and political affairs without them, are questions too weighty to be resolved here. We would like to suggest in these closing pages, however, that the mutual indifference which has replaced the explicit hostility between the field of political theory and the rest of the discipline has contributed to the theoretical impoverishment of political science and the enervation of political theory. In addition, we venture that the only way that theorists are likely to engage the serious attention of other political scientists is to seriously address themselves to the nature and implications of partisan politics.

215

Political science has been theoretically impoverished not so much because it has lacked theory, but rather because its theory has been lacking. Since political science has become a genuine social science, based upon the systematic testing of hypotheses rather than documented commentary, it has had three successively dominant conceptual frameworks: First group theory, then systems theory, and at present rational choice theory.[2] Despite their very real differences, each of these theoretical approaches consigns the goals of political actors to a subsidiary status, to what Carl Hempel referred to in his book, *Aspects of Scientific Explanation*, as the "antecedent conditions" of explanation as opposed to the explanatory regularities (1965, 249). For group theory subjective priorities enter as something for groups to organize, for systems theory they provide the demands to be processed, and for rational choice theory they constitute the ante which defines costs and benefits.

Group theory lost currency largely because it cannot explain why some interests become organized and others do not, while the most obvious theoretical flaw of systems theory is its inability to specify non-tautological system requisites. And because both attempt to provide essentially mechanical explanations for political phenomena, political conflict itself is just so much sound and fury, not something to be taken at face value.[3] Rational choice theory, on the other hand, being essentially about strategy, takes politics very seriously. It, too, is largely unconcerned with the origin of political ends or their relative priority. Moreover, it has difficulty accounting for such momentous decisions as the willingness to die for one's country in war or such relatively inconsequential ones as whether to vote. Nonetheless, rational choice theory has proven to be much more resilient than its predecessors, largely no doubt because many political phenomena can be understood as the result of competing strategies. More fundamentally, we think, rational choice owes its tenacious grip on the discipline to the fact that it is an interpretation of political conflict, and does not attempt to dismiss politics as somehow epiphenomenal.

If political theory is to reestablish its voice within the discipline of political science, it too must focus upon political conflict. Perhaps the subject matter of the discipline should be peace, stability, justice, or equality; in fact, however, most political scientists are largely occupied with partisan conflict. As the essays comprising this volume clearly indicate, there is a diversity of opinion among political theorists on the nature and implications of partisan politics. This is to be expected, and we certainly are not suggesting that political theorists must see intrinsic benefits in political competition. Yet if they are to be relevant to the discipline of political science an appreciable number of them are going to have to argue about the costs and benefits and the dangers and potential of political conflict rather than about the best means to limit or supplant it. Political theorists as a group cannot be accused of being apolitical; but whether acknowledged or not many of them are antipolitical. It is this, we submit, rather than their explicit discussion of normative matters, which tends to limit the relevance of their work to the discipline as a whole.

Political science needs political theory, but does political theory need political science? Why should we be concerned with our relevance to the discipline? What difference would it make if the serious study of political ends or principles were to take place primarily within departments of philosophy and literature, or schools of law, rather than within the discipline of political science? If political science were not concerned primarily with political conflict, there would be little difference indeed. As it is, however, political scientists are forced to develop a relatively keen sensitivity to the sources of contention and the practical tenuousness of authority, as well as to the fine and fragile line that often separates competition and coercion. Any discussion of political ends ignoring such essential elements of political context is bound to be incomplete and of questionable relevance to the political aspirations of our civilization. We are inclined to agree with John Maynard Keynes' oft cited estimate of the influence of "defunct economists" and "academic scribblers," but we suspect that theoretical ideas do not permeate the consciousness of "practical men" until they have been unified into a theoretical vision in which the particular and the immediate can be seen as manifestations of broader truths (Keynes 1935, 383). If our primary audience were confined to ourselves and other politically engaged intellectuals of a philosophical bent, our discussions of abstract principles and philosophical foundations, whatever our progress toward the truth of the matter, are unlikely to have much impact upon the political vision of either present or succeeding generations. We must convince those who are attempting to understand the details and implications of current political circumstances that their success depends in large part upon the adequacy of the abstract conceptual assumptions with which they necessarily begin. To do so, we must not only concern ourselves with the extent we think they fiddle, but also address ourselves to their subject matter.

NOTES

1. It is perhaps indicative that the only specialty journal in political theory that does not attempt to be interdisciplinary, *The Review of Politics*, is also the oldest. Compare *Political Theory*, *Political Philosophy*, and *History of Political Thought*.

2. The discipline has always been characterized by theoretical plurality, as well as theoretical indifference. By dominance we mean the theoretical option receiving a clearly disproportionate amount of attention among those who think about such things. Our historical assertions can, of course, be challenged, but we doubt that many would find them controversial, however overstated. Some meager support is provided in a popular advanced text of 1967. Eugene J. Meehan, *Contemporary Political Thought*, notes (101) that had he written the book ten years earlier he would have had to devote considerable attention to group theory, but that it had now been largely abandoned. He went on to lambast systems theory (under the rubric of "functionalism") at great length. He later explored "formalism," but described it as a "recent innovation" which was "important more for its potential than for its accomplishments" (288).

3. See Schattschneider's, *The Semisovereign People*, for an assessment of group theory (1960, 28). When systems theory was still prominent, skeptical political scientists often derisively referred to David Easton's "black box," because he graphically portrayed the political system as a rectangle in which "inputs" were processed into "outputs." The box was referred to as black apparently because Easton never discussed how this occurred, but simply represented the process as a wavy line within the box leading to "Authorities" (1965, 30).

REFERENCES

Brecht, Arnold. 1959. *Political Theory: The Foundations of Twentieth-Century Political Thought*. Princeton, NJ: Princeton University Press.

Easton, David. 1965. *A Systems Analysis of Political Life*. New York, NY: John Wiley and Sons, Inc.

Hempel, Carl G. 1965. *Aspects of Scientific Explanation: And Other Essays in the Philosophy of Science*. New York, NY: The Free Press.

Keynes, John Maynard. 1935. *The General Theory of Employment, Interest and Money*. New York, NY: Harcourt, Brace, & World.

McCoy, Charles A. and John Playford. 1967. *Apolitical Politics: A Critique of Behavioralism*. New York, NY: Thomas Y. Crowell Company.

Meehan, Eugene J. 1967. *Contemporary Political Thought: A Critical Study*. Homewood, IL: The Dorsey Press.

Morgenthau, Hans J. 1946. *Scientific Man vs. Power Politics*. Chicago, IL: The University of Chicago Press.

Schattschneider, E. E. 1960. *The Semisovereign People: A Realist's View of Democracy in America*. New York, NY: Holt, Rinehart and Winston.

Strauss, Leo. 1962. "An Epilogue." In *Essays on the Scientific Study of Politics*. Edited by Herbert J. Storing. New York, NY: Holt, Rinehart and Winston, Inc.

CONTRIBUTORS

William E. Connolly, (Ph.D., Michigan, 1965), Professor of Political Science, The Johns Hopkins University. Books: *Why I Am Not a Secularist*, (Minnesota, 1999); *The Ethos of Pluralization*, (Minnesota, 1995); *The Augustinian Imperative: A Reflection on the Politics of Morality*, (Sage, 1993); *Identity/Difference: Democratic Negotiations of Political Paradox*, (Cornell, 1991); *Political Theory and Modernity*, (Blackwell, 1988); *Politics and Ambiguity*, (Wisconsin, 1987); *Legitimacy and the State*, ed. (Blackwell, 1984); *Appearance and Reality in Politics*, (Cambridge, 1981); *The Politicized Economy*, (Heath, 1976); *The Terms of Political Discourse*, (Heath, 1974); *Social Structure and Political Theory*, ed. (Heath, 1974); *The Bias of Pluralism*, (Atherton, 1969); *Political Science and Ideology*, (Atherton, 1967).

Mary G. Dietz, (Ph.D., California-Berkeley, 1982), Professor of Political Science, University of Minnesota. Books: *Thomas Hobbes and Political Theory*, ed. (Kansas, 1990); *Between the Human and the Divine: The Political Thought of Simone Weil*, (Rowman and Littlefield, 1988).

Adolf G. Gundersen, (Ph.D., Wisconsin, 1991), formerly Associate Professor of Political Science, Texas A&M University. Currently an unaffiliated scholar and full-time father. Books: *The Environmental Promise of Deliberative Democracy*, (Wisconsin, 1995).

John G. Gunnell, (Ph.D., California-Berkeley, 1964), Distinguished Professor of Political Science, State University of New York at Albany. Books: *The Orders of Discourse: Philosophy, Social Science, and Politics*, (Rowman and Littlefield, 1998); *Regime and Discipline: Democracy and the Development of Political Science*, ed. (Michigan, 1995); *The Descent of Political Theory: The Genealogy of an American Vocation*, (Chicago, 1993); *The Development of Political Science: A Comparative Survey*, ed. (Routledge and Kegan Paul, 1991); *Between Philosophy and Politics: The Alienation of Political Theory*, (Massachusetts, 1986); *Political Theory: Tradition and Interpretation*, (Winthrop, 1979); *Philosophy, Science, and Political Inquiry*, (General Learning Press, 1975); *Political Philosophy and Time*, (Wesleyan, 1968).

Donald S. Lutz, (Ph.D., Indiana, 1969), Professor of Political Science, University of Houston. Books: *Colonial Origins of the American Constitution: A Documentary History,* ed. (Liberty, 1998); *A Preface to American Political Theory,* (Kansas, 1992); *The Origins of American Constitutionalism,* (LSU, 1988); (ed.), *Perspectives on American and Texas Politics,* (Kendall/Hunt, 1987); *American Political Writing During the Founding Era,* ed. (Liberty, 1983); *Popular Consent and Popular Control: Whig Political Theory in the Early State Constitutions,* (LSU, 1980).

Edward Bryan Portis, (Ph.D., Vanderbilt, 1973), Professor of Political Science, Texas A&M University. Books: *Reconstructing the Classics: Political Theory from Plato to Marx,* (Chatham House, 1994); *Handbook of Political Theory and Policy Science,* ed. (Greenwood, 1988); *Max Weber and Political Commitment: Science, Politics and Personality,* (Temple, 1986).

Arlene Saxonhouse, (Ph.D., Yale, 1972), Professor of Political Science, University of Michigan. Books: *Athenian Democracy: Modern Mythmakers and Ancient Theorists,* (Notre Dame, 1996); *Hobbes's Three Discourses: A Modern Critical Edition of Newly Identified Works by the Young Thomas Hobbes,* (Chicago, 1995); *Fear of Diversity: The Birth of Political Science in Ancient Greek Thought,* (Chicago, 1992); *Women in the History of Political Thought: Ancient Greece to Machiavelli,* (Prager, 1985).

Ruth Lessl Shively, (Ph.D., Wisconsin, 1993), formerly Assistant Professor of Political Science, Texas A&M University. Currently an unaffiliated scholar and full-time mother. Books: *Compromised Goods: A Realist Critique of Constructionist Politics,* (Wisconsin, 1997).

Thomas A. Spragens, Jr., (Ph.D., Duke, 1968), Professor of Political Science, Duke University. Books: *Reason and Democracy,* (Duke, 1990); *The Irony of Liberal Reason,* (Chicago, 1981); *Understanding Political Theory,* (St. Martin's, 1976); *The Politics of Motion: The World of Thomas Hobbes,* (Kentucky, 1973); *The Dilemma of Contemporary Political Theory: Toward a Postbehavioral Science of Politics,* (Dunellen, 1973).

INDEX